Reviews

Great and VERY unusual book. Helped me see myself more clearly.

— Frank Schaeffer, Author of *Crazy for God*

———

In *Shattered Diana: Downloading Malware*, Diana Lee gives a captivating narrative of her chaotic upbringing in an evangelical home in the 1950s. The book gives the reader an introspective look at how Diana-the-child felt and attempted to cope as she experienced the psychological and physical abuse of her home and the religious fear and shame indoctrination of growing up in evangelicalism. The book frequently interjects Diana's narrative— one that creatively blends prose with poetry—with the scoldings Diana so frequently experienced and the religious hymns, still widely sung today, that celebrate obedience and redemption through violent punishment.

—Eric Cernyar, JD

———

Your book will help those who have been saying "what's wrong with me?" change the question to "what's wrong with them?" It could help millions stop the self-blame they were taught and to put it back where it belongs, with the perpetrator!

Thanks, Diana, for telling it like it is.

—Pam Lampe

———

Thanks, Diana, for making us aware.

—Barbee James

Evangelical Fundamentalism is like going through life looking in a mirror. Everything is backwards.

—Paul Weis

Review of Susanna and John Wesley's Religion and Parenting Style

Wesley worshipped an ancient, revengeful warrior god who demanded total obedience. His god's goal was to control the universe with spells, sacrifices and gruesome punishments. He hated women and what he called their weaknesses: compassion, intuitive wisdom, love and creativity — including the ability to give birth. He also feared them because of their understanding and acceptance of the continual changes in nature; and therefore, the need for death. Those who still follow the rules of Wesley's god raise children who are generally obedient, yet carry the rage and wounds inflicted by the followers of this blood-thirsty god. Any wonder our earth and its creatures are in such distress.

Rev. Sylvia Falconer
Unitarian Universalist Minister

A Neuroscientist's Response to Susanna Wesley's Child Rearing Letter to John [1732]

Experimental neuroscience work shows that experience shapes behavioral adaptations by reorganizing neuronal maps/circuits in the brain. The emotional circuits in the brain are organized along a continual structural/functional axis. Bonding, love, safety, appetitive circuits exist at one end of this physical axis, and fear, anxiety, fight and flight are at the other end of this axis. It is also known that the neuronal circuits that "fire together wire together". Simply put, the circuits that are used/"fed" are the circuits that are built up and thus shape the particular behavioral adaptation.

This would suggest that an environment of "beatings" and "breaking" the soul would "feed" the fear, anxiety, and aggressive type behavioral adaptations and develop these respective neuronal circuits; by contrast, shaping the soul in the context of love, bonding, empathy, compassion, etc. would "feed" the circuits of the other end the emotional circuits and promote the accompanying adaptive behaviors.

Howard Nornes, PhD
Emeritus Professor of Anatomy and Neurobiology
Colorado State University
College of Veterinary Medicine and Biomedical Sciences

ShaTterED DianA

A Memoir Documenting How Trauma and Evangelical
Fundamentalism Created PTSD, Bipolar and Dissociative
Identity Disorder (Multiple Personality) in Me

Diana Lee M.A.

Book One - Downloading Malware

Child Advocate Press
Loveland, Colorado

First Printing 2015

ISBN 978-1-62967-055-3
Library of Congress Control Number: 2015955240

ATTENTION CORPORATIONS, UNIVERSITIES, COLLEGES, AND PROFESSIONAL ORGANIZATIONS:

Quantity discounts are available on bulk purchases of this book for educational or gift purposes. Special books or book excerpts can also be created to fit specific needs.

Table of Contents

I dedicate my memoir to my children and grandchildren!
You are in my heart—always!
Nana

And to Sam!
Thanks for being a true friend by hearing my fear, being there for me and by telling the truth!

Acknowledgments

From the bottom of my heart, I want to thank everyone who helped me discover truth and recover, especially my therapists and professors! You gave me a self and a life worth living!

I also thank my maternal grandmother for her enduring love, integrity and honesty. Aunt Bebe thank you for telling me painful family truth and for going to child protection on my behalf when you were only fourteen years old and for always being there for me! For alienated family members, I thank you also because unwittingly you dropped information that confirmed or filled in gaps in my own memory and provided documents that enabled my MDs and therapists to understand the destructive family and destructive religious system I was born into.

I am also grateful to Jeanise and Lou Brown. What an irony of life that you both — a handsome, distinguished, highly educated, respected, talented, successful, black couple — crossed my path just as I was struggling to cope with and understand KKK flashbacks! You simply spread your loving wings to include me, protect me, and help me recover from mental illness and also breast cancer by your love. And you exposed me to a different kind of Christianity.

Lovey, Scout, Susan, Georgia, Marina, Elizabeth, Paul, Sam, Kevin, John — and everyone who has met me — thank you for listening to my story *ad nauseam* and helping me bear my unbearable grief and come to understand and accept just how bizarre my story is. No wonder it made me ill! An IT friend set up my book computer and for that I am deeply appreciative. It truly has taken "a village" to help me recover and fulfill my child self's vow to survive, grow up and tell by writing a book.

I am indebted to Tom McCaffrey the FBI agent who helped ground me by explaining "relives" and making me aware I knew details about the KKK that are not common knowledge. Having a connection to a seasoned agent enabled me to survive the most terrifying memories so I could feel safe enough to continue therapy after Tom promised to pick up every time I needed to call — unless he was out of the country or in court testifying. (Take that scary people! I had the FBI!) Tom enabled me to trust my white therapist during years I wanted no contact with white people because my historian's mind knew how many had had/have KKK affiliations — even the loving maternal side of my family had that terrifying sociopathic history.

In addition, I want to acknowledge and thank the kindnesses of the following authors who have given me permission to quote them in my series and/or professionals who have helped guide me in some way. Lundy Bancroft; Colin Ross, M.D.; Julie Brand, M.S.; Lloyd deMause; Norman Doidge, M.D.; J. Vincent Felitti, M.D.; Steven Hassan, M.Ed., LMHC; Elaine Pagels, Ph.D.; Ellen Reilly J.D.; Gloria Steinem; Douglas Darnall, Ph.D.; Marilyn Van Derbur; Victor Vieth, J.D.; Richard Demarest, J.D.; James Fallon, Ph.D.; Joseph Atwill; Stephen Kohlbeck, allied ASID; Linda Watson, ASID; and an extra thank you to attorney Susan Lach, J.D., for helping me stand up for my human rights even though I didn't realize I had any at the time!

The following friends and professionals proofread all or parts of my book series and offered content and formatting insights that made my series much better, but in the end, all content was my choice and I alone am responsible. With deepest gratitude I thank you for sharing your valuable time and talents with me: Wayne Viney, Ph.D.; Howard Nornes, Ph.D.; Sally Kile, MSW, LCSW; Maggie Hayes, Ph.D.; Eric Cernyar, J.D.; Wayne Carpenter, M Div., MA, LMFT; Mary Walker, MA; Barbee James, allied ASID; Pam Lampe, Bob Stewart, ED.D.; Jim Smith; Paul Weis, M.S.; Rev. Sylvia Falconer; and Ann Perry, ASID. Thank you all for believing the themes addressed in my series were worthy of your gift of time and talent and to Brian Schwartz at Wise Media Group and his wonderful team who turned my dream into reality!

A special thank you to Paul Weis for working photoshopping magic on my therapy art so it could be included in my series and making old family photos print ready. And another special thank you to Marlene Winell, Ph.D. for giving me permission to include a photo of her painting, "He Must Increase, I Must Decrease" in my postscript.

My book is more credible thanks to permission from Gospel Publishing House to include my 4 year old Sunday school paper;

and Olan Mills Photography for giving me permission to use the photo of my family during my high school years. We all look like we are in a trance because we were!

Another special thank you goes to Jeanne Weiskopf for inspiring me to add book club discussion questions to help readers tie my experiences to current trauma research and recovery.

Marilyn, thank you for teaching me about shame and for calling evil, evil so I could connect the dots and escape! I had not used the word evil yet and I needed to because so much of my crazy environment was religious! Thank you for being the loving, understanding and wise support that you have been. We *Phi Beta Kappa* women are determined not to let the bad guys win by sweeping evil under the rug or the blood. We care deeply about protecting children and about helping survivors recover fully. Thanks for all you have done in spite of push back. You are my heroine!

There are no words to describe what Wayne Viney's presence in my life has meant. We met when he joined my senior honor's committee. He recognized what had been done to me and slowly but surely began suggesting books I might be interested in reading and by doing so helped my therapists walk me out of Evangelical Fundamentalism. Wayne started with the *Malleus Maleficarum.* I would come to understand I had been in the same system and damned-if-I-do and damned-if-I-don't crazy-making position of millions of innocent women hung, drowned and burned by the Lord's godly people. (E.g., if a woman was thrown off a bridge and floated she was a witch; if she drowned she was a good woman. Either way she was dead. Rev. Falconer made me aware that in some villages all women were killed.) I came to understand I had been born into and indoctrinated into a psychopathic system!

Howard Nornes taught me basic neuroscience that grounded my life and story in science and that gave me the stability I needed when others were trying to undermine me and telling people to ignore me because I'd "always been a problem child and hysterical." Of course! Hysteria is a symptom of what the very same people were doing to me! Howard introduced me to epigenetics, methylated genes, autonomic nervous system, conditioned fear, and neuroplasticity. "Neurons that fire together, wire together." Howard explained what my history meant for my brain and body and also explained why — with appropriate therapies — my brain recovered from my traumatic past. In short, thanks to neuroscience, I now know nature/genetics loads the gun but environment fires it. It often does not matter what genes we inherit as much as what our internal, social and physical environment does to our genes. Thank you Howard!!! You made science FUN!

Sally, what I can I say? You saved my life! How many licensed therapists are willing to literally stand in OR next to their patient during a bilateral mastectomy because the patient has a history of bad things happening when they are on tables, in bed asleep and the last bilateral triggered a massive breakdown? Thank you for committing me to the psych hospital against my will when you saw I'd given up and was deeply suicidal — and suicidal not because I was fighting breast cancer and mental illness — but because of how my family was treating me *while* I was fighting for my life. Thank you for keeping me safe so I could recover and tell my story! Maggie, you know how you helped! I love you both!!

After I learned cancer had returned, I could not have survived or completed this project without many friends (especially Elizabeth Metcalf, Suzanne Blanchard, Barbee James, Marina Dagenais and Paul Weis); many oncology social workers connecting me to numerous cancer foundations; Medicare, food stamps, Extra Help, DORA; my dermatologist Aaron Hoover, MD, Front Range Dermatology Associates; oncologist Scot Sedlacek, MD, Rocky Mountain Cancer Center; radiologist Gwen Lisella, MD, CU-North; surgeon Barbara Schwartzberg, MD, Western Surgical, and grief therapist, Renee Baker, MSW, LCSW, Pathways Hospice! After being misdiagnosed more than twice and hitting rock bottom, they and their nurses and social workers along with my Hope Lives massage therapist, Donna Corbett-Lewis, turned the Titanic around and are enabling me to live happily and fruitfully with a stage 4 breast cancer diagnosis that includes both estrogen positive and triple negative! I learned it is social workers who grease the healing machine for survivors in many ways!

Foreword

I am delighted to write the foreword for Diana's important book. I was her psychotherapist for the period from fall 1993 through November 2004 and then on an as- needed basis until early 2007. Diana's story and documents provide a window into a Christianity of which many are not aware.

I earned my MSW in 1969 and my clinical license in 1972. My practice specialty was working with adult women abused as children. The treatment, therefore, was often long and psychologically painful. The formal diagnoses were usually Post Traumatic Stress Disorder (PTSD) and/or Dissociative Disorders. The first step was to provide an environment where clients could feel safe and respected and heard.

Dissociation means disconnection. Dissociative Identity Disorder is the disconnection of one part of one's self from another. Symptoms include inability to remember personal information, and the presence of several distinct identities with differing ages, memories, styles, agendas, and perceived appearances. The goal of therapy is to slowly reintegrate these parts into the core person.

A child is born with both a drive to connect with a primary caretaker and a drive to disconnect from painful experiences. When a primary caretaker is both nurturing and hurtful, the child has a problem. So the child creates a part of itself that can forget the painful experiences and connect. Another part of the child is aware of the dangerous potential and learns to avoid the caretaker when necessary or possible. This is considered by many as the "primary split". Once a child learns this creative defense of dissociation, parts can be created to play many different roles, and there is often an amnestic barrier between the parts. The go-to-school-and-learn part may not know what happens at home, for example.

A "trigger" is something that begins to bring dissociated memories together. The full moon was a major trigger for Diana, as you will discover in Book 4. Sometimes sophisticated perpetrators deliberately enhance dissociation for their own purposes to keep certain incidents from being remembered by the victim, or to create parts within the subject that perpetrators could control for their own use. During the period Diana and I worked together some of those perpetrators attempted to discredit the diagnosis of DID to protect knowledge about their actions. That is a very complicated story beyond the scope of this book.

I was fortunate to be able to attend conferences, read books and articles, and consult with experts about cutting-edge treatment techniques for dissociative disorders. The International Society for the Study of Trauma and Dissociation was a very good resource. I am especially grateful for the work and generosity of Colin Ross, MD.

Diana was referred to me because she was not getting the help elsewhere that she needed regarding a troubling memory about a toddler girl on a white enamel table. In addition to abuse issues, Diana had intense fear of making her divorce transition alone because she would soon be a forty six year old displaced homemaker with no career history or suitable college degree. She came to the office with great energy and childlike enthusiasm.

In the beginning I was somewhat uncomfortable with the parental position of authority Diana sometimes afforded me. I kept trying to equalize the relationship. As I became acquainted with Diana's internal parts, I understood that it was her child parts and submissive wife parts who were expecting me to be an authoritarian adult instead of a partner in her quest for recovery.

The revelation of child abuse, particularly when it involves family members, is unpredictable and agonizing. The forces of denial are strong, but so are the cravings for truth. Diana gives a riveting description of how the uncovering felt from her side of the room in Book 4. It came in non-chronological bits and pieces from the experiences of internal parts created to cope with the unmanageable and the unimaginable. We needed to honor those parts who had taken the brunt of the abuse and help them heal. The flashbacks involved real time sensory overload and disorientation as to time and place and identity. Sometimes before she left the office I would need to make sure the part present could safely drive a car. Our big picture job was to make sense of all the shattered bits and pieces, the memories, the feelings, and the different parts, and then knit them together to understand the time line of Diana's life and produce a coherent whole self.

The integrated self ultimately holds all of the memories as well as the amazing specialized capabilities of the separate parts. When integration has finally occurred the client is able to think in broad concepts and make internally informed decisions about beliefs and life goals. And even write books!

Diana did every bit of homework I assigned. She read every book I suggested, lots of them! She never missed a weekly session, in spite of the very difficult nature of the work. She made great use of drawings to examine relationships and situations and to record flashbacks.

Diana and I were an interesting match with regard to our religious experiences. As a child I attended a garden variety Protestant church in the Midwest. My Congregational church Sunday school teachers taught us the basic tenets of Christianity, in particular the Golden Rule. Our Bible verses revealed how Jesus welcomed everyone, sinners included. We examined the idea of being our Brothers' Keeper. Our workbooks presented complicated situations, and we were asked to consider possible choices of behaviors. Some of the situations involved difficult feelings, such as anger and jealousy. The exercises were thought provoking. Listening, fairness, empathy, compassion, understanding, compromise, and generosity were words we learned to use.

When I was eleven, a nearby Congregational church burned to the ground. Our church was to vote on whether we would ask their congregants to join our services and Sunday school until their church could be rebuilt. I was excited about welcoming other children.

To my astonishment the plan was voted down. I asked the older woman sitting in the pew next to me, "Why?" She answered, "We don't want little visitors in our church."

I later learned the burned out congregation was Black. My church's response infuriated me. This was not the Christianity I had been taught. I began shopping for a new church by attending services with friends. My disillusionment led me away from organized religion and toward spirituality in other forms.

Many years later I understood the timing of that burned church in 1955 coincided with, Brown v. Board of Education, which led to school integration. I suspected the Black church had been torched. So I resonated with Diana's outrage toward the KKK.

Diana's religious experiences were radically different from anything I was aware of in spite of my tour of churches and a college class in comparative religions. She had to educate me about her evangelical and fundamentalist beliefs. When she talked about evil, the devil, demon possession, end times and the rapture, I was astounded. I thought the notion of demon possession was an artifact of Medieval times. Of course, it was not my job to challenge her religious beliefs. My professional code and personal philosophy required that I honor the beliefs of clients.

While studying for her undergrad and master's degrees in history, Diana had become aware of other ideas. Professors challenged her childhood information and began to shake the bedrock of much of what she had been taught before she began therapy. During our sessions, I watched her face as she tried to correlate new concepts with the religious teachings around which she had based her life.

At times, when Diana considered incompatible ideas, her eyes danced back and forth as she processed the discrepancies. I felt I was literally seeing new neural pathways form in her brain. Her academic experiences and extended therapy eventually allowed Diana to decide what to believe for herself.

Examination of her childhood churches revealed parallels to destructive cults. I had recommended William Sargant's *Battle for the Mind.* We met with a cult expert, and he corroborated the cult idea. He explained some families are run like cults and also explained ways in which her religious leaders, some of whom were family members, had taken creative license with Greek myths and Bible verses. Their interpretations gave them a rationale for enormous abusive power as well as an avenue to collect money (tithes) from parishioners.

Physical abuse was recommended by sect leaders for very young children and would have certainly have had the effects of causing them to dissociate and making them compliant and easy to manipulate.

Sometimes, as Diana reconnected with family members to try to validate childhood memories, she was drawn back to guilt and denial. Her journey was not only an intellectual exercise, but it created a serious crisis of conscience. She was often caught between guilt and potential freedom. This was not an easy road! She eventually lost her entire family in the process, and that resulted in enormous, gut-wrenching grief.

In particular, Diana was challenged by the concept that a husband and wife could have equal status in a marriage. She had been taught that she must follow her husband's ideas because he was the religiously designated head of the family. In her growing independence Diana could not always accept his ideas of how things should be. As Diana describes in Book 4, the law backed equality in her marital agreement, and that fact reinforced her courage and will, but resulted in a protracted legal battle.

Diana faced extreme health problems while in therapy. She had both precancerous ovaries removed which precipitated a very scary full blown manic episode that required psychiatric hospitalization. It was during her in-hospital stay that she received her three diagnoses from her psychiatrist. She had breast cancer that necessitated a bilateral mastectomy and chemotherapy, and another psychiatric hospital stay after she became depressed and suicidal. Each of her medical issues required treatments and medications that produced symptoms of their own.

Diana's ex-husband's notion that she could have somehow created these medical difficulties to avoid work is utter nonsense — as was his suggestion she could have recovered sooner. Diana wanted to work. She did everything she could to work. The legal issues were an energy drain and a distraction from her recovery — not to mention they kept her frightened and on the victim/perpetrator/rescuer splits she was working hard in therapy to recover from. Diana struggled to survive financially specifically because of the pressures her ex exerted on her as she documents in Book 4.

Even in the midst of all the legal, medical, and financial difficulties Diana determined to live a fun and normal life to the degree that she was able. She had made a commitment to her internal nine year old girl to do so. I was very concerned as she dated numerous men before all her child parts were integrated but as her therapist it was not my job to take control of her life.

When I reflect on our therapy process I am thoroughly impressed by Diana's enormous energy and enthusiasm, by her quest for truth, by her intellectual capacity, and by her research capabilities. Those assets carried her through therapy and illness to mental and physical health and now propel her in this new venture to inform a broad audience about destructive religious fundamentalism and evangelicalism.

Sally Kile, MSW, LCSW (retired)
Colorado, 2015

Introduction

Little did I know, or even suspect, when my gynecologist informed me in late October 1994 that my ovaries were precancerous and I needed a bilateral oophorectomy immediately, surgery would trigger a devastatingly bizarre psychological, physical, spiritual, and emotional odyssey that would hijack and dominate the next ten years of my life. Life as I had known it was over!

I learned in our local psychiatric hospital I was suffering mental illness: Post Traumatic Stress Disorder (PTSD), rapid cycling Bipolar 1 Disorder and Dissociative Identity Disorder (DID), formerly known as Multiple Personality Disorder (MPD). I was assured, however, by my psychiatrist, that I was not crazy as I assumed. My symptoms were the result of what had been "done to me!" "This is not where crazy people come, Diana. This is where victims of crazy people come!"

As my journey unfolded over the next decade, numerous flashbacks containing slivers of memory functioned like helter-skelter puzzle pieces my therapist and I had to piece together so I could understand exactly what had been "done to" me. I then had to integrate these memories and their unexpressed, forbidden, frozen emotions into my highly educated, middle-aged, adult personality — my authentic self. I often felt like I was looking through a kaleidoscope that someone else was turning. It was horrific and left me looking and feeling unstable — because I was! I would discover my instability actually functioned to undermine my credibility and, thus, protect those who had harmed me.

In other words, creating mental illness in me provided a perfect smoke screen for what many would call evil — the belief that one is free to do anything to anyone after a tribal, military, religious or political conversion experience. In spite of the very best therapy, I did not understand my flashbacks were not the result of demons and/or Satan in my head (demon possession) until a seasoned FBI agent told me in 1999, "Diana, they are relives — experiences you've had." The most gut-wrenching part of therapy was learning

1

that the people I had loved the most were the very ones who had made me ill and then losing them as I recovered and began standing up for myself and telling the truth.

Not until I recovered was I able to think for myself and deconstruct Evangelical Fundamentalism and discover it is rooted in trauma — including child abuse. It shares harsh religious parenting practices with Puritan childrearing, Catholicism's frightening Hell, St. Augustine's born-in-sin theology, Wesley's personal Jesus mixed in with Luther's anti-Semitism, Calvin's authoritarian Geneva, propaganda, etc., etc. In short, it is a hodgepodge. Distilled it is authoritarian mind control.

Gabor Mate, M.D., addiction researcher and lecturer, says the Puritan's were "appalled" by Native American parents because they did not spank their children and because they picked them up and comforted them when they cried. He explains that Native Americans were not perfect parents but they were much more in tune with their children's developmental needs than the Puritans. In some circles, Evangelical Fundamentalist parenting, very similar to my story, is considered an important and necessary foundational aspect of America's moral history and culture. Religious trauma is one of the dirty little secrets we, as Americans, have been sweeping under the rug — and under "the blood"— at children's and taxpayers' expense.

For me, and millions of children, being born into Evangelical Fundamentalism is like being born into a parallel universe. Because of the religious gloss we actually have fewer legal rights than secular children! [See: *Breaking Their Will: Shedding Light on Religious Child Maltreatment,* Janet Heimlich] After therapy I realized it was as though I'd been playing a bit role in the movie *Star Wars.* I was expected to fight evil daily — actually moment to moment — in myself and in the "evil world." The Bible was my script, my sword, and my protective combat uniform-costume thanks to both Old and New Testament military propaganda. The Bible as my script and my sword in my imaginary cosmic battle explains the point of the weekly Bible verses I had to memorize. I was being conditioned to live my entire life in that surreal world. I did not know it was actually cult brainwashing!

I thought I was becoming one of the chosen ones — God's precious daughter — who would wear a jewel crown in heaven and have a new name that only God and I knew — a special child. After recovery and extensive research I came to understand what I was actually doing as a child and adult was using this same imaginary world to both survive and to rid myself of the shame created by child abuse and the symptoms of chronic toxic stress on my brain and body. I was attempting to recover from the mental illness symptoms created by child abuse — by using destructive religion to cope and heal — which only justified and reinforced what I was experiencing in my family and vice versa. I had been an innocent child but I carried the shame my perpetrators should have been carrying. Thus, I had been their scapegoat and all the religious rites and rig-a-ma-roll was just that and nothing more. They could not "save" or "heal" me because I didn't need any form of religious salvation; I needed licensed therapy that would enable my brain to recover!

As a child I had no way of knowing children's songs like The B*I*B*L*E were programming my mind to believe an altered reality because I was developmentally too young to understand and challenge it; thus, fundamentalist reality is all I knew way into adulthood because I was kept relatively isolated from the allegedly "evil world." Isolation dogma dovetailed with — and hid — child abuse from me and provided a glass wall around me that prevented others from understanding and helping me. I am deeply grateful for my public school education that provided contrast and made me aware there was something better even though I'd been taught it was evil and to be shunned.

I am deeply grateful the love from my mother's family enabled my infant and toddler brain to wire in love and empathy. Without that experience my story would have ended much differently. Given the kinds, timing, duration and degree of traumas I experienced, I could have become part of "the Lord's army" — a violent, shame-based, fear-fueled princess-soldier for that god — lacking in empathy and mindlessly replaying and justifying Old Testament conquest stories of genocide — ancient war propaganda — in our contemporary society — as many Evangelical Fundamentalists are currently doing.

Writing My Story

I wrote my memoir to honor the tenacious nine-year-old me who vowed to survive with God's help and grow up to tell the truth. I vowed to pay attention so I could write a book because I truly believed in my child's heart-of-hearts that adults would have helped me if they had understood the devastating confusion and suffering I was enduring. As an adult, I simply could not break my promise to my former helpless, innocent and trapped child self. And it is timely given fundamentalisms are on the rise worldwide.

Books 1 through Book 4 document my story of yearning for truth and health as I'm being undermined by family and destructive religion. My series reveals what I'm being taught as well as my commitment to survive and recover from what was once considered impossible — chronic emotional, physical, intellectual and spiritual traumas that determined how my brain wired and how it functioned — because symptoms like mine had been viewed from a medical model rather than a trauma model. In other words, Bipolar Disorder!

My licensed, Ph.D. psychologist told me, "We've known fundamentalist children were being programmed but we didn't know how it was being done." The first book in my series, *Downloading Malware,* provides a window into aspects of how it is often done. At the core is the belief that adults are entitled "to break children's will" (and often their spirit) and indoctrinate and shape them into being what the adults want them to be — the child has no choice. It is a simple formula: traumatize and indoctrinate — just like military boot camp.

Deceptive emotional and spiritual abuses are at its core because children are not born in sin or sinners. Corporal punishment is a foundational breaking technique. Incest is not uncommon. Withholding what children need and desire is not uncommon so that they turn to the eye in the sky to rescue them. Bottom line, fundamentalisms are about control — they are political movements — not spiritual movements. Religion functions to distract what is really going on behind the scenes as victims are manipulated into doing what they are programmed to do — including acting against their own best interests to the point of unwittingly sacrificing their own children's mental and physical health and well-being — to a hero's death on a battlefield. When I asked a professional artist friend, who also grew up in Evangelical Fundamentalism, what his canvas would look like if he painted what it felt like to grow up in fundamentalism he replied immediately, "It would be filled with tears."

———

My intention is to tell the truth to the best of my knowledge and ability. In order to write and make sense of all the memories, I created a historical timeline with the help of three supportive aunts and numerous documents.

My memoir series — *Shattered Diana* — is based on my extensive archive of therapy journals, therapy art, signed interviews with my Aunt Bebe, dated photographs, old letters and cards, journals, scrapbooks, canceled checks, airline tickets, hospital records, hymns, a returned Sunday school paper from age four, Evangelical Fundamentalist books and church counselor handouts, newspaper clippings, yearbooks, family genealogy records, court transcripts and other legal documents, report cards, bills and receipts, souvenirs, my own memories, my sisters' and other relatives' memories, what I learned from psychologists, therapists, psychiatrists, neuroscience and psychology profs, my own extensive research, and some of my childhood trauma art saved by my maternal grandmother, whom I affectionately called "Mom."

All of my childhood memories described in Book1 *(Downloading Malware)* came back as individual visual, tactile, emotional or auditory flashbacks. Each represents one compartment in my mind that had been walled-off due to overwhelming trauma. These compartments — or "parts" of my mind — were not integrated into my conscious awareness or adult understanding — but they were unconsciously influencing my adult choices and behavior while I remained clueless. All were indelible memories because they were made with stress hormones and, thus, were not made like normal fallible memories — they were trauma memories made in my limbic system's amygdala by fear! [See: *The Body Keeps the Score*, Bessel Van Der Kolk, MD]

Shattered Diana *Series Synopses*

Book 1, *Downloading Malware*, in my *Shattered Diana* series, is my child's voice and represents my child-self's understanding of her world. I've employed reflections to add information that occurred before the book begins at age six, but I did not reflect as a child. I was always in the present or fogged out or confused and often depressed longing for a better future. I was not able to make sense of my life, although I'd begun to question our religion by age nine — before more traumas forced me to use it as my primary defense mechanism so I could simply survive day to day by creating my relationship with "Jesus" and "God." I believed what adults told me, even when something felt wrong or odd. I was trained to override my own sense of right and wrong in deference to authoritarian adults and fundamentalist dogma and to endure.

Book 1 *Postscript* includes a signed interview with my loving and supportive Aunt Bebe describing the vicious physical and emotional attack I experienced before age two at the hands of my father. I include Susanna Wesley's letter to her son John who created the Methodist religion known as Evangelicalism. Because Wesley's advocated beating babies and toddlers with a rod, I came to slowly understand many of my most chilling, psychologically and physically destructive childhood experiences, were rooted in the authoritarian ideology advocated in this 1732 letter with a religious gloss.

The postscript, therefore, links many of my experiences with current scientific research that has discovered most mental illnesses are due to trauma's effect on inherited genes rather than the previous model that assumed victims inherited faulty genes associated with psychiatric disorders. Nurture has triumphed in the nature v. nurture debates. Emotional abuse is actually the most lethal form of trauma and, therefore, is often the genesis of Bipolar Disorder and Schizophrenia. In the postscript, I also offer a quick review of cutting-edge scientific Israeli archaeology that debunks Evangelical Fundamentalist theology. Book club discussion questions are included. My exhaustive series' bibliography will be offered free on shattereddiana.com as soon as it is available.

Book 2 *(Malware Playing in the Background)* continues the brainwashing saga as I document how women are undermined and kept confused and how my former husband built upon the foundation instilled during my childhood — that was often reinforced with a belt so that I learned to confound love with pain and suffering. As an astute friend commented, "Diana, are you saying the Bible Belt means, 'Believe the Bible or get the belt?'" "Yes! Or worse, emotional abuse!" During my marriage I recognized something was wrong but I did not understand what. I did not realize fundamentalist demands for wifely submission, suffering in silence, personal sacrifice, purity, unattainable perfection, fear of non-fundamentalists and distrust of normal human emotions had completely undermined my sense of self. I was taught not to trust my own emotions — and what they were telling me — in deference to so-called biblical truth aka propaganda and programming.

Because Evangelical Fundamentalism is a patriarchal misogynistic system, woman are often scapegoats ("Evil Eve don'chya know! She brought sin and death into the world. Can't trust 'em. Gotta keep 'em barefoot and pregnant! Control 'em! That's whachya gotta do!") and that is why I falsely assumed it was only me who was messed up — not the system I was in — that turned out to be just another version of what I'd grown up in with a shiny, new-to-me analytical, theological-grad-school-glossy façade that left me believing I was finally on the right path. But, unfortunately for me, I was not becoming more intellectual — it was pseudo intellectualism based on literal interpretations of the Bible. (I swear these folks spend their lives trying to make sense out of nonsense and then call it theology!)

Actually, my brain and mind were steeping in brainwashing and cultic control, like a tea bag in hot water, as I was being sucked even deeper into fundamentalist mind control and insanity. In fact, one of my former church's intern minister's "ministry" is now recognized as a hate group by the Southern Poverty Law Conference as are a number of religious organizations that crossed my path. Yikes!

Book 3 *(Systems Crash)* documents my sudden breakdown in November 1994 and the family dynamics that guaranteed it would happen. "Diana," my therapist told me, "you would have found yourself in a psych hospital even if you had had a perfect childhood because of how your husband treated you." Big WOW! "But, but, but, HOW?" "WHY?" "He never even saw you! He had no idea what he had!"

Book 4 (*Reprogramming*) provides a window into the therapy that helped me recover my mind and documents the forces that colluded to make my recovery all but impossible — frivolous litigation and warped family dynamics. I would come to view my divorce as an example of how courts can be used to continue domestic violence — at taxpayers' expense — when men truly believe — or at least apply — Evangelical Fundamentalist delusions to justify it. From my point of view, I really was in an epic battle between good and evil; and thus, it made it more difficult to get into reality and out of the surreal Evangelical Fundamentalist world view. Keeping me terrified kept me dissociated and unbalanced and then I was blamed for not recovering as quickly as some demanded.

My divorce actually set a legal precedent in Colorado. Book 4 is, therefore, written in two separate fonts to give readers a choice of reading the therapy narrative, the legal narrative, or both. I'd eventually learn MDs were not exaggerating when they told me and others that some were trying to kill me and that I'd gotten breast cancer because of how my family had treated me the previous 10 years. Who would have thought this information was based on hard science — not simply kindness and support — as I assumed at the time! (Exaggeration? NO!)

Book 5 (*Defragging*) gives insight into my intellectual quest to understand why these things happened to me and to nail down what had happened with hard evidence. More had been going on than the child "me" or the wife "me" understood. I became ill because I'd been born into a psychopathic system. All my attempts to seek help were futile, before licensed therapy, because it was like my family and religion had blindfolded me, spun me around a few times and then told me to pin the tail on the donkey and I'd feel healthy and also get to go to heaven. Alas, I was only bumping around in the darkness of the same destructive system I'd been born into and, not surprisingly, to no avail. To recover I had to leave that system and not look back! But that was not easy because it was all I knew. It was my identity and gave me purpose for living — or so I'd been conditioned to believe. There was no way to integrate delusions and propaganda with recovery. As Alice Miller wrote, "The brain needs truth."

Book 5 also recounts my indefatigable struggle to break the brainwashing licensed psychologists call "religious programming" or "cult programming." I used my historian's skills and curiosity to deconstruct Evangelical Fundamentalism and place it within its historical context so I could break its destructive maniacal grip over my mind and reclaim my life.

———

My intention is to provide readers the opportunity to experience my world, to help them understand trauma-induced mental illnesses — which accounts for at least 92% of all mental illness in women — and to evoke empathy for victims of both mental illness and cult indoctrination rather than confusion, contempt, disgust, and rejection – which is the norm. My hope is that my story will lead to better protection for children's minds as well as their bodies.

My psychologist explained that it generally takes a person 20 years to escape fundamentalism — IF they escape — because it is like we are born into a box wrapped in tight cording. We need others to help us cut the cords that are preventing us from flying out of the box — by giving us truth and love. I want, therefore, to share what I learned so the road will be easier for others. I hope my story will encourage those still in the recovery process by giving them hope, even if they are told — as was I by one of my psychiatrists — that they will never recover and live psychotropic-med free and happy. I also want to inform anyone trying to understand and support a loved one suffering mental illness and enable therapists working with victims of Religious Trauma Syndrome gain more insight into this system. [See: Marlene Winell, Ph.D., *Leaving the Fold*]

Reading My Story

My story is formatted as a journal because people remember stories more easily than other genres. Some entries are in one font style and most in another. That gives a visual image of the reality of multiple personality disorder also recognized as split mind and compartmentalization of the mind. It is not unusual for each "part" to have its own handwriting style, own name and function within the mind's survival system, as well as, differing visual acuity. [See: Dorothy Otnow Lewis, M.D., *Guilty by Reason of Insanity*, p. 223] For the integrity of my book's interior design I have added only a few examples to remind readers what I was dealing with. A vertical line of words signifies the day child/night child split I had. In other words, the trauma was so great and my need to survive so great that I had two totally different realities — personas — that knew nothing about each other. Most hymns are centered and italicized. Headings and subheadings are provided to guide readers. I definitely did not have this clarity until way after therapy.

———

Because my books are memoirs, I request that readers and the press respect the privacy of my friends and my alienated family, as well as the doctors, mental health care providers, professors, and attorneys who helped me recover.

———

I often reflect on Gloria Steinem's insight: "In a crazy world, sane looks crazy."

———

I do not ask you to believe me. I ask that you listen and then do your own homework.

Diana Lee, M.A.
Colorado 2015

Diana Lee, M.A.

Book 1
(Downloading Malware*)

*Malware is defined as 'software intended to damage a
computer, mobile device, computer system, or computer
network, or to take partial control over its operation.'

If I had a world of my own, everything would be nonsense. Nothing would be what it is, because everything wouldn't be what it isn't. And contrary wise, what is, it wouldn't be.

And what it wouldn't be, it would. You see?

Lewis Carroll
Alice's Adventures in Wonderland

———

Evil was defined as the use of power to destroy the spiritual growth of others for the purpose of defending and preserving the integrity of our own sick selves. In short it is scapegoating. We scapegoat not the strong but the weak...It is no wonder, then, that the majority of the victims of evil...are children. They are simply not free or powerful enough to escape.

M. Scott Peck, M.D.
People of the Lie

———

Do you think I came to bring peace on earth? No, I tell you, but division. From now on there will be five in one family divided against each other, three against two and two against three.

Jesus
Luke 12:51-53 (NASB)

Elementary School Years
(1953-1959)

First Grade School Photo
Photographer: Anonymous

I am a little girl. I am now six years old because my birthday was in December. I have short, light-brown hair that my mommy perms with Toni permanents. I really hate that! Mommy told me my eyes are hazel. That means sometimes they look green and sometimes they look blue. I weigh 48 pounds.

It is 1953, and I am in first grade at Mae M. Walter's elementary school. It is spring time. I did not go to kindergarten because I could not pass the test that I took just after I turned five in Denver, Colorado. But I got to go directly to first grade when I moved to Florida a few months later. (It really hurt my feelings that I didn't pass that test. I thought I was smart!)

I live in a stucco rental house in Hialeah, Florida, near Miami. It is painted white with bright blue trim. It has a single-car carport, two bedrooms, a bathroom, living room, and kitchen.

In the daytime, I like to play house outside in the sunny weather. Sometimes I pretend I am building a house with a pile of cement blocks that are in my backyard. I love looking at the beautiful yellow, trumpet-shaped flowers on the allemande bush. I like my green parakeet, but I feel sorry for myself when Mommy makes me take his perches outside and clean them off by rubbing them with a piece of coarse sandpaper.

And I do not like it when Mommy saves the dollars I receive in birthday cards by putting them in "my sock" on the top shelf in the hall closet. My sock is really just one of daddy's big old socks tied with a knot at the top. I don't have a big pig bank like my girlfriend down the block. Just a sock!

Tonight as I lay asleep in my twin bed, I am awakened by Mommy's soft voice. "Diana, we need to check you for worms." As I open my eyes, it is very dark. I can tell my father is standing next to her and that he is holding some sort of light. My two younger sisters are asleep in their own twin beds in the same room.

I am lying on my back as I begin to feel the bottoms of my baby-doll pajamas being pulled down. Immediately I think, "I do not like what happens next!" Suddenly, I am no longer aware of what happens to my body. I cannot see what is happening. I cannot feel what is happening. I cannot hear what is happening. I am no longer here.

I am gone!

Scrambling My Brains

Abusive men, according to counselor Lundy Bancroft, turn reality on its head. They confuse women and children and make them feel crazy.

Why Does He Do That?

———

Today I love school. I feel excited as I walk home. I want to show my mommy and daddy what my teacher gave us. It is a little plastic case with my very own small tube of toothpaste and a new toothbrush. It says, "Pepsodent Toothpaste Company." We each got one!

"Look what I got in school today," I am excitedly saying to my family. "The teacher told us to brush our teeth after EVERY meal."

"Diana, that is not true. You are supposed to brush your teeth BEFORE you eat, not after. If you listen to your teachers, you will go to Hell" my father exclaims.

I feel shaken. I no longer feel happy and excited. I feel confused. What do I do? Do I brush my teeth before or after I eat? I don't want to go to Hell! I love my daddy. I really like my teacher. Something feels very wrong. What is true? My head is swimming.

I think being a kid is hard!

"Diana, stop talking with your hands!"
(Yes, Mommy.)

"Say, please."
(Yes, Daddy.)

"And thank you."
(Yes, Daddy.)

"Do you want me to skin you alive?"
(No, Daddy.)

"Do you want me to shake you until your teeth rattle?"
(No, Daddy.)

Pirates and Treasure Chests:
Compartmentalizing

I wore my red and white gingham dress to school today. It is my favorite dress. I LOVE the color red!

I go to first grade in the afternoon. I walk to school by myself. I walk to the end of the block and then turn left and walk along the canal. The road is called Red Road. Then I turn and walk a long way down another road that leads to my school. There are not many houses along Red Road and no houses along the road that leads to my school. I am almost always alone. Sometimes I feel scared, and Mommy walks with me part of the way, but mostly, I am alone. I feel very little.

I also feel confused because I do not understand why I have to go to school since Daddy tells me I will go to Hell if I listen to my teacher. But I still LOVE listening to her! I want to believe what she is telling me. I want to be like her. But I am afraid of going to Hell. How do I know what is true?

Today the teacher is talking to us about pirates and treasure chests. She has just drawn a pirate's chest on the left blackboard. "I know what I can do. I will put all of the ideas my teacher tells me, the ones that feel good but are ones I think Daddy and God would not like, into my own little pirate's chest in my head. Then when I grow up, I will be able to open it up and have all of the ideas that I like, but while I am little I will do what Mommy and Daddy tell me. Being a grown-up will be much easier," I think to myself.

"Children are to be seen and not heard."
(Yes, Daddy.)

"Do you want me to knock your block off?"
(No, Daddy.)

Family Stories Challenge My Conscience

Relatives are in town. They live in another state. We are going to go visit them tonight. They are at my great-grandparents' house on the other side of town. I am starting to feel really sick to my stomach, but Mommy said I still have to go. I feel like I am going to throw up! We stop at the drug store, and Mommy buys Milk of Magnesia. Uuuuuugggghhhhhhh! But my tummy feels better.

The adults are talking. The visiting aunt is saying, "He flew up over the windshield." "He was just an old alcoholic on a bicycle."

Something feels wrong. They are pastors. They speak for God. Something feels so wrong to me, but everyone else just listens.

Now they are laughing about how my daddy used to throw cats into boiling water when he was a boy. Something feels wrong again!

Daddy is talking now. He is telling about how he makes his girls mind him. He is talking about how he used to haul me out of church when I was a baby to spank me whenever I made any noise. I guess I had to learn that was God's house and I cannot make noise in God's house.

Mother's Lack of Empathy: Objectifying Me

I feel sad. I have just walked home from school. A girl was mean to me today. Mommy is standing at the stove. She is making apricot tarts to send to her brother. He is in a war in Korea or Africa or someplace. I tell Mommy what the girl said to me. "Diana, you never could keep a friend." I feel crushed. Mommy doesn't even turn away from her work to look at me. I am worse than I thought! I feel devastated and unlovable.

"Do you two want me to knock your heads together?"
(No Daddy!)

Nightmares

I have lots of nightmares. When I get up, Mommy is in the kitchen alone. She tells me to kneel at a kitchen chair. She prays for Jesus to protect me. Then she tells me to go back to bed.

Flying Trees

I don't always like school. I feel REALLY dumb. First grade is hard!

My class is in a white, wooden, one-room building with wooden floors. There are windows on the left side and blackboards in front. My desk is the second desk in my row, one row from the center of the room on the right side. It is a really old, wooden desk with an ink well and curvy wrought iron legs, but I love it! I like seeing all the names and doodles that have been carved into it by other kids. Somehow it makes me feel connected to them. I wonder if I will be able to pass first grade like they did.

I sit in back of Freddy. If I get a "U," he sees it before I do. When he passes my papers back to me, he smirks and says, "Failed again!" Those are my arithmetic papers. I feel humiliated. I truly hate school. I do not feel like I belong. I feel odd. In the reading group, I feel so stupid because I cannot figure out what I am supposed to do. Often, my eyes feel blurry, and I get headaches.

Something weird sometimes happens to me. Like when we were supposed to draw trees, I knew that trees have roots that go down into the ground, but that is not how I drew my trees during art class. When the weird feeling came over me, I did what I wanted to do and not what the teacher told us to do. Instead of drawing my roots into the ground, I drew mine curved up into the air. I don't know why I did that, I really don't, but I did! All I know is that a very strong force came over me, and I just felt like I HAD to draw them that way. Now I look stupid…again. I don't understand why I sometimes do things that make me look stupid when I know better.

Recreation based on drawing saved by Mom and lost in a fire.

In music, we are singing a song about "washing my hide." I feel VERY uncomfortable! Sweaty! Lightheaded! I think it is a

DIRTY song. I am thinking, "I don't want to be here. I don't like feeling DIRTY. I want to be a GOOD girl! I want to run away from this place!"

Purity

My family and I are in our car driving to church. It is Sunday. My mother is helping me with my weekly memory verse from the Bible.

"Blessed are the prrrr in heart."
"No, Diana, the word is 'pure' not prrr."
"Blessed are the prrrr in heart."
"Say, pure, Diana, not prrrr!"
"Blessed are the peerrrr in heart."

"What does prrrr mean?" I ask.
"It means very good. It means very clean," my mother says.
"Oh," I think, "that is what I want to be." "I want to be good."
"I want to be clean." "I want to be prrrr. Prrrr! Prrrrrr! Prrrrrrr!"

Real Live Lady Doll Flashbacks

I am lying in my bed. My sisters are still asleep even though it is light outside our windows. I know I should stop my dream. I know it is wrong. It makes me feel good and bad at the same time.

In the dream, I have a real-live lady doll. The lady doll is very beautiful and is always naked. She wants me to touch her and play with her. It is exciting to see a real-live, naked lady doll, but when I start feeling tingly feelings down there, I start thinking that I am not supposed to dream this dream.

Sometimes I wake up right away, but sometimes, like today, I like to keep on dreaming the dream because it feels good. After I wake up, I feel like I have done something very bad. I am a bad little girl!

Diana Lee, M.A.

Sunday School Lessons: Programming

In Sunday school, I learn about God, His Word and God's people.

The B-I-B-L-E
YES!
That's the book for me.
I stand alone on the
Word of God
the
B-I-B-L-E.

The B-I-B-L-E...

LED BY A CLOUD

God's people left Egypt. They had to cross a sea. God pushed back the water and led them through the sea on dry land. The Egyptians followed them. God took the wheels off their chariots, and they were drowned. God was taking His people to a new land. They did not know which way to go. God put a big cloud in the sky. God's people followed it. The cloud was a pillar of fire at night. They could see it all the time.

Published quarterly by the Gospel Publishing House, Springfield, Mo. Price, U. S., 8½ cents per quarter; Canadian and Foreign, 10½ cents per quarter. Entered as second-class matter, Dec. 4, 1941, at the post office at Springfield, Mo., under the Act of March 3, 1879. Printed in U. S. A.

Little Folks' FRIEND

Vol. 11   Third Quarter, 1952   No. 3
Part 3, for July 20, 1952

God's People Follow the Cloud
Memory Verse: In him will I trust.—*2 Samuel* 22:3.

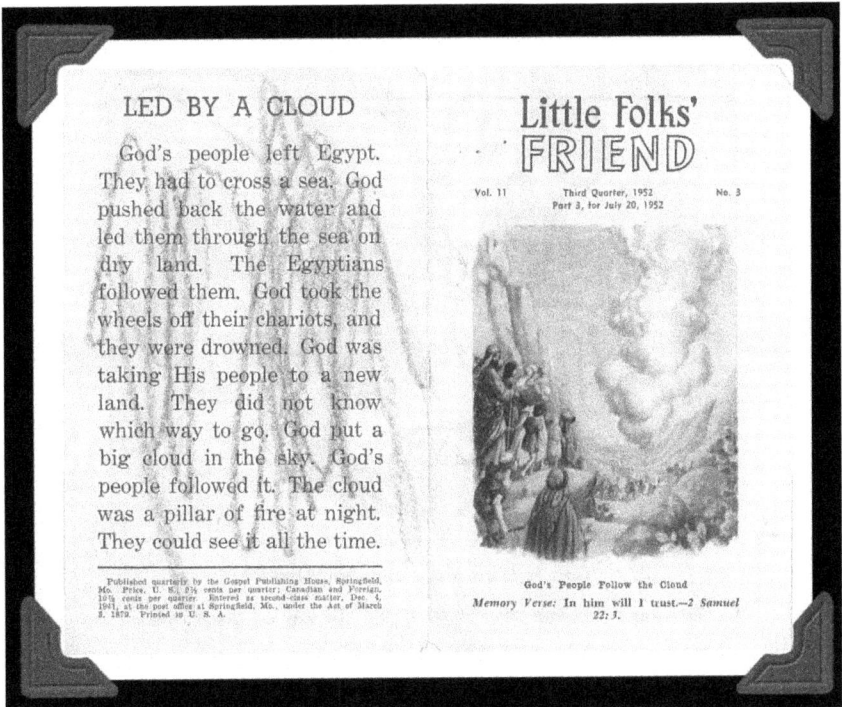

Used with permission, Gospel Publishing House

God is With Me: I Am Not Afraid

"God Is With Me; I Am Not Afraid"

MEMORY VERSE FOR NEXT SUNDAY: Thou God seest me.—*Genesis 16:13.*

Memory Verse: Thou God seest me. – Genesis 16:13

Diana Lee, M.A.

Sunday School Songs: Programming

Jesus loves me this I know
For the Bible tells me so
Little ones to Him belong
They are weak but He is strong

Yes, Jesus loves me
Yes, Jesus loves me
Yes, Jesus loves me
The Bible tells me so

Jesus loves the little children
All the children of the world
Red and yellow, black and white
They are precious in his sight
Jesus loves the little children of the world

A sunbeam a sunbeam
Jesus wants me for a sunbeam
A sunbeam a sunbeam
Jesus wants me for a sunbeam

This little light of mine
I'm gonna let it shine
This little light of mine
I'm gonna let it shine
Let it shine let it shine

Hide it under a bushel
No!
I'm gonna let it shine
Hide it under a bushel
No!
I'm gonna let it shine
Let it shine
Let it shine.

If you're happy and you know it
Clap your hands
If you're happy and you know it
Clap your hands
If you're happy and you know it
And you're not afraid to show it
If you're happy and you know it
Clap your hands
Clap! Clap!

I've got the joy, joy, joy, joy
Down in my heart
Down in my heart
Down in my heart
Down in my heart to stay.

I've got the love of Jesus
Down in my heart
Down in my heart
I've got the love of Jesus
Down in my heart
Down in my heart to stay.

Bedtime Stories: Fairy Tales and Bible Stories

Nothing is ever the same in my family. Some nights my Mommy and Daddy read to me and my sisters as we lay in bed, but most of the time they just tell us to GO TO BED!

Sometimes Mommy reads us Bible Stories from a big black book. Daddy only listens. Other times she reads fairy tales from our *Childcraft* book number three. I LOVE it when she reads and we are all together in my and my sisters' big bedroom!

Tonight the story is *The Princess and The Pea*. The princess is so prrrrr and good that even with lots of mattresses she gets bruised by a small pea that is on the bottom mattress. "I want to be like the princess," I think. "I want to be so prrrr that I can tell when anything is bad."

Tonight Mommy is reading us TWO stories! God flooded the whole world because people did not obey Him. EVEN the children and animals died! But Noah was saved because he listened to God and believed God and obeyed God. "Jesus, please help me obey God."

"Diana, stop talking with your hands!"
(Yes, Mommy.)

Child Prayer and Magical Thinking

I can hear my parents fighting. I am lying in my bed. I am supposed to be sleeping, but I cannot sleep. I feel scared. I wish they would stop fighting!

"Dear Jesus, please give my daddy gold so he will stop fighting with my mommy." Mommy has read me the story about spinning straw into gold. God can do anything! God will help my mommy and daddy.

———

I am lying in bed on another night listening to Mommy read our bedtime story, *Sleeping Beauty*. Now I am thinking about *Sleeping Beauty*. It would be good to be able to go to sleep and not wake up until I am big. I wonder how I could do that? Maybe God can help me.

———

"Diana, we are here to check you for worms."

———

"Shut your trap or I will shut it for you!"
(Yessss, Daddy.)

I remember I was only four when my daddy taught me to sing, "sticks and stones will break my bones but words will never hurt me." It made no sense to me then or now. I don't think people should throw rocks at other people or hurt them with words.

"Do you want me to beat you black and blue?"
(No, Daddy.)

Perfection

Be ye perfect [Matthew 5:48]

"I signed you up for 4-H, Diana," my mommy is telling me. "What is 4-H?" "It is for people who live on farms. It teaches skills." "But I don't live on a farm." "I think it will be good for you." "The first project is to hem a tea towel." I wonder what a tea towel is. I do not ask because I don't want to look stupid.

My mother hands me a light pink piece of fabric. It has little square patterns woven in it. She is showing me how I am supposed to thread a needle and how to make little stitches.

I try. "Like this?" I feel very proud. "No." "You need to make very small and very straight, even stitches." "It has to be PERFECT for 4-H." "Rip those stitches out and start over." I try again. And again! And again! "Like this?" "No. It still is not good enough for 4-H." I am feeling bad. I am feeling stupid. I am not good enough for 4-H. Mommy takes the fabric away from me. We do not talk about 4-H ever again.

Jesus loves me this I know for the Bible tells me so.

The Boxcar Children

School is still hard for me. I often feel confused and dumb. The other children know things I don't know. I can't figure out how they know so much! They always seem to just know what to do.

I still like my first-grade teacher. I still like the things she is teaching me: alphabet letters and numbers and reading to us, but I have trouble reading. It makes me get sweaty. It makes no sense to me. "THUH? cat…"

Today she is reading to us from *The Boxcar Children*. I would LOVE to run away from home and live with my sisters in a boxcar. I think it sounds like fun to hunt for vegetables like carrots and onions and then bring them home to the boxcar and cook them into a stew over a fire.

"If you keep crying, I'm going to give you something to cry about."
(Yes, Daddy.)

———

I love playing house and mommy. When my Betty doll acts up, I pull her panties down and spank her.

———

I Love You

My mommy and daddy went out tonight. I think they went to a church banquet, whatever that means. The word banquet sounds like something very special and fun! I'd like to go to a banquet!

I want to show Mommy how much I love her, so I have decided to clean the house for her. I have the cleanser, and I am scrubbing the bath tub and the bathroom sink. This is so much fun! I feel really grown up!

"Does your mother let you do that?" It is the older woman who is babysitting me and my two younger sisters.

"Yes," I reply, even though that is not true. I've never cleaned before. I am only six years old!

It is now morning. "Diana! WHY did you do that?" my mommy is asking me. She is very upset with me."

I am trying to tell her that I love her, but she is only upset with me.

"I had the house perfectly clean so it would be nice when the babysitter was here, and then you covered everything with Ajax cleanser!"

I feel bad. I thought I was doing something good. I guess I really am too bad to even know how to say I love you.

———

"Children are to be seen and not heard."
(Yes, Daddy.)

"Spare the rod and spoil the child!"
(Yes, Daddy.)

Comfort

Jesus loves me this I know
For the Bible tells me so
Little ones to Him belong
They are weak but he is strong

Yes, Jesus loves me
Yes, Jesus loves me
Yes, Jesus loves me

Diana Lee, M.A.

The Bible tells me so

Jesus loves the little children
All the children of the world
Red and yellow black and white...

Children's Church: Military Conditioning

Today in Children's Church, the teacher is telling us that we can trust whatever the Bible says because it is God's word.

Now we are all marching around and singing. I love singing, but I feel kind of silly marching and singing.

Onward Christian soldiers
Marching as to war
With the cross of Jesus going on before.

We are using our arms to look like we are riding a horse and shooting a gun and saluting.

I may never march in the infantry,
Ride in the cavalry,
Shoot the artillery.
I may never fly o'er the enemy,

But I'm in the Lord's army. (Yes, sir!)
I'm in the Lord's army, (yes, sir!)
I'm in the Lord's army, (yes, sir!)
I may never march in the infantry,
Ride in the cavalry,
Shoot the artillery.
I may never fly o'er the enemy,
But I'm in the Lord's army. (Yes, sir!)

Now it is time for candy. "Who knows their memory verse?"

When we sing I will make you fishers of men, we act like we are fishing. That is fun. I LOVE fishing!

———————

"Do you want me to blister your fanny?"
(No, Daddy.)

> *Jesus...loves.....me......this........I...........*
> *know........for.........the............Bible..........*
> *tells.............me..........so!*

Uuuuuuuuhhhhh! Uuuuu! Uuuuuh!
"Stop crying or I'll give you something to cry about!"
Uuu!
(Yes, Daddy.)

"Diana, stop talking with your hands!"
(Yes, Mommy.)

Remembering Life at Four Years Old

When I was four years old, I lived in a very nice apartment near First and Grant, not far from downtown Denver. We had older neighbors named Mr. and Mrs. Escher. They were very kind to me but they told my mommy I use bad words like, "suuuum thilly jackass!" Another neighbor complained because I lifted her dress while she was hanging up clothes and told her, "My mommy's legs are only this big," as I used my hands to show her.

I could sometimes see a man who sold peanuts from a cute cart as I looked out from my bedroom window. When I looked through my bedroom window the screen made it look like there was a cross on the moon. The cross made me think of Jesus and feel him close to me.

Sometimes at night when it was snowing, my daddy and I walked across the bridge over Cherry Creek and got chocolate shower ice cream at the Purity Creamery. That was fun! I LOVE chocolate shower ice cream!

I also remember one night after dinner. It was dark outside. I was playing with my daddy in the living room. He made bubbles for my sister and me by making soapy water in a small bowl and then using an empty wood thread spool like a pipe to blow bubbles. It felt really good to be playing with my family!

After playing bubbles, Daddy started wrestling with me on the floor and tickling me until I screamed for him to stop. It was horrible when he kept tickling me and I was crying for him to stop.

Then he started saying, "Diana, I was actually born a little girl." I knew he was teasing me by the look in his eyes. "No, you weren't!"

But he kept it up. His eyes got serious. "Yes. I am telling you the truth. All boys are actually little girls before they become boys. I wore a dress just like you."

Because he started talking seriously, I felt confused. I wondered, "Is it really true?" Something did not feel good. My head started hurting bad. BAD!

Blaming His Victim?

Today is Saturday. I am feeling very sad and lonely. Something bad has happened. Daddy was sitting on a kitchen side chair in the living room. I love Daddy, so I climbed up onto his lap and faced him and started hugging him. I felt very close to him, just like we were one person. I felt HAPPY and SILLY. I was only teasing, kidding, being a little kid.

That is why I feel so EMBARRASSED now, HUMILIATED, even though I don't understand why what I did was so wrong. Sniff. Sniff.

I really wasn't trying to make him mad. I was playing. I was really trying to show him how MUCH I love him. How close I feel to him! I thought it would be funny, not bad. I thought he would laugh, not get ANGRY!

I had been eating a cherry Popsicle, and I still had a little piece of ice in my mouth. When I kissed Daddy on the lips, I shot that little piece of ice into his mouth with the tip of my tongue. I thought he would start laughing, but he did not. Instead, VERY disgusted, he yelled, "DIANA!" and he THREW me off of his lap and walked away.

Now I feel brokenhearted. My daddy is mad at me. Why am I such a bad little girl? Why don't I know how to do things right like other kids? ALL the other kids seem to know things that I do not know. How do they know what I don't know? How can I learn what they know? Why isn't God helping me? I pray to Jesus to help me all the time. I don't LIKE being STUPID! I don't like not knowing what to do. I don't like always being WRONG!

―――

"Stop your crying or I will give you something to cry about!" (Yes, Daddy.)

―――

Jesus loves me this I know
For the Bible tells me so
Little ones to Him belong
They are weak but He is strong

Funny Eyes

I still don't understand what happens to me! At school, my eyes get blurry and my head feels fuzzy and I get headaches. It is hard to see and hard to pay attention to the teacher. I don't feel good when this happens. My head feels funny. I sometimes feel dizzy and like I might throw up. I don't feel like myself. It comes and goes, and I cannot figure out what makes it happen. Sometimes I do not feel like I am in my body. Isn't that silly? Sometimes I feel like a balloon flying in the sky or a really little person too tiny for my BIG body.

Mommy and Daddy took me to the optometrist my middle sister goes to for her crossed eyes. He said there is nothing wrong with my eyes. He thinks it is eye strain. I now have light pink glasses with silver sparkles. I look funny in them, and they do not help. I don't like wearing them, so I often set them on top of my school desk.

I wish I could figure this out. I feel odd because I don't know when the blurriness will come or what makes it go away. I sometimes have very clear eyes. I like it when that happens. It makes me feel really good and like I'm okay, but then they go back to blurry again.

My head does the same thing. Most of the time it feels fuzzy, but sometimes it feels very clear. I feel dumb when it is fuzzy, and I feel smart when it is clear!

———

Every night before I go to sleep, Mommy comes and sits on the edge of my bed. "It is time to say your prayer." "Now I lay me down to sleep, I pray the Lord my soul to keep. If I should die before I wake, I pray the Lord my soul to take." This prayer scares me. I do not want to die in my sleep. I say it because I am afraid of the boogie-man who I'm afraid is under my bed.

Choosing the Kind of Person I Want To Be

Tonight we are all in our bedroom and it is one of the happy nights that Mommy is reading stories to us and Daddy is sitting on the bed listening. Both of them are sitting on my middle sister's bed, and I am in my bed. My youngest sister is on her bed near the foot of ours.

My mommy is reading *The Emperor's New Clothes*. It is so funny that the Emperor is walking around with no clothes and he doesn't even know it. That is silly! Why doesn't anyone tell him? Why do they pretend he is okay when he isn't? That does not make sense!

"Dear Jesus, I want to be smart and good like the little boy who saw the Emperor had no clothes and was brave enough to tell him."

Thinking in Pictures like Temple Grandin

"DON'T give me that look, sister!"

"But...but...but...I don't understand."

"DO I (sigh) **HAVE** to DRAW YOU a Picture?"

(I must be stupid.)

Obey Parents or Die!

"Children, obey your parents that your days upon the earth may be long." This was our Sunday school lesson today. It is in the Bible, so it is true. I don't want to die, so I obey. Mostly!

"Diana, stop talking with your hands!"

(Yes, Mommy.)

"Diana, stick a sock in it!"
(Yes, Daddy.)

"I was so happy until…."

"WHAT DID YOU SAY TO ME?"

"Nothing."
(I didn't think he could hear me mumbling to myself.)

A sunbeam, a sunbeam
Jesus wants me for a sunbeam
A sunbeam, a sunbeam
Jesus wants me for a sunbeam.

I've got the joy, joy, joy, joy

Mommy Is Our Doctor

I am not going to school today. I feel sick. "Diana, roll over on your stomach," Mother is saying. She is giving me an enema. She is filling me with water. It hurts. She does not care. I get lots of enemas. My baby sister says we get them every time we sneeze!

Two days have gone past. I have been in my bed all alone. All I've had to eat is orange juice. I am SO hungry! I am tired of being in bed and all alone. I can smell dinner. Everyone is in the kitchen eating but me. I want to eat!

I get out of bed and walk from my bedroom through the living room and into the kitchen where my parents and two sisters are seated at the table eating dinner. "I am hungry. I want some fried shrimp, too." "You cannot have any because you are sick, Diana. Now go back to bed," my mommy says. "I will bring you some more fresh-squeezed orange juice after we finish eating." "But I am HUNGRY now!" "Diana, go back to bed," she says again.

I am back in bed, and now I feel worse because I know the rest of the family is eating some of my favorite foods: fried shrimp, pork and beans, and vanilla cake with coconut frosting. I feel sad. I feel alone. I feel hungry. This is awful!

_____

I sing my Sunday school songs in my head when I feel sad and lonely.

Little ones to Him belong
They are weak but HE is strong...

Crawfish: Above the Law

I am still living in the rental house. Tonight I got awakened because Mommy wanted me to see the crawfish that are crawling around on the grass in our backyard. LOTS of them! They are crawling out of a big canvas bag that daddy is holding on the ground. My mother has a large pot of water boiling on the stove.

My father gets the crawfish from traps in the ocean. The crawfish are really big and scary looking. They walk funny and have a fat tail and EYES at the end of a long spiky thing. Daddy doesn't own the traps, but he explains that there is a special law, so it is okay if he takes them. My daddy is SO smart. He knows EVERYTHING!

He likes to listen to country music on the radio. There is a song I like about crawfish pie and gumbo or something like that. I think it is a fun song, even though it is not a church song. It makes me want to dance, but dancing is a sin. So I NEVER dance. That jumbo-gumbo pie song was on the radio the time I saw Daddy open the refrigerator door and I saw a bottle of wine. It was about half full. But ASSEMBLY of GODERS are NOT SUPPOSED to drink WINE. It is BAD! He will go to HELL!

I am not eating crawfish. Just they are. I have to go back to bed. My sisters are still sleeping. They do not even know what was in our backyard tonight, but I do 'cause I'm the oldest.

———

The wise man built his house upon the rock
The wise man built his house upon the rock
The wide man built his house upon the rock
And the rain came tumbling down

Oh the rain came down
And the floods came up
The rain came down
And the floods came up
The rain came down
And the floods came up
And the wise man's house stood firm

The foolish man built his house upon the sand
The foolish man built his house upon the sand
The foolish man built his house upon the sand
And the rain came tumbling down

Oh, the rain came down
And the floods came up
The rain came down
And the floods came up
The rain came down
And the floods came up
And the foolish man's house went "splat!" [clap hands once]

I Need My Loving Grandmother

I want to talk to Mom. Mom is my grandmother who lives in Denver. She loves me.

I want to tell her I do not like what happens at my house. I have decided to draw a secret coded message like the ones on Saturday morning kid TV shows. I want her to come get me!

I drew a picture of me, but it doesn't make any sense! I drew a big circle on my tummy because I THOUGHT I had a hole in my tummy, but when I pulled my shorts down and looked at my tummy, I didn't see the big hole! I feel confused. Why would I draw a hole when I don't have a hole?

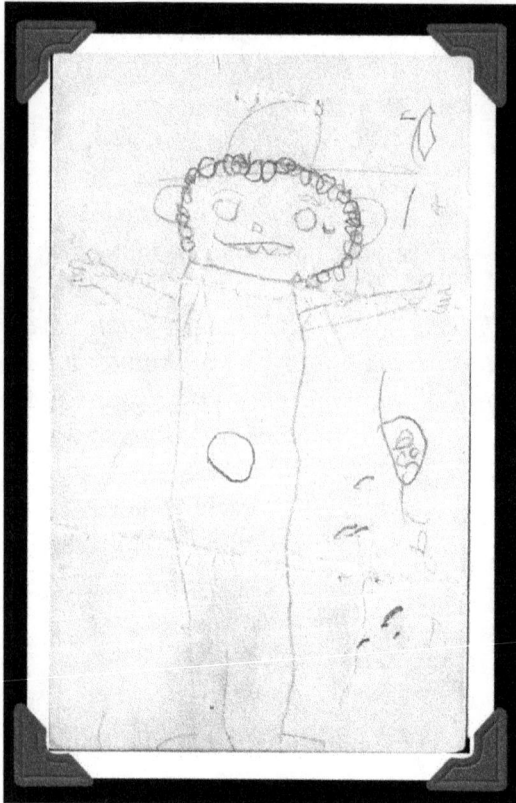

Original primary source document returned in 1989 when Mom died

I am trying to think of how else I can do this. How can I draw a picture so Mom will understand?

I am walking around my room thinking. Now I am sitting at the head of my bed with my back up against the white wall. I am drawing on the little piece of thin white cardboard that was inside the package my Three Musketeers candy bar came in. (That is my FAVORITE!)

I feel very frustrated. I don't know how to draw my body. How do I draw INSIDE me when I don't know what it looks like? Where is that HOLE that goes inside me?

After thinking for some time, I decide to try to draw what my inside FEELS like. As I close my eyes, I focus my attention on what it FELT like. I just let my pencil draw. When I stop, I am surprised to see that it is many circles, one inside of the other. So SO THAT is what my inside looks like!

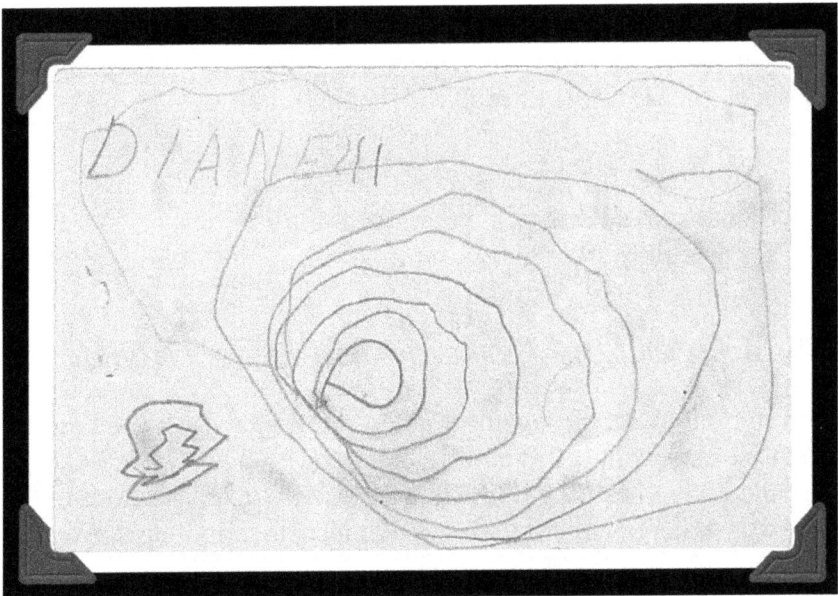

Original primary source document returned when Mom died in 1989
[Notice: I have already changed my name from Diana to Diane. This is common for traumatized children "The trauma is happening to her – not me!"]

I ask my mommy to mail my drawing to Mom. Today is June 8, 1953.

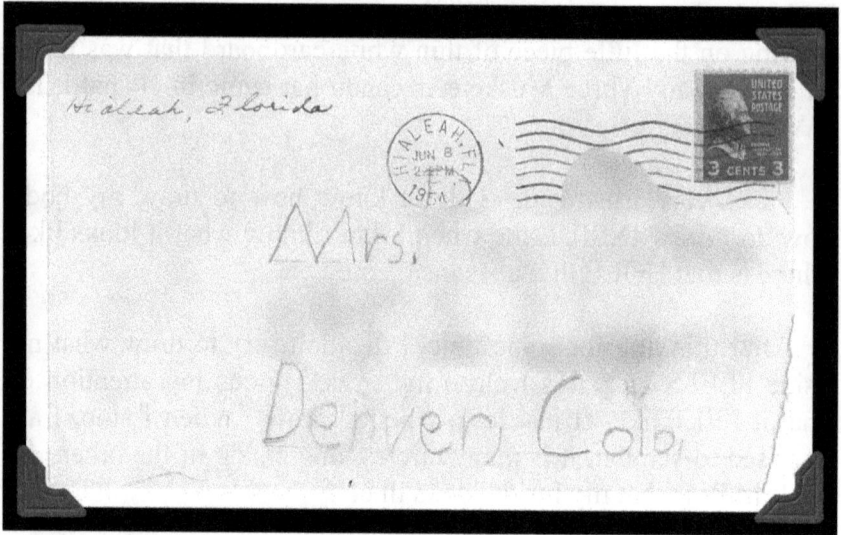

Dear Jesus, please help Mom understand my secret coded message. Please tell her to COME GET ME. NOW!

———

"Diana, stop talking with your hands!"
(Yes, Mommy.)

Sunday School Lesson: God Uses Tricksters

I am in Sunday school again. I am here every week! I am sitting around a table with all the other children my age. My teacher is very nice. She is sitting in the middle. There is a big cutout in the table top where she sits, so she is close to all of us. We are working on our paperwork, cutting with little scissors, pasting and coloring. I am still thinking about the story we heard in the big room with all the other children. The teachers use a flannel-graph board with colored pictures to tell us Bible stories.

Today when the other teacher told us about how Rebecca and Jacob tricked blind Isaac into blessing Jacob instead of Esau, something inside my chest felt sorry for Isaac and Esau. But the teacher told us God WANTED Isaac to bless Jacob because that was His plan. Jacob valued the birthright and blessing, and Esau didn't. Esau was not a good person. He did not trust God. So God took away his special gift, just like that, but I still feel sorry for him. I wouldn't want Rebecca and Jacob to treat me like that! I don't like them! To trick an old, blind man is MEAN. I don't understand why God wants people to be MEAN. Why didn't God make a better plan? I feel confused. I just don't understand God. Why punish Esau for being hungry? I get hungry!

God Tests Peoples' Love and Obedience

I didn't like the story Mommy read about God letting Satan hurt Job, either! Job was such a good person! I felt sorry for all of his children who died and were replaced with new ones, just like they never even existed. I would miss them!

A Fountain Flowing with Blood?

Deep and wide
deep and wide
there's a fountain flowing
deep and wide.

This is my most favorite Sunday school song! We stretch our arms as wide as we can and then as high and low as we can, and that is fun.

"Mommy, what does it mean?"

"There is a deep and wide fountain of blood flowing from the sword wound in Jesus' side. It is flowing to cover all the sins of the world."

"Oh! BLOOD! A fountain of blood! I was picturing a huge fountain of clean, fresh water rising high into the sky and little children playing under it. I wonder how I got that so mixed up," I think to myself.

Mom Left Me Behind: Rage!

I really love my grandparents. They are my mommy's parents– Mom and Grandpa. I really love my two aunts, also. I can tell they love me, too. They buy me candy, and they send me pretty dresses and birthday cards with dollars for my sock, and they hold me on their lap and give me hugs and kisses.

They live a long way away in Denver, where I used to live and where I was born in 1947 in Saint Luke's Hospital. I have not seen them for a LONG time, and I have really missed them! I have been so HAPPY because they have been here visiting us for the last whole week.

When they left today in their car, I felt VERY sad. I wanted to go with them so badly. My middle sister wanted to go with them, too. When they started to get into their Chevy, they found her crouched on the floor behind the front seat trying to make herself little enough so she would not be seen, but they found her and told her she had to stay. They laughed. They did not understand.

I began to feel very, very, VERY angry because I did not want to be left behind. I cried as they drove out of our driveway. Then I ran to our backyard where I could cry without being seen.

When I got into the back, I saw a large turtle. It was about 6" long. Before I knew it, I picked up the turtle and began throwing it against the pile of cinder blocks that I use to make my playhouses. I could not stop myself. I just kept picking up that poor little turtle and throwing it as hard as I could against those cement blocks.

When I saw that it had blood on its back shell, I remembered that God stopped when he saw the blood on the Israelites' doorposts. He did not kill their baby boys, but I still threw it one more time. I stopped and looked at how helpless the turtle was, and then I picked it up again and threw it one more time.

Then I ran into my bedroom. Now I feel so bad and ashamed because the neighbor's Great Dane saw me. I have never killed anything before. Now I KNOW that I REALLY am a bad little girl. There is something VERY wrong with me! I NEVER want ANYONE to EVER know that I might have killed a poor little turtle. BAD, BAD, BAD little girl!

Will its ghost find me? Did GOD see? Will I go to Hell? Can I hide? No!

Don't Want to Be Left behind Again: Accepting Jesus as My Savior

Terrorism...n. (1795): the systematic use of terror esp. as a means of coercion. (Webster's)

I am still six years old. Tonight I am sitting on the front row center of my church with my girlfriend Pat. The preacher is telling us all about Hell. I listen to EVERY word and feel scared.

The fold-up seats are covered in a dark golden tan Naugahide that makes my legs sweat as I sit and listen. It is a hot sticky Miami, Florida, summer night. Our church does not have air conditioning.

The preacher is REALLY upset. He shouts REALLY loudly. The chrome microphone is almost as tall as he is, and he carries it in both hands as he paces back and forth across the wide platform. He has a large white handkerchief in his pants pocket, and he occasionally stops walking so he can wipe off the sweat that is pouring down his forehead. His jacket is off. His white shirt is wet. His red tie is crooked. His bald head is shining with perspiration.

Somehow he manages to carry his Bible along with his microphone and handkerchief. He looks scary and silly at the same time. He is saying I will go to Hell and burn in the flames that will never die if I have sinned ONE time. God cannot tolerate ANY sin because he is prrrr. He also tells me Jesus is coming back SOON, and if I have even one sin, I will be LEFT BEHIND and will not go to Heaven with Him. I will go through the end of the world and the bloody battle of Armageddon. He says a great FIRE is going to destroy the world.

"Stop and think!" "You must make a CHOICE -- TONIGHT!" "Do you want to go to Hell when you die and burn in the Lake of Fire where there will be weeping and wailing and gnashing of teeth, or do you want to accept Jesus as your savior?" "Jesus is coming back soon." "Do you want to be LEFT BEHIND when Jesus comes?" "What will happen to you if you should die before you wake up tomorrow?" "What will happen to you if Jesus comes TONIGHT?" "We are in the end times." "There is a nuclear science magazine with a big clock on the cover, and the time is now set at 5 minutes before midnight." "Even ATOMIC SCIENTISTS know the world is about to end." "Repent and be saved."

As the organist begins to play "Softly and Tenderly Jesus is Calling," I feel guilty. I know with a capital "S" that I have SINNED and that I am SINFUL. Yesterday I lied to my mother when she asked who cut paper with her fabric scissors. I didn't say, "Not me," and I didn't admit it was me. I just stayed quiet.

Now I am feeling guilty and afraid that I will go to Hell because I lied to my mother. As the organ continues to play, I lean over to ask Pat if she would like to walk forward to the altar with me. She agrees. We both walk the three or four feet to the wood altar and bend down on our knees "before the Lord" and ask Jesus into "our wicked hearts." I feel better. I feel clean. I feel safe. My parents do not say anything–ever.

*What
can
wash
away
my
sins?*

*Nothing
but
the
blood
of
Jesus!*

*What
can
make
me
whole
again?*

*Nothing
but
the
blood
of
Jesus!*

*Oh,
precious
is
the
flow
that
makes
me
white
as
Snoooooooow!*

No
other
fount
I know
nothing
but the blood of Jesus!

Escaping into My Head: Dissociation

I love the story of *Hansel and Gretel.* It scares me when the witch locks Hansel in a cage and tries to push Gretel into her oven. I do not like those parts at all. What I like is how they are able to run away from home and their mean stepmother. I like that they use the moon to see in the dark and that they learn to leave stones on the path so they can find their way back if they decide to go home to their loving father.

As I lay on my bed tonight listening to Mommy read, I am wondering if I could ever be smart enough to run away from home. My middle sister ran away when she was four, but someone found her and brought her back home. I felt sorry for her.

As I keep listening, I wonder if it is possible to run away in my head. What could I use instead of stones so I can find my way back? I don't want to get lost in there. Daddy tells me I have rocks in my head. I wish I did!

Now I am feeling scared because I am thinking what I am thinking. CAN people get lost in their own head? It seems pretty big in there, and DARK. That is SO scary!

I am going to just try it a little bit to see what happens. I will be very careful. I hope the Devil doesn't get me in there!

Diana Lee, M.A.

Scrambled Brains: Always Wrong!

It is a different Saturday morning. I am standing at the foot of my bed. Daddy just walked in. He is standing next to me. He looks down into my face. I am looking up at his. He says, "Diana, you need to know something. You don't understand things correctly. You ALWAYS get things mixed-up and wrong." Now he is walking back out of the bedroom. Something does not feel right, but I am not sure exactly what it is.

I feel shocked! I feel confused! I feel dumb! I feel humiliated! Part of me thought I was smart. I guess I was wrong.

I am SO glad I am not a boy. Boys have to grow up and work and take care of their family. I am too dumb to do that. I am so glad I am a girl. I LOVE my dolls and playing house!

———

"Wipe that look off your face right now!"
(Yes, Daddy.)

Why Do We Girls Have to Go to Bed so Early?

I am standing at my bedroom window. It faces the street. I see the neighborhood kids playing in the street. Some are jumping rope, some are running around, some are riding bikes. It is still very light outside, but my mommy and daddy say my sisters and I have to go to bed. I feel very sad. I don't know the other kids, but I want to. I want to be outside with them. I feel lonely. I want to be like the other kids. I feel brokenhearted. I feel trapped. I wish I could just climb out the window.

———

"Diana, we are here to check you for worms"

———

I don't understand. I feel confused as I wipe the sleep from my eyes. I have been sound asleep, but now Mommy is waking me up in the middle of the night, but not to check my worms.

"Brother and Sister Brown, our church friends, are here, and they brought Pat." (Why is she up in the middle of the night?) (Why do we have company in the middle of the night?) Pat is my friend who accepted Jesus with me. I am very surprised my parents woke me up to PLAY and have FUN. I didn't know they could do that! I am surprised they would only wake me up and not my two sisters. I feel special!

I am walking into the kitchen and am more surprised to see my FATHER has baked an applesauce CAKE. I didn't know my father COULD bake a cake! He says cooking is women's work. He NEVER does ANYTHING in the KITCHEN! MY FATHER BAKED A CAKE? This is SO confusing. Mommies are SUPPOSED to bake the CAKES. How did Pat know we had cake? In the middle of the night? We don't have a telephone!

More Undermining

"Diana, your younger sister is SO smart. She knows EVERYTHING. ALWAYS follow what she does," I hear my mother telling me. "Try to be like her." Splash, splash go my tears. I thought I was smart! What will I do when she is not around?

———

"Did you know people who hate green are crazy?" my smart sister is asking me. "I guess I better always like green," I think. I don't want people to think I'm crazy! I've overheard people at church talking. They say Rosa's husband tells her that she is crazy because she speaks in tongues and goes to our church. I wonder why he says that. Something makes me wonder if it is true.

"Diana, stop talking with your hands!"
Hhhhhhhhhmmmmmmmmppppppphhhhhh!
(Yes, Mommy.)

Aftershock

I am still the same little girl. I am standing on the black asphalt play area at my school with the rest of my class on a warm Florida day. The sky is blue with a few clouds. I am not feeling well. My head feels fuzzy. I feel sick to my stomach, dizzy. I am sweating. The teacher told us to make a circle. That was not hard for me to do, but now my hands are feeling sweaty too because I feel confused. Actually, if I tell the whole truth, I have to say I feel panicky. The teacher told us to move counter clockwise in our circle, and I do not know what that means. "That means move to your left."

Oh! But I do not know which way is right and which way is left. I quickly look down at my little hands hoping to figure it out. "Which is which," I wonder? "Is this my left or my right hand?" Because I know that I am "NOT smart," and know "I always get EVERYTHING wrong," and am not smart like my sister, I do not trust myself. I really do not want to make a mistake in front of my entire class. As I look at both of my hands trying not to let anyone see me, I am trying to figure out which to choose. I know that no matter which one I choose, I will choose the wrong one because "I always get EVERYTHING wrong."

I make my choice, and then I do the opposite. That way I should be right. I move. I am wrong. I feel embarrassed. I feel stupid! My head is spinning. I hurry to catch up with the other kids hoping no one has seen my mistake. Nobody says anything. I am safe for the moment. (Thank goodness Freddie is not around.)

ShaTterED DianA

Why can't I be like a normal kid? Why can't I be like all the other kids? How do they know EVERYTHING -- all the things I do not know? I HATE being STUPID! I HATE school! I want Jesus!

———

I've got a home in Glory land that outshines the sun
I've got a home in glory land that outshines the sun
I've got a home in glory land that outshines the sun
    Way beyond the blue.

Do Lord, oh do Lord
Oh do remember me
Do Lord, oh do Lord
Oh do remember me
Do Lord, oh do Lord
Oh do remember me
Way beyond the blue.

Stained Glass: Compartmentalizing

My sisters are outside playing because it is Saturday. I am sitting on the asphalt-tile floor in our bedroom. I love to draw what I call stained glass. I take my sheet of paper and my black crayon, and I draw lines all over it. They crisscross over each other and create little boxes. I like to make them different sizes and shapes. Inside each little box, I color in a different color. When I finish the entire page, I think it looks very beautiful. I don't remember when I first started drawing like this, but I do it often now. It is fun, and it makes me feel good.

Recreation; no originals survived.

Terror

It is summer. I am in my bedroom alone with my mother. She is cleaning and telling me about a man who killed all of his children while they slept because he did not want them to have to live in such an evil world. I do not say anything. Is she going to kill me while I am asleep? My little sisters too?

I cannot feel anything. I am numb. I am frozen. I am like Lot's wife who turned into a pillar of salt. I cannot simply walk away. I cannot even FEEL my body.

I remember when I was four, she told about a mother who killed her little boys and chopped them up and put them in bags for the garbage men to take away. I am AFRAID of my mommy!

———

It is still summer. Mommy is busy cleaning the kitchen. She SAYS she found some candy she did not know she had. I have never seen any candy like this before. The pieces are chunky golden squares and are sprinkled with powdered sugar. It makes me think of mothballs. I KNOW mothballs are POISONOUS. My sisters are happy to get candy. I tell Mommy I do not want any. Part of me DOES NOT TRUST HER! I am afraid she IS trying to KILL me! But I don't understand where that thought came from. Part of me knows it is PROBABLY candy, but I still say no, just to be SURE.

———

"Diana, do you want me to hit you in the head with a ball-peen hammer?
(No, Daddy.)

Jesus loves me this I know
For the Bible tells me so
Little ones to Him belong
They are weak but HE is STRONG!

Jesus with children Wikimedia 2013

My Church

My church is a big, two-story, white, stucco building. It has big, red, neon letters on the roof that say, *The wages of sin is death.* Sometimes, one of my great-grandmothers plays the piano. My other great-grandmother puts grape juice in all the little cups for Communion. In Sunday school and children's church, I learn lots of songs.

O be careful little eyes what you see
O be careful little eyes what you see
There's a Father up above
And He's looking down in love
So, be careful little eyes what you see

O be careful little ears what you hear
O be careful little ears what you hear
There's a Father up above
And He's looking down in love
So, be careful little ears what you hear

O be careful little hands what you do
O be careful little hands what you do
There's a Father up above
And He's looking down in love

So, be careful little hands what you do

O be careful little feet where you go
O be careful little feet where you go
There's a father up above
And He's looking down in love
So, be careful little feet where you go

O be careful little mouth what you say
O be careful little mouth what you say
There's a Father up above
And He's looking down in love
So, be careful little mouth what you say

———

"Diana, curiosity killed the cat!
(Yes, Daddy!)

The Fire Truck: Programmed Not to Fear Death

I am walking home from school. It is a nice day. I am walking along the canal by myself. There is no one around. I am almost ready to cross Red Road when I see a fire truck coming toward me. I wonder what will happen if I run out in front of it instead of waiting for it to pass? There are no other cars, just the fire truck. I run out in front of it. It honks at me in an angry way. Why did I do that? Why wasn't I scared?

———

"Do you want me to smack you in the face?"
(No, Daddy.)

Isolating from the Evil World
Protects Predators

Mommy tells me I am not supposed to make friends with "the world." "The World" are all the people who do not go to my church. We are in my bedroom and talking as she is making my sister's bed. She is telling me our church is the TRUE church and only the people in our church will go to Heaven when they die. So I am not supposed to be around the other people who will be going to Hell.

This makes me feel sad. I wonder if the nice neighbors who invited us over to play in their outdoor pool are going to Hell? I never got to see them again, and I had SO MUCH FUN at their house! There were lots of mommy's and children and cookies and Kool-Aid.

What about the kids whose daddy works with my daddy? They invited us over for yummy spaghetti, and we played on their very own merry-go-round, but I never saw them again either. What about the other kids whose daddy works with my daddy — the ones we went to the beach with? That was SUCH a FUN day! I never saw them again. What about my friends at school? They are very nice! Their mommy's give me juice. They sometimes drive me to school. What about little Ann down the street? Her parents let me play on her swings whenever I want, even if they are not home. (That's where I was swinging when I saw the HUGE full moon and decided it didn't look scary to me!) SOMETHING about this does not FEEL right.

———

"Do you want me to whip you until you can't sit down?"
(No, Daddy.)

I've got the joy, joy, joy, joy
Down in my heart
Down in my heart

47

Down in my heart
Down in my heart to stay!

"Do you want me to skin you alive?"
(No, Daddy.)

If you're happy and you know it
Clap your hands

"Diana, you are cruisin' for a bruisin'!"
(Yes, Daddy.)

Mom's House

I have been having SO MUCH FUN in Denver at Mom's! Today she made us spice cake with brown sugar frosting. Oh, yummy! It is the best cake I have ever tasted! And for lunch, we had Franco-American spaghetti out of a can. I LOVED it! I'm eating things I've never had before. And in Mom's refrigerator there is a very BIG clear drawer that is filled to the top with oranges.

My sisters and I played outside with Pal all afternoon. Pal is Mom's collie. He looks just like Lassie! Yesterday, Mom asked me to cut Pal's hair. Well, that did not turn out so good. Pal now has ridges. Everyone was surprised I didn't know how to cut his hair, but it is okay. Everyone just laughed and said, "It will grow out."

I love being around my grown-up aunts and uncle. This house feels so good. It is fun here. We are spending the ENTIRE summer here. My mommy packed ALL of our clothes in big round cardboard missionary barrels. ALL of our clothes! Daddy didn't come, just we three girls and Mommy.

My uncle has a brand-new black and white 1955 Chevy.

Uh, oh! Something bad just happened, and Mom and Mommy are very upset with my middle sister. (My SMART sister.) Mom asked her to do something, and my sister, who is 11 months younger than me, said, "No! You cannot tell me what to do. You are just an old nigger washerwoman!" Mommy is washing her mouth out with soap.

The phone is ringing. It is my aunts' friend from church. He called to talk to them, but he asked to talk to me first. He is silly-teasing me and making me laugh. He tells me that when I grow up he is going to marry me. He gave me a ring from the Crackerjacks box. I am only seven! My aunts are getting dressed up. They are going to something called a rodeo in Cheyenne. I don't know where Cheyenne is, but I really want to go there someday. I love the word Cheyenne. Cheyenne! Cheyenne!

I am now sitting on the porch waving goodbye to my aunts as they leave with their boyfriends. It is a beautiful evening. Mom has me and my sisters snuggled up in a blanket next to her as we sit on her yellow metal glider and talk and laugh. I like the candy corn she is feeding us. Mom is always fun! She makes me feel good.

Across the street, I see the Rio Grande train roar past the gravel pit. I love hearing its whistle. I can see all the way to the Gates Rubber Plant!

This is a perfect world. A loving place! "Yes. I'd love another piece of candy corn. Thank you, Mom!"

———

"Diana! I've told you before! Stop talking with your hands!" (Yes, Mommy.)

ShaTterED DianA

No Laughing

My
sisters
and
I
are
acting
silly
and
laughing.

My
mother
interrupts
our
fun.

"Don't
laugh
too
hard
or
soon
you
will
be
crying."

Is
fun
a
sin,
also?

Bedtime in Denver

I don't like it when the grownups – Mom, grandpa, my uncle, my two aunts, and Mommy – make my sisters and me go to bed so they can sit up and talk and laugh. I really don't like it because they close the door tight. I am afraid of the dark. I am also afraid because they tell me someone might peek in the window – Mexicans.

It helps that they play records for us. When they ask me which ones I want to hear, I always say Gene Autry's *Peter Cottontail* and *The Old Rugged Cross*.

Here comes Peter Cottontail hoppin' down the bunny trail...

On a hill far away stood an old rugged cross, the emblem of suffering and shame...for a world of lost sinners was slain...so I'll cherish the old rugged cross till my trophies at last I lay down; I will cling to the old rugged cross, and exchange it someday for a crown...

The Old Rugged Cross helps me think about Jesus, and that makes me feel safe. Thinking about Peter, makes me feel happy.

I can hear the grownups laughing.

"Oh, Lord!"

Now Mommy is talking, "I can move just one thing in a room, and Diana will notice as soon as she walks into the room."

I didn't know she did that! I think that means there is something good about me. I hope I can keep doing it!

Keep Family Secrets or Hurt the Lord's Work

Mom is in her bedroom when I come out of the bathroom across the hall. (Her bathroom always smells like soap – nice soap.)

"Diana, come here. I want to talk to you a minute." I am now in her bedroom. Her curtains are shut because she has been resting. "Diana, never tell anyone what happens in your family. If people find out, it will hurt the ministries of your aunts and uncles."

I shake my head okay and walk out. I don't know what she is talking about. I would never hurt the Lord's work!

———

Today my aunts and their best girlfriend from church drove up into the mountains to Buffalo Bill's grave and a place called Berthoud Pass. They bought me and my sisters a silver bracelet with REAL turquoise in it. It is a REAL Indian bracelet! I love it! It was a cool day, and Mom made homemade applesauce for us. I love this place!

Confused and Confusing

I love listening to my aunts sing because they harmonize:

> *Give me oil in my lamp*
> *keep me burning*
> *burning, burning*
> *burning*
> *till the break of day!*

"What does oil in my lamp mean?" I ask my Aunt Bebe. "Diana, it means that we are the lamp and the Holy Spirit is the oil that lights us up and directs us and gives us the energy we need to do the Lord's work."

In Sunday school, I sing:

This little light of mine
I'm gonna let it shine
This little light of mine
I'm gonna let it shine
Let it shine
Let it shine
Let it shine.

Hide it under a bushel?
NO!
I'm gonna let it shine.
Hide it under a bushel?
NO!
I'm gonna let it shine
Let it shine
Let it shine
Let it shine.

Yes! This is what I want to be – a lamp that Jesus lives in and shines out into "the world" like a sunbeam.

Time to Leave Denver

It is time for us to leave Mom's house and go back home. EVERYONE feels very SAD.

Mom fried chicken for us to take with us on the Trailways bus, and she also packed green grapes and brownies. My uncle drove us to the bus station, but he drove too fast and got a ticket. I liked riding in the back seat of his new Chevy!

The bus is now driving along the highway, and I can look out the window, but I feel SO SAD. I and my sisters are crying. The chicken and grapes make us think of Mom and how much we miss her already.

We cannot stop crying. WE DO NOT WANT TO GO HOME. Mommy is sad, too. The bus stops at a little town called Springfield, Colorado. Mommy is asking the bus driver if he will let us off and get our barrels. He says, "Yes. Of course, I will." We get to go back to Denver and Mom's house! Hurray!

Evangelical Fundamentalist Child's Understanding of Salvation

Accepting Jesus as my savior and asking him into my heart means I have been washed in his blood. When God looks at me now, he sees I am covered with Jesus' blood instead of covered in sin. I am prrrr because of Jesus precious blood!

What can wash away my sin?
Nothing but the blood of Jesus!
What can make me whole again?
Nothing but the blood of Jesus!

Oh! Precious is the flow
That makes me white as snow;
No other fount I know,
Nothing but the blood of Jesus!

I love Jesus…becaaaaauuuussseeee He first loved me.

Brand New House

I no longer live in the rental house. Mommy and Daddy bought a brand-NEW house! A real house in a new subdivision! It is so beautiful! We have three bedrooms, a beautiful pink and maroon bathroom, a living room with really big jalousie windows that go almost to the ceiling and all along the wall that looks out on the backyard, a beautiful copper colored kitchen, and a utility room. All the floors are terrazzo. I LOVE THIS HOUSE!

My job will be to clean the pink and maroon bathroom tile every Saturday with Bon-Ami to keep it shiny.

Mommy says I get a room of my own because I am the oldest. My two sisters share the big pink room that is right next to mine. My room is Wedgwood blue. That means it is kind of gray blue. Mommy is busy making pinch-pleated curtains for ALL the windows. (She must be smart.)

I can hardly sleep tonight because I feel so happy and excited. This new house smells good! Tonight, Mommy gave me a beautiful chenille bedspread for my new BIG double bed. The bedspread is white with pink trim and flowers that are yellow and pink with green vines and leaves. I think my bed looks like a big birthday cake. I love it! Everyone is in my room looking at my new bed spread. I am jumping all around with joy.

Tinkerbelle's Fairy Dust: Dissociating

I am very scared as I lie in my bed tonight. I am TOO SCARED to go to sleep. But tomorrow is a school day; I must get to sleep. "Dear Jesus, please help me get to sleep." I am lying very still. I am on my back. My arms are by my side. I am imagining that Tinkerbelle's fairy dust is floating down from the ceiling. The flakes look like little sparkles of gold glitter. Slowly, slowly they begin to cover me up. I keep imagining them falling all around me until I am fully covered up and am no longer frightened and feel safe in my bed. Now my eyes are getting heavy, and I am feeling drowsy. I am falling asleep.

———

I prefer standing with the men instead of the ladies. Tonight we are having dinner at one of my aunt's and uncle's house. My uncle asks my father, "Are you ready to go coon hunting?"

55

I know that coon means colored people but I don't know how I know. This feels bad! "Daddy, what…" "Curiosity killed the cat, Diana." (Yes, Daddy.)

"They have the mark of Cain," is what my daddy says. "God turned Cain's skin black. The Bible says…."

———

The neighborhood girls have taught me if I step on a crack in the sidewalk, I will break my mother's back. Our sidewalk is brand new, so we count the marks between the sections as cracks. I never step on one because I would never hurt my mommy.

We have fun playing hopscotch. The older girls taught us younger kids how to be blood buddies. So we did it. Now I have friends forever.

Weird Mirrors

My little sisters and I are with our mother. Today we are having our pictures taken. This time it is in a studio instead of the photographer coming to our house like before.

It is now my turn and I am sitting in front of a strange mirror. I can see lots of me. At first I feel shocked! And confused! Scared! Dizzy! Off balance! But after I get used to it, I am thinking it would be very good if there really were lots of me. One Diana could go to school. One Diana could go to church. One Diana could just play. One Diana could....

1955
Photographer: Anonymous

Weird Bathroom Conversation

This is very unusual! My mother called me and my sisters to come into the bathroom with her while she is going to the toilet! This has never happened before, and it feels icky. I am forcing myself to look up at the really cute curtains at the window that Mommy made. They have a large needle-punch white rabbit on a soft pink background. But what she is saying makes me focus on her now, and it really surprises me. "How would you three like a new daddy?"

My two sisters and I are speechless. What does this mean? I think it would be very good. I shake my head yes. WE ALL DO!

Faith Healing

I feel embarrassed! I am now eight years old. I don't want anyone to see me HERE. I want to hide. Oh, no! There's May from school. Oh, no! She sees me. I am going to ignore her so she won't think it is really me. How did I get here? Jack Coe's tent revival meeting! Faith healing! Parents!

Lots of people are hiking across the field to get to the big white tent. I hear a man saying the tent holds about 20,000 people. That must be a lot because it is huge. "It is the biggest tent revival," I hear him saying. I am surprised this many people come to something like this. I feel humiliated!

He is preaching now. He is a fat man who yells. Well, I guess he is like our pastor – especially on Sunday nights.

Now people are going forward to be healed just like Oral Roberts on TV! They are in wheel chairs and on crutches. It makes me think of church: "Do you believe Jesus can heal you?" "Jesus can heal anybody." "Just put your faith in him." "Raise your hands!" "I said, raise your hands!" "Praise Jesus!" "Thank you, Jesus!" "Praise God!" "Hallelujah!"

God heals people when Jack puts his hands on them and asks them if they believe and then prays for them in Jesus' name. Just like Jesus healed the sick.

Everyone around me raises their hands and praises Jesus every time someone gets healed. Some people speak in tongues, like at church. My hands are raised, but I feel dishonest because I really feel uncomfortable. I feel bad that this feels strange to me, but it does. I know it is good that people get healed. But I don't think most of my girlfriends' parents believe like this. I'm pretty sure our neighbors don't. I think my parents are pretty dumb. I would rather be Baptist or a Methodist than full gospel. I want to be like other people! I don't like being strange just because that is what God says I have to be!

––––––

It is another day. Wednesday, February 8, 1956. My parents are upset. "Look at the paper! They have arrested Jack Coe for practicing medicine without a license. Atheists! Communists! They are fighting against God and his work. It is certainly a sign we are in the end times!"

(I think he looks funny behind bars. The paper says he hurt a little boy with polio. My cousin has polio. That is serious.)

Terror: The Russians are Coming! Maybe Tomorrow! Terror!

My mommy is sitting on the edge of my bed. "Diana, tomorrow is May 1, and we think the Russians might attack us because it is a special holiday for them. We need to pray that if Jesus comes tonight, he will take you with Him to heaven."

I'm scared! After Mommy's prayer, I bury myself in fairy dust.

Easter Chicks: Sadism

"Where are your Easter chicks? Can't find them? Guess what? You ate them yesterday at the church's Fourth of July picnic! Your great-grandmother killed them and fried them. Ha! Ha! Ha!"

I feel numb as I listen to my father. At first it seems too horrible to be true. But I know it is. Why did he tell us?

———

"Do you want me to wring your neck?"
(No, Daddy.)

Self-Hypnotizing: Numbing Out

Saying my memory verses over and over helps me not feel so frightened.

"Thy word have I hid in my heart that I might not sin against thee.
Psalms 119:11"

"Thy word have I hid in my heart that I might not sin against thee.
Psalms 119:11"

"Thy word have I hid in my heart that I might not sin against thee.
Psalms 119:11"

"Proverbs 3:5
Trust in the Lord with all thine heart; and lean not unto thine own understanding."

"Proverbs 3:5
Trust in the Lord with all thine heart; and lean not unto thine own understanding."

"Proverbs 3:5
Trust in the Lord with all thine heart; and lean not unto thine own understanding."

"Proverbs 3:5
Trust....."

"I'm coming, Mommy!"

Daddy Is My Beach Savior

My family goes to the beach a lot. It is called Baker's Haulover. I love the water, and I really like it when I ride on my daddy's back as he swims along the top of the water. I pretend he is my alligator.

But today was scary for me. There were two lady teachers walking out into the water talking about very interesting things. I followed behind them. It was fun listening to them talk. They did not know I was behind them.

It started getting a bit deep for me, and then I stepped into a hole and the water went over my head. My daddy pulled me out, and I coughed out all of the water. "I saw you following those ladies, Diana. But I decided to wait until you were in over your head before I got you," my father is saying.

If HE KNEW I would get into trouble, why didn't he just tell me that the water sloped down and would get deeper and that there were holes? I feel embarrassed and stupid and humiliated.

Today when Mommy and Daddy took my picture in my swimsuit, I raised my hands over my head like a model. I felt the tingly feeling when my swimsuit top began to slide down. But I didn't care. Then I felt bad that I didn't care.

Faith Healer

I am listening to my parents talk. They have just learned the faith healer preacher, Jack Coe, died. Of polio! Today is December 17, 1956. He was teaching my parents and everyone not to use any medicines or go to doctors. That is why we don't go to doctors. Our religion is the Bible, and the Bible says God heals people if they have enough faith.

"He was only 38." "I guess the Lord needed him in Heaven more than on earth." "Some people say he was a heavy drinker." "Oh no! That cannot be true. Not after he accepted the Lord! The Lord healed him in the military."

I feel confused. My little cousin who had polio is okay now because everyone prayed for her. My mommy went to visit her in the hospital and took her a cute little tea set. But, but, but… This isn't supposed to be the way Jesus works! Her family does not believe in Jesus. They write Xmas, not Christmas. They do not go to faith-healing tent meetings (I have more fun at their house!).

Fanny Farmer's Cookbook for Children

I finally found a book at the school library that my mommy will let me keep. I am not allowed to read any of the children's classics. My Bible is all I read when I am feeling bored and lonely on Saturdays – well, until Mommy subscribed to a social studies magazine for me. It comes with lots of colorful stamps and I enjoy pasting them onto the right boxes in the stories. But I think the stories are pretty boring. (I close my bedroom door so I am in my own little world. I don't have to listen to my father.)

My mother even made me take back the books I bought **with my own money** at the five and ten-cent store: *Tom Sawyer* and *Huckleberry Finn*. That broke my heart because I wanted to be like the kids at school. But she let me buy some adult earrings.

Learning to cook with Fanny is okay. I am very excited. Today I'm making scrambled eggs again. My father just walked into the kitchen and is whispering something in my left ear. "Diana, I like your scrambled eggs MUCH better than your mother's." Then he walked away.

ICK! I do not like him talking like that to me. It does not feel good. It makes me feel as if I am sneaking behind mommy's back. I love my mommy!

But she did hurt my feelings when she made me throw out all my biscuit dough the other night. How was I supposed to know the sifter held two cups of flour instead of one? She didn't even let me try again.

Just like the accordion lessons – I only had one or two, and she didn't think I did good enough, so that was that. No more accordion lessons.

Be ye perfect, even as your Father which is in heaven is perfect.
Matthew 5:48
Be ye perfect, even as your Father which is in heaven is perfect…

Thinking In Pictures: Confusion

"What do you mean?" "DO I (big sigh) have to draw you a picture? (No, Daddy.)

———

My parents still have over-stuffed, brown furniture in our living room. I really like the new modern furniture with straight lines. I LOVE the color turquoise! That is the kind of sofa I would buy. We do not have many decorations in our house, but everything is always spic and span. Our living room is pretty large. The walls are all forest green. I like them. We have a picture of Jesus, a landscape picture and a plaque that someone gave my parents for a wedding gift:

Trust in the Lord with all of your heart
And lean not unto your own understanding.
In all thy ways acknowledge him
And He shall direct thy paths.

I read that plaque often and try to trust Jesus, especially when I do not understand why things are the way they are in my family.

The picture of Jesus has a door without a door knob. I have been taught at Sunday school that means only I can open the door to my heart for Jesus. He is a gentleman and will knock on the door of my heart, but he will never push the door open and barge in on me. I have to be willing to let him come into my heart, and I have to keep asking him to come in and stay.

Come in to my heart
Come in to my heart, Lord Jesus.
Come in today.
Come in to stay.
Come in to my heart, Lord Jesus!

Daddy tells me that one sin is all it takes for Jesus to leave my heart and leave me alone and to burn me up like pruned tree branches. I try very hard to be a very good little girl, but I'm always afraid of Jesus leaving me all alone. How would I survive without him helping me get through each day?

Classical Conditioning:
Trust and Obedience and Ice Cream

When we walk with the Lord
in the light of His word,
what a glory He sheds on our way!
While we do His good will,

He abides with us still,
and with all who will trust and obey.

Trust and obey, for there's no other way
to be happy in Jesus, but to trust and obey.

Not a burden we bear,
not a sorrow we share,
but our toil he doth richly repay;
not a grief or a loss,
not a frown or a cross,
but is blest if we trust and obey.

Trust and obey, for there's no other way
to be happy in Jesus, but to trust and obey.

Oh, good! Church is finally over and I can go get my ice cream money from my great-grandfather. He always stands at the back of the church with dimes for me and my sisters. At night, like tonight, we stop for ice cream on the way home. Hurray! It is hot tonight. I'm gonna get a hot fudge sundae at Jack Himmer's ice cream shop!

Sadism

This feels wrong to me. My baby sister is crying. She is three years younger than me. She is the one EVERYONE loves. THAT is WHY I cannot understand what is happening. It IS mean!

"Yes. We found you under a cabbage leaf," my mother is teasing her as our family drives home from Sunday night church. My family calls it teasing, but it feels wrong to me. It feels like my little sister is being tortured. She doesn't know what to believe, and I am afraid she doesn't feel loved and wanted when they talk to her like this.

She still wets the bed and sucks her thumb. So Mommy puts hot pepper sauce on her thumb, but that does not stop her. And they tease her about wetting. I think they should just leave her alone. She is so sweet.

She has reading problems, like I do. They are making her feel stupid, too. I love her, but I was jealous when she got the cute little red cowgirl boots for Christmas and the cowgirl skirt and vest. She looked so cute.

She asked my parents to get her a pet skunk. When mommy explained that it would smell bad if it got upset, my sister asked why she couldn't just get it de-skunked. It was so cute the Miami newspaper printed it. This sister is the one who makes everyone laugh for fun. I guess that is why what they are doing now hurts my heart.

———

I hate the way my father runs around the house wearing only his Jockey shorts. It feels icky. I think it is arrogant. And I feel uncomfortable when my mother wears nightgowns that show her nipples. I wish she'd wear a robe!

Mommy CAN Cry!

Today is a summer day. I am at home with my mother and sisters. My mother is a homemaker, like all of my friends' mothers. There is one nurse at the end of the block, but we do not know her.

My mother is crying her heart out today. When she backed the car out this morning, she learned a kitten had hid under the hood of the car. It was hit by the fan when she turned the ignition on. It totally DEVASTATED my mother that she killed the kitten. She couldn't even go to the store after that. I did not know she could feel bad and cry about ANYTHING. I have NEVER seen her cry because she trusts Jesus. So I am very surprised by her reaction.

Mommy is the one who always buys us baby chicks or a baby duck or a baby bunny for Easter. Easter and Christmas are fun times at my house. Those are the BEST times. EVERYONE is happy then. And Daddy is quiet. NOBODY yells. NOBODY gets beaten.

Mommy is also the one who says, "It doesn't matter who your relatives are. All that matters is who you are!"

Chaos: Parents Do Fun And Scary Things

When my sisters and I get home from school around 3:30, we watch television until dinner time. We are not allowed to eat any snacks because it might spoil our dinner. We are not allowed to open the refrigerator – ever.

Mommy lets me make pudding for dessert a lot. It gets hot cooking it on the stove. I get tired stirring it.

Mother likes to cook and bake. She makes dinners that are Cuban, Italian, Chinese, Mexican, and American. I really like the Cuban black beans over rice. She makes yummy cakes. My favorite tastes like a Peter-Paul Mounds candy bar because it is dark chocolate with coconut inside. We also have lots of steaks – and fish that my daddy catches. Mommy makes peanut butter fudge for my school class Christmas parties. It is SO good! Being a perfect homemaker is important to Mommy.

We cannot leave the table until our plate is clean because of the starving children in China. And we cannot use a big size fork until we learn to hold a salad fork correctly. Daddy doesn't allow ANY talking at the table, so we hear him slurping his food.

My daddy likes to barbeque chicken Saturday evenings and make homemade ice cream. My favorite is strawberry! His chicken is the best I've ever tasted. He likes to do things with his younger cousin. They water ski at the two lakes not far from our house. But the rest of us just have to watch them from the shore. I think it looks like fun. "I'd love to water ski," I think.

Sometimes I have to walk around the house with a book on my head to practice my posture. As Christians, we have to look good so others will want to know Jesus.

Today I decided to see what would happen if I put the end of my barrette into one side of the bathroom socket. I got shocked! I jumped! It scared me! It did not hurt as much as when I was four and wanted to see what would happen if I put my hand into Mommy's wringer washing machine. It hurt! She got mad at me. The older neighbor lady fed me pears. Mommy has a modern washer now.

Compulsive Drawings: Child Communication

I don't draw stained glass pictures so much now, but I do draw the same picture over and over just like I used to draw stained glass over and over. It ALWAYS has two coconut palm trees and the ocean with a little sail boat.

Reproductions made in therapy. No originals survived. All were done only in Florida and in the new house.

Mommy still reads us Bible stories sometimes. I still like the story about Samuel.

God came to him at night. Samuel learned not to be afraid. He learned to say,

"Lord, here am I!"

———

I've got the joy, joy, joy, joy
Down in my heart
Down in my heart
Down in my heart
I've got the joy, joy, joy, joy
Down in my heart
Down in my heart to stay.

I've got the peace that passes understanding down in my heart
Down in my heart
Down in my heart
I've got the peace that passes understanding down in my heart
Down in my heart today!

My Sunday school teachers have taught me that JOY means: **J**esus first, then **O**thers, then m**Y**self. If I want to be happy and joyful, then I must always put Jesus first in my life by obeying His Word

Too Dissociative To Think Clearly

My parents are not home this afternoon. I know bad things are happening in my family. I feel very upset. We need help!

Even though I am nine, I am not allowed to use our one black telephone. I do not really know how to use it, but today I must try to get help. I am the oldest. It is my duty. I am very frightened and nervous as I dial "0" for the operator. "Can you tell me if there are people who help children?"

"Dial Oxford blah blah blah." I dial "0"x.

"Operator. May I help you?" I slam the phone down. I feel embarrassed.

"How did I get the operator?" "I am dialing Oxford….."

I feel even more frightened. "What will happen? What will my parents do to me? But I am the oldest. It is my duty to get help."

I dial again. "0" x…….."

"Operator. May I help you?"

I am feeling even more nervous, frightened, and stupid now. I am shaking. I cannot make my head work. It feels fuzzy. What is wrong with me? Why can't I dial correctly? I try to concentrate harder.

One more time. "0" x.

"Operator. May I help you?"

I am sweating and nervous and very scared and shaky. I don't feel like me.

I hear our family car. My mother is home. I give up. I run back to my bedroom. I am too stupid to get us help. I feel sad. And scared! What would Mommy do if she found out?

———

"Diana, why do you follow me around the house like my shadow? Go away! I'm busy! Go play!"
(I don't know why, Mommy; I didn't realize I was.)
I feel crushed!

Mother's Blood-Curdling Scream

I am standing in the hallway next to my mother. I am trying to tell her that something bad is happening to me. I feel it very strongly. But I cannot find the words I need to communicate. I am silent. I begin waving both of my arms. My hands are moving together as if I am holding an imaginary ball while the ball keeps growing and getting bigger. So I keep moving my hands further and further apart.

I am nine years old and I feel very grown up most of the time, but I do not know how to explain this. Why don't I know the words? She is not understanding me! I am now crying. I need help! I feel completely and totally overwhelmed. I feel helpless. I feel hopeless. Why can't she understand me?

I thought she and Jesus can read my mind. I thought Jesus sees everything. WHY isn't Jesus telling her? WHY isn't Jesus helping me? I'm praying. I'm being a good little girl!

My sisters are playing in their room, the pink room. Actually, they are jumping on their twin beds and having silly-fun. My mother just walked into the hall from the living room and saw them. I am standing at my bedroom door ready to walk into the hall. Mother just let out a bloodcurdling scream like I have never heard before.

"STOP JUMPING ON YOUR BEDS, YOU TWO!"

I know that something very bad has happened to my mother. I have never seen her act or sound like that before. I don't know why she is so upset. I can tell it is more than my sisters jumping on their beds. It sounded like something deep, very deep, inside her just ripped apart. I KNOW bad is happening. I just don't know what it is. BUT I CAN FEEL IT!

My mommy has started having something called asthma. It makes her cough in church. She sometimes has a hard time breathing. I feel embarrassed when she interrupts the sermon and singing with her coughing. Then I feel guilty.

I am not a loving daughter. I KNOW I should feel sorry for her. Why don't I?

Creating An Imaginary Friend

I am standing in front of my church congregation in Miami along with all the other kids who did all of their work in Vacation Bible School. I got the award for perfect attendance. The Sunday School Superintendent gave me a beautiful framed picture of Jesus surrounded by sheep. It is a picture of Psalm 23. I love my picture! I will hang it up in my bedroom.

I feel better when I look at this picture and remember that no matter what, Jesus loves me and I can always talk to Him anytime I want to by praying. That is what my Sunday school teacher taught me. Prayer is simply talking to God. I often feel all alone and sad, but talking to Jesus helps me feel better.

Psalms 23
The Lord is my shepherd;
I shall not want.
He maketh me to lie down in green pastures:
he leadeth me beside the still waters.
He restoreth my soul:
He leadeth me in the paths of righteousness for his name's sake.
Yea, though I walk through the valley of the shadow of death,
I will fear no evil:
for thou art with me;
thy rod and thy staff they comfort me.
thou preparest a table before me in the presence of mine enemies:
thou annointest my head with oil;
my cup runneth over.

Surely goodness and mercy shall follow me all the days of my life:
and I will dwell in the house of the Lord forever.
[KJV]

Overwhelming Spasms: Wedding Ritual

I have run into my sisters' bedroom to get away from everyone as quickly as I could. Something is VERY wrong with me. I am standing with my back next to the pink wall. I'm pushing against it to try to get my body to stop making very strong movements inside me. I never remember this happening to me before. I am having very unusual feelings from my waist down to my bottom. They are coming up from between my legs and into my tummy. They are very, very strong feelings. They feel like huge tight waves washing over me. What is happening to me? In some ways it feels good, but in other ways it feels so strong that it is scary and agonizing.

I don't know what is happening, but I do know there needs to be a wedding. I don't understand why I know that, but it is just this other very strong feeling that I have inside me. It feels like a force that is pushing me to have a wedding. I do not have a daddy doll, but I have two girl dolls, and I can pretend. Many girls have bride dolls, but I've always thought they were stupid, so I've never wanted one.

I know there are always parties after weddings and there is food and usually candy and nuts. My mommy always keeps nuts in the living room during the holidays from Thanksgiving to Christmas. I am now cracking open a lot of Brazil nuts, which Daddy calls nigger toes. And for some reason, I am also washing them with water – lots of water – even though I know we usually just crack them open and eat them. But this is a wedding, and I want to do everything right. EVERYTHING needs to be clean – and pure.

I am surprised the strong feelings went away after I did the wedding, but I feel sick to my stomach now because I ate too many of the washed Brazil nuts. Ugh!

I now think of myself as a woman. I just turned nine. When mommy took my picture this morning, I posed like TV model Bess Myerson.

Church Service

I really like it when the whole church starts singing and clapping. I feel like dancing. Too bad it is a SIN!

I can see the Sunday school attendance board. 453 in Sunday school this morning. There are more in church.

When the roll is called up yonder I'll be there
When the trumpet of the Lord shall sound,
and time shall be no more,
And the morning breaks, eternal bright and fair,
When the saved of earth shall gather
over on the other shore,
And the roll is called up yonder I'll be there.

When the roll is called up yonder,
When the roll is called up yonder,
When the roll is called up yonder,
When the roll is called up yonder I'll be there.

"Hallelujah!" "Praise the Lord!" "Bless you, Jesus!"

On that bright and cloudless morning when the dead in Christ
shall rise,
And the glory of His resurrection share;
When His chosen ones shall gather to their home beyond the skies,
And the roll is called up yonder, I'll be there.

When the roll is called up yonder,
When the roll is called up yonder,
When the roll is called up yonder,
When the roll is called up yonder I'll be there.

Let us labor for the Master from the dawn till setting sun,
Let us talk of all His wondrous love and care;
Then when all of life is over, and our work on earth is done,
And the roll is called up yonder, I'll be there.

When the roll, is called up yonder…

Someone has interrupted and is speaking in tongues. Now they are saying, "I am coming soon. The end is near. Watch and wait. Be prepared for the great and terrible day of the Lord."

SCARY! But part of me also thinks they are playacting! It is always the same stuff! It feels silly to me!

On Christ the solid rock I stand, all other ground is sinking sand…

Mother's Hi-Fi: Programming

Down from his glory
Ever living story
My God and savior came
And Jesus was his name

Born in a manger
To his own a stranger
A man of sorrows
Tears and agony

Oh how I love him
How I adore him
My great creator
My all in all

ShaTterED DianA

The great creator
Became my savior
A man of sorrow
Tears and agony

Lying in bed at night, I hear my parents' new hi-fi playing the records they just bought. All of them sing about Jesus. I am happy we have these new records. I love listening to them as I fall asleep. Mommy plays them all the time, but I never get tired of them. They are very comforting.

Someone told me the music to this song matches one called *It's Now or Never*. I don't get to listen to much popular music – Daddy calls it the devil's be-pop music. So I didn't know the music is really from a worldly song. It is BEAUTIFUL! I would LOVE to dance to it! Now when I imagine being covered in fairy dust, I also have music to help me feel close to Jesus. They both make me feel not afraid.

On a hill far away stood and old rugged cross,
The emblem of suff'ring and shame;
And I love that old cross where the dearest and best
For a world of lost sinners was slain.

So I'll cherish the old rugged cross,
Till my trophies at last I lay down;
I will cling to the old rugged cross,
And exchange it some day for a crown.

Oh, the old rugged cross, so despised by the world,
Has a wondrous attraction for me;
For the dear Lamb of God left His glory above
To bear it to dark Calvary.

In that old rugged cross, stained with blood so divine,
A wondrous beauty I see,
For 'twas on that old cross Jesus suffered and died,
To pardon and sanctify me.

Diana Lee, M.A.

To the old rugged cross I will ever be true;
Its shame and reproach gladly bear;
Then He'll call me some day to my home far away,
Where His glory forever I'll share.

Sing the wondrous love of Jesus;
Sing his mercy and his grace.
In the mansions bright and blessed
he'll prepare for us a place.

When we all get to heaven,
what a day of rejoicing that will be!
When we all see Jesus,
we'll sing and shout the victory!

While we walk the pilgrim pathway,
clouds will overspread the sky;
but when traveling days are over,
not a shadow, not a sigh.

When we all get to heaven,
what a day of rejoicing that will be!
When we all see Jesus,
we'll sing and shout the victory!

Onward to the prize before us!
Soon his beauty we'll behold;
soon the pearly gates will open;
we shall tread the streets of gold.

When we all get to heaven,
what a day of rejoicing that will be!
when we all see Jesus,
we'll sing and shout the victory!

When we walk with the Lord
in the light of His word,

ShaTterED DianA

what a glory He sheds on our way!
While we do His good will,
He abides with us still,
and with all who will trust and obey.

Trust and obey, for there's no other way
to be happy in Jesus, but to trust and obey.

Not a burden we bear,
not a sorrow we share,
but our toil he doth richly repay;
not a grief or a loss,
not a frown or a cross,
but is blest if we trust and obey.

Trust and obey, for there's no other way
to be happy in Jesus, but to trust and obey.

But we never can prove
the delights of his love
until all on the altar we lay;
for the favor he shows,
for the joy he bestows,
are for them who will trust and obey.

Trust and obey, for there's no other way
to be happy in Jesus, but to trust and obey.

Then in fellowship sweet
we will sit at His feet,
or we'll walk by His side in the way;
what he says we will do,
where he sends we will go;
never fear, only trust and obey.

Trust and obey, for there's no other way
to be happy in Jesus, but to trust and obey.

———

"Diana, stop talking with your hands!"
(Yes, Mommy.)

I Never Know What to Expect: Anxiety

Sometimes Mommy takes me and my sisters to Funland Amusement Park. The tilt-a-whirl is my favorite ride! One time she even took my little sisters and me on a picnic all by ourselves without Daddy! We got to eat pork and beans right out of our own little can! We also went to the alligator farm and saw the Seminoles rub the tummy of the biggest alligator to make him fall asleep. And we've been to the bird and deer farm, the doll museum, and Vizcaya. My sisters and I got to be on the local kids' TV show.

I'll never forget Mommy taking me to the Denver Museum of Natural History when I was four. One of our ministers had just moved to Alaska, and she pointed to the window that had snow and polar bears and told me that is what Alaska looks like. I want to go there someday!

Daddy is the one who says, "I'm hungry for watermelon or cheesecake." Then he takes us to the bakery or to the fruit stand. That is fun if he doesn't get upset with Mommy in the car. Sometimes he is hungry for Royal Castle hamburgers, so we get to go there. I love how they fry the onions and pile them on!

Mommy takes us shopping and we have lunch at Woolworths. I get corn dogs. Yummy!

Sometimes Daddy needs a Yoohoo chocolate soda, so we stop at the U-ToTE'm. Daddy is the one who takes us to Homestead AFB air shows and Bayfront Park to watch the big fishing boats come in, and he even took us on a REAL submarine and destroyer! It is good to live in Miami!

Going to our annual church picnics at Crandon Park is fun, but most often we go to the beach and grill hamburgers and play in the water. We still go fishing in the Keys. Sometimes my uncle lets me steer his big inboard boat. It is fun when we park at an island and grill the fish we just caught.

"Diana! I told you to turn left and you turned right! You steered us right into the sandbar!"

"I'm sorry!" Stupid again!

I enjoy going to my cousin's house. We play paperdolls – Natalie Wood and Robert Wagner. It is more fun at unbelievers' houses!

Unconsciously Acting Out The Secret

I am visiting my grandparents in Tennessee. I am with my great-grandmother. She is my father's paternal grandmother.

She often invites me to her house on the weekends to watch TV and just be with her. It is better than being at home, so I am glad to get away. On Saturday nights, we watch *Perry Mason*, *Gunsmoke* and the *Twilight Zone*.

Today we have taken a drive to Cumberland Gap National Park. We ate lunch in a very big beautiful log building. I liked the feel of it – RUSTIC! It had huge picture windows that looked out over the mountains. Our lunch was served family style. I never heard of that before in a restaurant!

Now we have stopped by a little stream. I am lying on a large flat rock out in the water. My Grandfather is getting ready to take a picture of me. He is looking through his camera lens. For some reason that I cannot explain, I feel an urge to spread my legs apart as far as I can. I KNOW my mother would tell me to be "lady like," but the urge to be bad is so STRONG. I normally want to do what is good, so I am deciding to spread them but not so much. "What is THAT URGE?" "Is that the devil in me?" "Is it my sinful nature?" It makes me feel EMBARRASSED. AND tingly good down there!

Scapegoating

I am still in Tennessee. My great-grandmother and my grandmother are sitting under the trees in my grandmother's BIG back yard that looks like a park relaxing and talking. I am at their neighbor's house. She is a school teacher. She is nice to me. She lets me come over and talk with her. I like just being around her. It feels good. I like the way she talks to me and treats me like I'm grown up.

Today she asked me why I always call Daddy "My Father" when I talk about him. I don't know. I wonder if that means something.

My grandmother and great-grandmother took me shopping at J.C. Penney's. My great-grandmother bought me a really pretty dress. It is lavender on the top with lines of little flowers up and down the skirt. She tells me that I eat like I have a straight gut – whatever that means. But it is still fun here. We have Ritz crackers with Cheese Whiz while we watch TV at night! Fun!

After dinner last night when we were all watching TV and eating dessert, I went to the kitchen to get myself a drink of water from the faucet. I noticed a little bit of water had dripped onto the floor under the sink, probably from my grandmother washing the dishes. I thought it would be funny to make a joke about it. I yelled out to my grandmother, "You've got a mud puddle on the floor by the sink!"

I had barely closed my mouth when I felt my paternal great-grandmother's hand smack me in the mouth HARD from behind! "Don't you dare criticize your grandmother's housekeeping, young lady!" I did not know that was a criticism. I thought it was a joke.

I was teasing my grandmother because I love her. She makes me real strawberry milkshakes!

My great-grandmother hurt my feelings and embarrassed me. I went to our bedroom and cried for my mommy. I miss her!

Confusing Thoughts

I'm still in Tennessee with my great-grandmother. I am in the bathroom at my grandparents' house. I am sitting on the toilet, and I notice that I have several little brown hairs growing – down there. I am shocked! I feel shaken! I feel embarrassed!

"THEY ARE NOT GOING TO LIKE THIS," I think. Now I'm wondering, "WHY am I thinking THAT?" There are some large scissors on the back of the toilet. I take them and snip off the little hairs. Now I feel better.

————

It is still summer 1957 and I am still in Tennessee and I am still nine years old. I have been here a LONG time. I have found the most beautiful dolls. The bakery sells them. They are for sitting on the bed, not to play with. I wrote and asked Mommy to send me money. She didn't.

Today is Sunday. My grandparents took me to a different kind of church. It is called Methodist. It was HUGE – two stories with a big balcony and lots of beautiful stained glass windows and dark stained wood trim and spindles. I like this church. It feels good to me.

The best part was when we sang a new song called *The Battle Hymn of the Republic*, written by a lady named Julia Ward Howe. She wrote this song about the War Between the States. She thinks like me. She was NOT on the slave owners' side. OH, NO! I would have liked her and felt safe with her. When I grow up, I want to be like her. I think God is like her. He helps people instead of hurting people. That song felt majestic and strong in my chest when we got to sing it with the large choir and the big pipe organ. I felt like marching into battle to help people.

Mine eyes have seen the glory of the coming of the Lord:
He is trampling out the vintage where the grapes of wrath are
stored;
He has loosed the fateful lightning of His terrible swift sword:
His truth is marching is on.

Glory, glory, hallelujah!
Glory, glory, hallelujah!
Glory, glory, hallelujah!
His truth is marching on...

In the beauty of the lilies Christ was born across the sea,
With a glory in His bosom that transfigures you and me;
As He died to make men holy, let us die to make them free,
While God is marching on.

Glory, glory, hallelujah!
Glory, glory, hallelujah!
Glory, glory, hallelujah!
Our God is marching on.

Mom and Jesus Are Not Coming: Creating A Lois Lane Survival Part

Today is a warm and partially cloudy Saturday afternoon. I am back in Hialeah. It is still 1957. I am still nine years old. I am wearing the green and purple plaid shorts set Mother made me. I love them. I love the colors. Mommy makes most of my clothes, but sometimes I get to wear hand-me-downs from the big girls at church – like sack dresses. I like that!

I am sitting alone on the swing in my back yard. I am looking at the numerous belt welts that stripe my legs like candy canes. I am wondering why no adult ever asks me about the welt marks.

That seems more than odd to me. "How can people just sit back and do nothing?" I ask myself.

I am thinking of Mom in Denver. "Why doesn't she get it?" I've been sending her secret coded messages for several years, but she has not come for me.

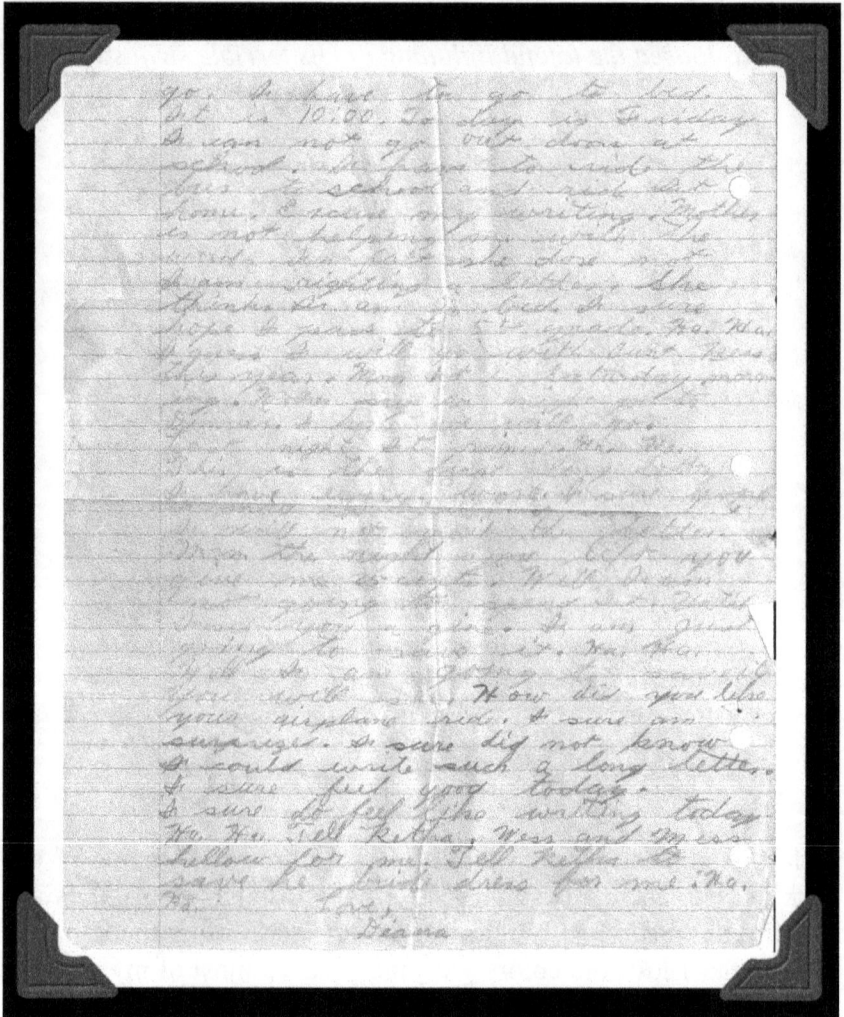

1957 - Original returned when Mom died in 1989 but not discovered until 2012.

I pray to Jesus for help and to send Mom to take me away. I don't understand why Jesus does not hear my prayers. I am doing everything my Sunday school teachers tell me to do!

I am looking up at the puffy, backlit clouds overhead as I continue to sit on my swing with my feet resting on the short Bermuda grass. The sun is mostly behind the clouds illuminating them with a golden glow that makes me think of Jesus and the pictures of Heaven in my Bible story book. Many nights I've prayed to Jesus to help me, but now I realize He is not coming to help me, and neither is my grandmother! I am completely alone. I have to figure out how I will survive.

Determined, I walk from our sunny backyard dotted with a couple citrus trees, the neighbor's six-foot hedge and my mother's tomato and zinnia garden to my own bedroom. I am told I was given a room of my own because I am the oldest, but I envy my two sisters who are together in the pink room next door. They seem happy.

As I walk into my Wedgwood blue room, I see my little toy typewriter sitting on the terrazzo floor where I left it the day before. I had decided to write a book on this Christmas gift. I realize that by most peoples' standards, my family looks normal. Many people would be quite surprised to learn what REALLY goes on behind our closed doors because we are Christians who are always going to church and to revivals – a handsome daddy, a beautiful mommy, three little girls, new dresses, new shoes, new hats or ribbons in our hair, new gloves, new purses, a white Bible in our hands, and a nice clean car to drive us to church.

I wanted to tell because I want the bad stuff to stop, but every afternoon when I get home from school, all of my hard work has disappeared. I don't KNOW what happens to it! So every day I've had to start again. Now I have finally given up in total and complete frustration.

Life is unbearable! I do not recall exactly what is happening. I just know that bad things are happening. I don't know the words to say what I need to say. I feel completely and totally overwhelmed. I want it to stop. I want a family like my friends have.

After looking at my toy typewriter and feeling my frustration, I move over to my bedroom jalousie window and look out onto 110th Street and up into the sky. I know I am in a hopeless situation. I realize no one is coming to rescue me. I have to do it on my own. Without any tears, I simply throw my shoulders back and make a vow to God that I WILL SURVIVE and I WILL GROW UP and become an adult and when I do, I WILL WRITE MY STORY. I feel VERY strongly that people would help me if they knew the truth, but I have no way to tell them.

As I look out my window, I begin talking to God. I vow to remember EVERYTHING that happens so when I grow up I can just sit down at a normal typewriter and type away without having to do any research. My story will just pour out of me. I will be like investigative reporter Lois Lane on the *Superman* TV show.

I suddenly realize my head can be my camera. Whenever I see something bad going on, I will "take a picture" by focusing my eyes on the scene and then blink them. I decide my ears will be my tape recorder, like the tape recorder in speech therapy. I know no adult will ever realize what I am doing.

Fairy Dust and Jesus: Dissociating

I am lying in my bed in my Wedgwood blue bedroom imagining fairy dust falling all around me and listening to my parents' hi-fi. I let the fairy dust fall until I feel no fear. I think of Jesus and how much He loves me, even though I don't understand why He is not coming for me or sending Mom. Maybe tomorrow he will come. Maybe tomorrow He will tell Mom.

What a Friend we have in Jesus,
All our sins and griefs to bear!
What a privilege to carry
Everything to God in prayer!
O what peace we often forfeit,
O what needless pain we bear,
All because we do not carry
Everything to God in prayer!

Have we trials and temptations?
Is there trouble anywhere?
We should never be discouraged,
Take it to the Lord in prayer.
Can we find a friend so faithful
Who will all our sorrows share?
Jesus knows our every weakness,
Take it to the Lord in prayer.

Are we weak and heavy-laden
Cumbered with a load of care?
Precious Savior, still our refuge—
Take it to the Lord in prayer;
Do thy friends despise, forsake thee?
Take it to the Lord in prayer;
In His arms He'll take and shield thee,
Thou wilt find a solace there.

'Tis so sweet to trust in Jesus,
Just to take Him at His word;
Just to rest upon His promise;
Just to know, Thus saith the Lord.

Jesus, Jesus, how I trust Him,
How I've proved Him o'er and o'er,
Jesus, Jesus, Precious Jesus!
O for grace to trust Him more.

O how sweet to trust in Jesus,
Just to trust His cleansing blood;
Just in simple faith to plunge me,
'Neath the healing, cleansing flood.

Yes, 'tis sweet to trust in Jesus,
Just from sin and self to cease;
Just from Jesus simply taking
Life, and rest, and joy, and peace.

ShaTterED DianA

I'm so glad I learned to trust Thee,
Precious Jesus, Savior, Friend;
And I know that Thou art with me,
Wilt be with me to the end.

Down from His glory
Ever living story,
My God and Savior came,
And Jesus was His name.
Born in a manager,
To His own a stranger,
A Man of sorrows, tears and agony.

O how I love Him! How I adore Him!
My breath, my sunshine, my all in all!
The great Creator became my Savior,
And all God's fullness dwelleth in Him.

What condescension,
Bringing us redemption;
That in the dead of night,
Not one faint hope in sight,
God, gracious, tender
Laid aside His splendor,
Stooping to woo, to win, to save my soul.

O how I love Him! How I adore Him!
My breath, my sunshine, my all in all!
The great Creator became my Savior,
And all God's fullness dwelleth in Him.

Without reluctance,
Flesh and blood His substance
He took the form of man,
Revealed the hidden plan.
O glorious myst'ry,
Sacrifice of Calv'ry,

And I know Thou art the great I AM.

No Longer A Room of My Own

Mommy took my blue bedroom away from me and gave it to my middle sister. (The smart one.) That is okay. I like being in the pink room now with my youngest sister. We each have our own twin bed. Mine is under the front window, and hers is on the side under the window near the front porch. We have open space in between for our toys and dolls. That is where we play.

Today I was at Evelyn's house. Her daddy is a Presbyterian minister. I have FUN at Evelyn's. Today we got into her brother's old car and pretended we were driving. We accidentally made the car roll toward the canal that runs behind her house, but Evelyn knew how to stop it. I didn't feel scared, just numb.

When I am at Evelyn's house, I feel something really good. It feels warm. I like that feeling. I do not really believe what my mommy says about "the world." EVERYBODY'S house feels good but ours! HOW CAN WE BE GOD'S CHOSEN PEOPLE? God sure is STRANGE! I KNOW I would rather be in the world!

More Great-Grandparents!!!

My OTHER great-grandfather and his wife are driving up in front of our house. Sometimes they come to visit us on Sunday afternoon and then take me home with them. They have a beautiful art deco home with huge gardens all around. He used to own a drug store on Miami Beach before the crash of 29, whatever that is.

She and I play like I am a princess, and she puts a satin blanket around me for my robe and makes me a crown and wand out of tin foil. We have fun playing together and with their big orange cat named Alexander. He is named after Alexander the Great, some important man.

Usually my parents pick me up at their house on their way home after night church. We go to different churches. They go to

Little River Baptist Church. She told me that I needed to accept Jesus in their church, also, SO I DID!

The last time I spent the night with them, she cooked hot dogs by boiling them in water. I never saw hotdogs cooked like that. When I looked down from the stairs and saw them in the pan, I got sick to my stomach. The smell made me gag and want to throw up. I had to go upstairs and lie down. I could not eat them. She said, "I've never heard of a child getting sick from looking at hotdogs boiling in a pan." I did! I got VERY sick. Ughhhhishhhh!

What can wash away my sins?
Nothing but the blood of Jesus!
What can make me whole again?
Nothing but the blood of Jesus!

Mommy's Music

The only time it is quiet in our house is when Mommy is asleep at night and the hi-fi is off!

Have you been to Jesus for the cleansing pow'r?
Are you washed in the blood of the Lamb?
Are you fully trusting in His grace this hour?
Are you washed in the blood of the Lamb?

Are you washed in the blood,
In the soul-cleansing blood of the Lamb?
Are your garments spotless? Are they white as snow?
Are you washed in the blood of the Lamb?

Are you walking daily by the Savior's side?
Are you washed in the blood of the Lamb?
Do you rest each moment in the Crucified?
Are you washed in the blood of the Lamb?

When the Bridegroom cometh will your robes be white?

90

Are you washed in the blood of the Lamb?
Will your soul be ready for His presence bright?
And be washed in the blood of the Lamb?

Lay aside the garments that are stained with sin,
And be washed in the blood of the Lamb;
There's a fountain flowing for the soul unclean,
O be washed in the blood of the Lamb.

———

I'm sitting in children's church with about 40 or more kids. The teacher just asked if anyone has a biblical name. I KNOW she wants the kids named: Matthew, Mark, Luke, John, Paul, Peter, Timothy, Andrew, Mary, Martha, Dorcas, or Priscilla to raise their hand. BUT I am feeling ornery and cannot resist this. I raise my hand. "What is your name?" "My name is Diana." "Are you SURE that is a Bible name?" I was named after the goddess Diana in Ephesus." (Yuk! Yuk! Yuk!)

"Uh, does anyone else have a biblical name?" Sometimes a different ME pops out and surprises even ME!

———

A few weeks ago I ran my new bicycle into my youngest sister. I wasn't going fast, and she didn't cry, but it was intentional. Now I feel bad that I did that. Only a BAD girl would hurt someone. I think I might have a demon. I KNOW my middle sister does! She was so mad she KICKED a hole in my bedroom door when I lived in the blue room!

Visual Trigger

After Sunday morning church, we often go out for lunch. Today we are at Jumbo's family restaurant. I always get the fried shrimp with French fries. I love fried shrimp! I really don't care a lot for fried fish.

Usually we go home. Often Daddy watches football on television, and I play dolls at Judy's three doors down or stay in my bedroom by myself. Now that I am older, I sometimes get to go home with a friend from church – Roberta, Pat or Judy. It is FUN!

I am surprised to hear that today we all are going to an aunt and uncle's house. I really don't know them very well, so I don't feel comfortable. He is actually my father's uncle, although he is not that much older than my father. My great-grandmother got married when she was only sixteen and pregnant. They had five or six children. It turns out my father actually grew up with some of his aunts and uncles because my grandmother was one of their oldest children. She got married at sixteen, also. I get confused about who is who.

For some reason that I don't understand, we don't see most of these people very often. I am not sure, but I think it is because they do not go to our church. Even if they are relatives, we have to stay away from them if they are going to Hell. My parents don't want them to influence us because Satan is very sneaky. Some of them smoke, some of them drink, some of them go to movies, and some of them DANCE! The ladies wear red lipstick and red fingernail polish. Mommy says they have not accepted Jesus as their savior. That is why they SIN.

Now I am sitting in front of their television watching *Walt Disney's Wonderful World of Animals*, or something like that. I don't really like it, but there is nothing else to do. They are showing a close up of some sort of bird. I didn't hear the name. It has this bag thing hanging under its neck. It is a big bird. I see that bag puff up. Oh, no! Suddenly, I feel like I am going to throw up. I feel horribly nauseated. Why did seeing that bird's bag thing puff up and get bigger make me feel like throwing up? That makes no sense to me.

Rescue the perishing, care for the dying,
Snatch them in pity from sin and the grave;
Weep o'er the erring one, lift up the fallen,
Tell them of Jesus, the mighty to save.

Rescue the perishing, Care for the dying;
Jesus is merciful, Jesus will save.

Though they are slighting Him, still He is waiting,
Waiting the penitent child to receive;
Plead with them earnestly, plead with them gently,
He will forgive if they only believe.

Rescue the perishing, Care for the dying;
Jesus is merciful, Jesus will save.

Down in the human heart, crushed by the tempter,
Feelings lie buried that grace can restore;
Touched by a loving heart, wakened by kindness,
Cords that are broken will vibrate once more.

Rescue the perishing, Care for the dying;
Jesus is merciful, Jesus will save.

Rescue the perishing, duty demands it
Strength for your labor the Lord will provide;
Back to the narrow way patiently win them,
Tell the poor wand'rer a Savior has died.

Rescue the perishing, Care for the dying;
Jesus is merciful, Jesus will save.

Pain and Suffering Prove Love

"For whom the Lord loves he chastens."
"For whom the Lord loves he chastens."
"For whom the Lord loves he chastens."
[Hebrews 12:6 KJV]

Reciting my memory verses over and over is the only way I can keep them in my mind. Sometimes I write them over and over. I feel closer to God when I memorize His words.

"Mommy, what does chastens mean?"

"Look it up in the dictionary."

Ummm. "Discipline. Purify. Punish." "So GOD punishes people he loves!"

Oh! I understand. GOD WANTS ME TO SUFFER! THAT is why Jesus has not come for me! THAT is why Jesus did not tell Mom to come get me! GOD is making me a good little girl because he loves me. It is for my own good. GOD is making me PURE!

———

"Pull your shorts and panties down and bend over the bed so I can spank you with Daddy's belt."

("Yes, Mam.")

———

I like singing to myself. Sometimes I sing out loud when I walk to the dime store because it is a long way away. Sometimes I invite all of my neighbor friends and my two sisters to sit on a bench that I made outside with cinder blocks and a plank. I teach them my Sunday school stories and songs.

When We All Get to Heaven

Sing the wondrous love of Jesus;
Sing his mercy and his grace.
In the mansions bright and blessed
he'll prepare for us a place.

When we all get to heaven,
what a day of rejoicing that will be!
When we all see Jesus,
we'll sing and shout the victory!

While we walk the pilgrim pathway,
clouds will overspread the sky;
but when traveling days are over,
not a shadow, not a sigh.

When we all get to heaven,
what a day of rejoicing that will be!
When we all see Jesus,
we'll sing and shout the victory!

Onward to the prize before us!
Soon his beauty we'll behold;
soon the pearly gates will open;
we shall tread the streets of gold.

When we all get to heaven,
what a day of rejoicing that will be!
when we all see Jesus,
we'll sing and shout the victory!

"Everything gets made right in heaven, IF I can survive until then,"
I think to myself.

If you're happy and you know it
Clap your hands
If you're happy and you know it
Clap your hands
If you're happy and you know it
And you're not afraid to show it
If you're happy and you know it
Clap your hands
Clap! Clap!

There is a name I love to hear,
I love to sing its worth;
It sounds like music in mine ear,
The sweetest name on earth.

Oh, how I love Jesus,
Oh, how I love Jesus,
Oh, how I love Jesus,
Because He first loved me!

Oh, how I love Jesus,
Oh, how I love Jesus,
Oh, how I love Jesus,
Be—caussssse Heee first loved meeeee!

Classical Conditioning Interrupts My Thinking

It is Saturday afternoon. I'm lying in the pink bedroom on my twin bed that rests against the wall with a big jalousie window above it. I'm thinking about the girls at school who wear Ten Commandment charm bracelets. I'm puzzled because my parents and church tell me that "we" are the "true church" and everyone else is going to Hell, but they have not talked to me about the Ten Commandments or bought me a bracelet to remind me to follow the Ten Commandments.

I'm now in fifth grade, so it was easy for me, well, almost easy, to find the Ten Commandments in the book of Exodus in my little white Bible that my daddy's parents bought me when I started school. As I read them, I really don't see what the big deal is! I really think I am strong enough to keep these and make God happy with me. They do not seem that hard!

I don't want to lie, steal, or kill anybody. I don't know what adultery means. But my church teaches me that without Jesus in my heart it is IMPOSSIBLE to follow God. I don't understand why it should be IMPOSSIBLE to not lie, steal or kill. Something inside me feels like this is something I can do. Does it mean I am bad if I think I can keep these and my church says it is impossible? Is there really something bad inside me that won't let me be good?

I am now hearing a very shrill sound. I wonder where that is coming from? I look outside and Daddy is mowing the front yard. I don't see anyone else, but I still hear the noise. "Where is it coming from?" I am wondering if anyone else can hear it. Daddy doesn't appear to hear anything unusual.

I was thinking about God when I started hearing it. I wonder if this is how God talks to people. Bible stories tell me God talks directly to people if they are good people. I REALLY want to be

GOOD ENOUGH to talk to God. Like Samuel! The noise is still there. Hmmm! "Lord, here am I!"

I am now sitting on the end of my bed and looking upward toward the ceiling above my double closet because that seems to be where the shrill noise is coming from. I can still hear it. I am picturing the RKO radio tower at the end of old movies on TV. It shows sound waves going out from the tower. Maybe God talks like that tower. Maybe God is glad I want to be a good child and follow the Ten Commandments. I don't know for SURE if this shrill noise is God, but what else can it be?

> *I can hear my Savior calling,*
> *In the tend'rest accents calling;*
> *On my ear these words are falling,*
> *"Take thy cross, and daily follow me."*

> *I will take my cross and follow,*
> *My dear Savior I will follow,*
> *Where He leads me I will follow,*
> *I'll go with Him, with Him all the way.*

Gun: Control

My daddy always has a gun with us. Sometimes it is under the front seat of our car. At night it is under his pillow in his and Mommy's bed. Guns scare me!

> *Jesus loves me,*
> *"Little ones to him belong*
> *They are **WEAK** but **HE** is **STRONG!**"*

Baptism Of The Holy Spirit

I am almost ten years old. My daddy takes me to Sunday night church. My mommy and sisters stay home. Mommy says my sisters are too young and need more sleep before school.

Tonight I decide I want to be filled with the Holy Spirit. I want to be the best person I can be! I have walked to the front of the church and knelt at the altar. An older lady – a prayer warrior – someone I do not know – has knelt down beside me. I am surprised that neither of my great-grandmothers came to pray with me! I am surprised a complete stranger is here with me at this important event in my life!

She tells me to simply repeat da-da-da until it happens. After a very brief time, I find myself hesitantly and very quietly bubbling out the sounds. I feel embarrassed and shy. The older woman tells me that I am doing it. I am now filled with the Holy Spirit who will help me be a good little girl. The Holy Spirit will be the oil in my lamp. I will shine, shine, shine! I feel surprised it is that easy (something does not feel right about this).

When I get home, I tell my mommy. She is happy and calls Aunt Bebe. I fall down on the floor and speak in tongues like Jesus. I tell my mother, "I must be about my father's work." But…but….where did THAT come from? Now I feel embarrassed and dishonest.

———

I have decided it is best that I be a religious little girl. I have a very hard time dancing in my phys ed class because my head gets fuzzy and I feel light and awkward. I have a hard time remembering and following the instructions. My religion does not allow me to dance. So it is good for me to be religious since I am not like the other kids.

My pastor wrote me a note to excuse me from dancing. This does not feel good, but I do not know what else to do.

———

My sisters and I fight A LOT. We scream, hit each other, wrestle, and pull each other's hair. I am becoming mean!

———

I'm lying on my bed listening to Mommy's music:

Diana Lee, M.A.

When we walk with the Lord
in the light of His word,
what a glory He sheds on our way!
While we do His good will,
He abides with us still,
and with all who will trust and obey.

Trust and obey, for there's no other way
to be happy in Jesus, but to trust and obey.

Not a burden we bear,
not a sorrow we share,
but our toil he doth richly repay;
not a grief or a loss,
not a frown or a cross,
but is blest if we trust and obey.

Trust and obey, for there's no other way
to be happy in Jesus, but to trust and obey.

But we never can prove
the delights of his love
until all on the altar we lay;
for the favor he shows,
for the joy he bestows,
are for them who will trust and obey.

Trust and obey, for there's no other way
to be happy in Jesus, but to trust and obey.

Then in fellowship sweet
we will sit at His feet,
or we'll walk by His side in the way;
what he says we will do,
where he sends we will go;
never fear, only trust and obey.

Trust and obey, for there's no other way

ShaTterED DianA

to be happy in Jesus, but to trust and obey.

What a fellowship, what a joy divine,
Leaning on the Everlasting Arms!
What a blessedness, what a peace is mine,
Leaning on the Everlasting Arms!

Leaning, leaning,
Safe and secure from all alarms;
Leaning, leaning,
Leaning on the Everlasting Arms.

O how sweet to walk in this pilgrim way,
Leaning on the Everlasting Arms!
O how bright the path grows from day to day,
Leaning on the Everlasting Arms!

What have I to dread, what have I to fear,
Leaning on the Everlasting Arms!
I have peace complete with my Lord so near,
Leaning on the Everlasting Arms!

All hail the power of Jesus' name
Let angels prostrate fall,
Let angels prostrate fall,
Bring forth the royal diadem,

And crown Him, crown Him,
Crown Him, crown Him;
And crown Him Lord of all!

Ye chosen seed of Israel's race,
Ye ransomed from the fall,
Ye ransomed from the fall,
Hail Him who saves you by His grace,

And crown Him, crown Him,
Crown Him, crown Him;

And crown Him Lord of all!

Let every kindred, every tribe,
On this terrestrial ball,
On this terrestrial ball,
To Him all majesty ascribe,

And crown Him, crown Him,
Crown Him, crown Him;
And crown Him Lord of all!

———

It is my father talking. "The only good nigger is a dead nigger." He talks this way all the time. I prefer listening to the record at my girlfriend's house.

He's got the whole world in His hands,
He's got the whole wide world in His hands.
He's got the whole world in His hands
He's got the whole world in His hands.

This song feels good. My daddy's talk feels bad – VERY bad. I wish he'd shut up!

Mendacious: Consciously Creating A Trigger

My mother will not tell me how to spell memorable. I am wondering if it is m-e-m-O-r-a-b-l-e or m-e-m-E-r-a-b-l-e. "Look it up in the dictionary, Diana."

I am sitting in our living room on the floor with our 1936 dictionary opened in front of me. The terrazzo is cold, so I have scooted myself onto the gray wool area rug. My legs are crossed in front of me so I can hold my notebook and write while I look through the dictionary. I really don't like looking up words, but I just found some VERY interesting words: mendacious and mendacity. They mean being dishonest and lying.

They make me think of my father. I know he lies. I am memorizing the word "mendacious" so when I grow up and hear that word, I will remember I knew my FATHER IS A LIAR! I just don't know how I know. But I know that I know. Something inside is telling me. I guess it is the Holy Spirit!

I will look up mendacious every day so I NEVER EVER forget. I KNOW my father is a liar!

Would you be free from the power of sin?
There's power in the blood, power in the blood;
Would you o'er evil a victory win?
There's wonderful power in the blood.

There is power, power, wonder working power
In the blood of the Lamb;
There is power, power, wonder working power
In the precious blood of the Lamb.

Would you be free from your passion and pride?
There's power in the blood, power in the blood;
Come for a cleansing to Calvary's tide;
There's wonderful power in the blood.

Would you be whiter, much whiter than snow?
There's power in the blood, power in the blood;
Sin stains are lost in its life giving flow.
There's wonderful power in the blood.

Would you do service for Jesus your King?
There's power in the blood, power in the blood;
Would you live daily His praises to sing?
There's wonderful power in the blood.

Repercussions: No Sexual Boundaries

I am sitting in my bedroom reading my Bible. It is Saturday. I wish I had a girlfriend who would like to ride bikes with me. I think it would be fun to take a little picnic and have a great adventure.

I spend many Saturdays in my bedroom alone. I feel bored. I don't have anything to do. I have read all the stories in my social studies magazine that Mommy gave me and pasted all the stamps in place.

Sometimes I get invited to Judy's house. She lives a few houses away. I used to like going to her house. We used to make cookies and play with our dolls. It used to be FUN.

But now I have funny feelings about going to Judy's. The last time I went, she asked me if she could look between my legs. I never had a friend ask that before. I didn't know what to do. I wanted to say NO! BUT I didn't know HOW. So I let her. It felt icky.

I am bothered that I didn't know how to say no. What is wrong with me? Why did I do something I really didn't want to do? That scares me. Now I feel bad and don't want to go to her house to make cookies or play dolls because I don't know what she will ask me next time. I feel sad.

Singing to myself helps me not feel so sad.

> *He's got the whole world in His hands*
> *He's got the whole world in His hands*
> *He's got the whole world in His hands*
> *He's got the whole world in His hands*
>
> *He's got the little bitty baby in His hands*
> *He's got the little bitty baby in His hands*
> *He's got the little bitty baby in His hands*
> *He's got the whole world in His hands*
>
> *He's got everybody here in His hands*
> *He's got everybody here in His hands*
> *He's got everybody here in His hands*
> *He's got the whole world in His hands*

Coping: GOD Is My Protector

I am in my pink bedroom laying crumpled up on my bed. I am on top of my bedspread, not under it, because it is in the afternoon. I feel terrified! I learned a long time ago that if I think of GOD, I don't feel so scared. And if I think of God and still feel scared, I've learned to close my eyes and just imagine God growing bigger and BIGGER and getting meaner and MEANER until I don't feel scared any more.

It is when Daddy yells at ME that I have to make GOD BIG.

"Do you want me to chop you up and use you for fish bait?"
(No, Daddy.)
"Do you want me to knock your heads together?"
(No, Daddy.)
Turning to God is how I feel safe. I just keep making God bigger in my head until my scary feelings go away.

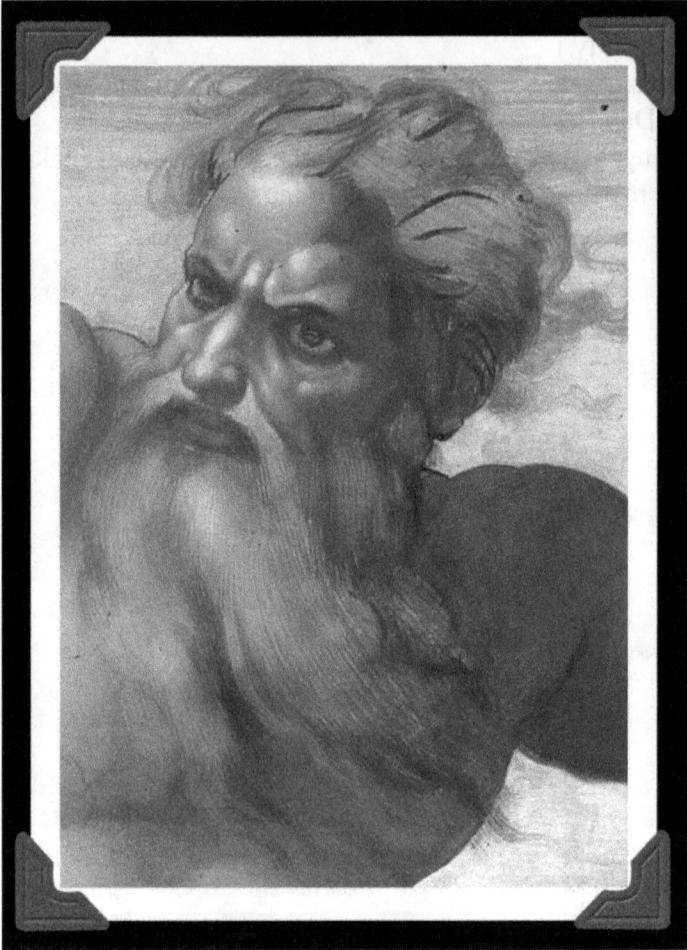

Michelangelo Sistine chapel Photographer Unknown Wikimedia Commons

I've also learned to blur my eyes when I am trying not to see something that I don't think I am supposed to see. And I've learned to put pressure on my ear drums to help me not hear what I am not supposed to hear.

> *Oh be careful little eyes what you see…*
> *Oh be careful little ears what you hear…*
> *There's a Father up above…*

I often have to jab my fingernails into the underside of my wrist when I feel frightened. It helps me not feel so frightened or angry because I can only feel the pain.

Self-hypnotizing Helps Me Escape Bullying

At my house, my daddy is always picking on my mommy, and that upsets me. Over the top of Mommy's religious music, I can ALWAYS hear his big mouth exclaiming, "OOOOOOOH, Jilllllllllllll!" He treats my mommy like she is stupid. He thinks men are smarter than women. He thinks I am stupid just because I'm a girl. I can never say anything, or do anything, he disagrees with.

Mommy just ignores him after she says, "BS!" But I have to run to my room or into the bathroom and dig my fingernails into my wrist until my fear goes away and I can make God bigger. I HATE him! Sometimes I even pray that he will not return from his fishing trips. Then I feel bad and have to ask Jesus to forgive me of my sins and come back into my heart.

When we are in the car, Daddy usually picks on Mommy. I can't stand it. I've learned to lay my head down on the backseat arm rest and to focus on the sound of the car engine and the sound of the tires hitting the pavement. That takes me away so I don't have to listen to Daddy.

Pigheaded

"Diana, you are so pigheaded!"
(I wonder what Daddy means. Ugly???)

———

The older kids at church taught me this version. I LOVE it. Yuk-yuk!

A sunbeam a sunbeam
Jesus wants me for a sunbeam
A sunbeam a sunbeam
Jesus wants me for a sunbeam
I'll be a toaster for Him!

ShaTterED DianA

Mommy's music helps me feel strong. It helps me know that things will get better in Heaven…or when I grow up. I've noticed adults don't pick on each other like they pick on kids. So growing up will be good.

I never want to forget how awful my life feels. Gray! Fuzzy! I can tell there is a wall between me and other people. It is like a glass wall. I can see out. Others can see in but we do not talk with each other. Nothing I want to do is allowed because I am a Christian and God wants me to suffer in this life to prove I can resist Satan and deserve Heaven. Thinking about Heaven helps me feel happier and hopeful.

Sing the wondrous love of Jesus;
Sing his mercy and his grace.
In the mansions bright and blessed
he'll prepare for us a place.

When we all get to heaven,
what a day of rejoicing that will be!
When we all see Jesus,
We'll sing and shout the victory!

While we walk the pilgrim pathway,
Clouds will overspread the sky;
But when traveling days are over,
Not a shadow, not a sigh!

Let us then be true and faithful,
Trusting, serving every day;
Just one glimpse of him in glory
will the toils of life repay.

Onward to the prize before us!
Soon his beauty we'll behold;
Soon the pearly gates will open;
We shall tread the streets of gold.

Diana Lee, M.A.

Safety Patrol

I'm VERY surprised I was chosen to be a safety patrol guard at school. I tell the younger children when to cross the street. But I do not like this responsibility. I feel nervous because my head is always fuzzy, gray, and lightheaded! What if I make a mistake? What if one of the little kids gets hurt? What would I do? I wonder if other guards worry like I do. I don't think their heads are fuzzy!

———

Daddy says I make him get mad. It is my fault when he gets mean. "Do not provoke me, Diana!" When I ask Mommy questions, she asks, "Are you writing a book?" (Of course I am! I AM Lois Lane reporter!) "Just the facts Mam!"

———

I've got the joy, joy, joy, joy
Down in my heart
Down in my heart
Down in my heart
I've got the joy, joy, joy, joy
Down in my heart
Down in my heart to stay

I've got the peace that passes understanding
Down in my heart
Down in my heart
Down in my heart
I've got the peace that passes understanding
Down in my heart
Down in my heart today!

Other times, I remember and think about my Sunday school lessons. I like the one about Jesus asleep in the boat during the storm when everyone else was terrified. That is what God wants me to do. Don't worry! Just go to sleep! Trust Him! He is in control. "Dear Jesus, please give me the kind of faith you had."

109

"I've told you before and now I'm going to tell you again, no talking at the dinner table. Just eat your dinner, then ask to be excused when you are finished."

(Yes, sir.)

Blind Faith: Coping Mechanism

"Do you want me to knock you in the head like a mullet and chop you up and feed you to fish?" (No, Daddy)

The day after Thanksgiving, my father always takes the rest of us fishing. He goes fishing a lot, but the Friday after Thanksgiving is always our turn. Mommy packs turkey sandwiches in the brown cooler along with fruit and Pecan Sandies and Kool-Aid. We get up early in the morning, and my sisters and I climb into the back seat of the car and fall asleep because the fishing place is far away in The Keys.

Today we are far out in the water. I cannot see any land. The top of the side of the boat is close to the water. I feel scared when I think of all the big fish in the water. What if they tip us over? Our rental boat is wooden and very small. We sit on plank seats that go across the little boat from side to side. There are no life jackets.

"Mommy, what will happen to us if a big fish knocks our boat over?" I ask.

"Diana, Daddy will save us," my mother responds immediately.

I just got goose bumps on my arm. This answer does not make sense to me! How could one person – even a daddy – save four other people when we cannot see land and we do not have any life jackets?

I feel troubled. I guess something is wrong with ME! Nobody else seems worried. I think of Jesus and know HE will save us.

Last time I caught a really big fish! It was more than three feet long! Daddy said it was a sand shark. Actually, I didn't catch it all the way. It snapped my line just as Daddy and I were pulling it into the boat.

I love being on the water with the sun shining. We never see any other boats out here. Just us! They call it The Keys, but I don't understand. My head keeps picturing house and car keys. But daddy tells me, "NOOOOOO, Diana! IT MEANS LITTLE ISLANDS. DO I HAVE TO DRAW YOU A PICTURE?"

So I just try not to think about it because it makes my head feel like it just melted. I don't know why MY head can't understand what keys mean.

Dear Jesus, please help me be a smarter girl. I don't like being dumb.

More about Jesus would I know,
More of His grace to others show;
More of His saving fullness see,
More of His love who died for me.

More, more about Jesus,
More, more about Jesus;
More of His saving fullness see,
More of His love who died for me.

More about Jesus let me learn,
More of His holy will discern;
Spirit of God my teacher be,
Showing the things of Christ to me.

Walking in sunlight all of my journey;
Over the mountains, through the deep vale;
Jesus has said, "I'll never forsake thee,"
Promise divine that never can fail.

Christmas

I
love
Christmas –
Mommy's
cookies;
a
turkey
dinner;
the
beautiful
tree
with
lights,
glass
ornaments
and
tinsel;
a
new
dress
for
church;
Silent
Night
Holy
Night
and
Joy
to
the
World
the
Lord
has
come;
But

never
anything
that
is
on
my
wish
list.

Bebe

I love lying in bed looking up at the white, plastic candles with red lights in my bedroom window before I go to sleep. Silent night, holy night. Tomorrow is Christmas. I wonder what Santa will bring me. I got to open one present tonight. I chose the one from my Aunt Bebe because I love her so much. This year, everyone drew names instead of buying everyone a present because Bebe is married now. She gave me a new white slip with a skirt that sticks out – a crinoline. I wore it to bed. I wanted to feel close to Bebe. Thinking of Bebe makes me feel loved and happy. Oh, those red lights are so pretty! Joy to the world the Lord is born!

———

I love going to the Orange Bowl Parade! It is so beautiful! It is at night. I would like to be one of the beautiful ladies on the floats when I grow up. We go every year. Hurray!

Gyroscope: Using Everything In My Environment To Cope

I'm in fifth grade and sitting at my desk at DuPruis Elementary School listening to my first man teacher. I REALLY like him! He talks to us like we are grownups instead of babies. He taught us about the men who climbed Mount Everest and what they did when they got trapped in an avalanche. I would NEVER have thought of THAT! My head doesn't think like that. It is too fuzzy. I would have DIED!

My teacher also told us about a book he just read called *Fail Safe*. It would be fun to fly a jet, but I know I am too dumb. Today he is telling us about gyroscopes. They keep submarines balanced when they are underwater. This gives me an idea.

Without drawing any attention to myself, I am praying to Jesus as I sit and listen to my teacher. "Dear Jesus, please be my gyroscope." I don't know why I think I need a gyroscope, I just know I do.

Not very often but sometimes when I walk to school, my head feels clear and that feels SO good! I wish it could be that way ALL the time! I still don't understand why I can't keep it that way.

I also don't understand why I have to learn ALL the multiplication tables if Jesus is coming back soon. My teacher took me and some boys out into the hall yesterday and told us, "No more goofing around. You HAVE to learn the tables NOW." I guess I better do it! That was embarrassing!

Blessed assurance, Jesus is mine;
Oh, what a foretaste of glory divine!
Heir of salvation, purchase of God,
Born of His Spirit, washed in His blood.

This is my story, this is my song.
Praising my Savior all the day long.
This is my story, this is my song,
Praising my Savior all the day long.

Perfect submission, perfect delight,
Visions of rapture now burst on my sight;
Angels descending, bring from above
Echoes of mercy, whispers of love.

Perfect submission, all is at rest,
I in my Savior am happy and blest;

Diana Lee, M.A.

Watching and waiting, looking above,
Filled with His goodness, lost in His love.

I love to tell the story
Of unseen things above,
Of Jesus and His glory,
Of Jesus and His love.
I love to tell the story,
Because I know 'tis true;
It satisfies my longings
As nothing else can do.

I love to tell the story,
'Twill be my theme in glory
To tell the old, old story
Of Jesus and His love.

I love to tell the story;
More wonderful it seems
Than all the golden dreams,
I love to tell the story,
It did so much for me;
And that is just the reason
I tell it now to thee.

I love to tell the story;
'tis pleasant to repeat
What seems each time I tell it,
More wonderfully sweet.
I love to tell the story;
For some have never heard
The message of salvation
From god's own holy Word.

I love to tell the story;
For those who know it best
Seem hungering and thirsting
To hear it like the rest.

And when, in scenes of glory,
I sing the new, new song,
'Twill be the old, old story,
That I have loved so long.

Oh Jill: Emotional Battering!

My daddy is still mean to my mommy. "Ooooooh, Jiiiillllll!"
Sometimes she just wants to do something fun like miniature golf after we pray in the New Year at church.

I feel sorry for her – for us. I still HATE him! (And feel guilty for hating him!)

Bunnies and Easter Eggs For Me!

Sixth grade is FUN! I was chosen to be one of the artists who got to draw the Easter scenes with colored chalk on the blackboards in the back of the room because of my grade on our last social studies test. There is a Christian scene with Jesus dying on the cross, and one with the Easter Bunny and lots of pretty eggs.

I chose to draw bunnies and eggs. (I DON'T LIKE TO THINK OF CHURCH AT SCHOOL!) So did Evelyn! She taught me how to draw bunnies. I didn't know I could draw. I really like Evelyn. She is kind to me and helpful.

I almost didn't get to be one of the artists because my teacher made an error and didn't catch one of my mistakes on our test. I was going to ignore it because I really wanted to be an artist, but the boy in front of me – not Freddie – was looking at my paper and said he was going to tell the teacher. He wanted to be one of the artists too. So I went up and told the teacher that he made a mistake. He thanked me for being honest and told me I could still be an artist because I'd been honest. That really surprised me! It made the boy in front of me MAD!

———

"Diana, pull your shorts and panties down and bend over the bed so I can spank you with Daddy's belt." (Yes, Mam.)

116

Jesus loves the little children
All the children of the world
*Red and yellow **black** and **blue**…*

Trust and obey
for there's no other way
to be happy
in Jesus
than to trust and obey!

How Can I Know What I Don't Know?: Dissociation

Saturday morning. My sisters and I have gotten our own cereal and are watching cartoons and *Sky King*. Mommy and Daddy's bedroom door is closed. I KNOW what that means, but I don't know how I know. I can't see through their door! I know it is about the douche bag and why the bathroom will smell like vinegar. Knowing this gives me an icky, sick-to-my-stomach feeling. I just want to grow up. Life will be good then.

It bothers me when I know things I don't know. It confuses me. I can't tell if Jesus or the Holy Spirit is telling me things that I don't know OR if Satan is in my head telling me BAD things. HOW can I know?

Have you been to Jesus for the cleansing power?
Are you washed in the blood of the Lamb?
Are you fully trusting in His grace this hour?
Are you washed in the blood of the Lamb?

Are you washed in the blood,
In the soul cleansing blood of the Lamb?
Are your garments spotless? Are they white as snow?
Are you washed in the blood of the Lamb?

ShaTterED DianA

Are you walking daily by the Savior's side?
Are you washed in the blood of the Lamb?
Do you rest each moment in the Crucified?
Are you washed in the blood of the Lamb?

Oooooohhhhhhhh, Jjjjjjjjjjjjiiiiiiiiiiiiiillllllll!

Are you washed in the blood,
In the soul cleansing blood of the Lamb?
Are your garments spotless? Are they white as snow?
Are you washed in the blood of the Lamb?

Oooooooooohhhhhhhh, Jjjjjjjjiiiiiiiiilllllll!

When the bridegroom cometh will your robes be white?
Are you washed in the blood of the Lamb?
Will your soul be ready for the mansions bright,
And be washed in the blood of the Lamb?

Ooooooohhhhhhh, Jiiiiiiiiiiiillllllllll!

Are you washed in the blood,
In the soul cleansing blood of the Lamb?
Are your garments spotless? Are they white as snow?
Are you washed in the blood of the Lamb?

Lay aside the garments that are stained with sin,
And be washed in the blood of the Lamb;
There's a fountain flowing for the soul unclean,
O be washed in the blood of the Lamb!

Oooooooooohhhhhhh, Jiiiiiiilllllllll!
There he goes again. I try to drown him out with the hi-fi music.

Are you washed in the blood...

Now I am feeling REALLY crazy! First I KNOW what my parents are doing behind closed doors, but I really don't. But I do, kind of. But HOW?

NOW after listening to my father's BIG mouth and my mother's "BS" reply, I am thinking, "HOW could they do THAT and then start fighting almost immediately afterwards?" What is happening with my head? Where are these thoughts and feelings coming from? This feels so incredibly icky. My tummy is flip-flopping, and I want to crawl out of my skin. I need to take a nap. I just need to go away. *Sleeping Beauty*, here I come!

"Wipe that look off your face or I am going to knock it off."

(Yes, sir.)

Mother's music just keeps playing.

> *Trust and obey for there's no other way*
> *to be happy in Jesus*
> *than to trust and obey...*

I feel CRAZY. Maybe this is what it means to have demons in me.

———

"Diana, I want you to walk around with this thick dictionary on your head. You need to learn to stand straight."

(Yesssss, Mam.)

"And stop talking with your hands."

(Yessss, Mam.)

"Have you noticed how funny you look when you drink from a glass, Diana? Your lips look like a car trunk."

(Nooooo, Mam.)

I Don't Want To Be A Woman!

I am eleven years old. I just finished sixth grade. My family and I are back in Denver for the summer. It is 1959. Daddy came with us this time. We are living at Mom and Grandpa's. I still love it here!

I am old enough to make money mowing their lawn with the old push lawn mower. I make twenty-five cents each week. After mowing in the afternoons, I walk to the Dairy Queen by myself. It is about six blocks down Mississippi. It makes me feel grown up to go off by myself. I always get my favorite: medium strawberry sundae!

This morning very early before anyone else was up I felt funny and went to the bathroom. My mother came immediately. There was blood in my panties. I did not know what was happening to me, but Mother did. She helped me.

I am now a woman. BUT I DON'T WANT TO BE A WOMAN! Women are weak. I don't want to be weak! I want to stay strong. Women don't get to have FUN. I want to have FUN! I DO NOT LIKE WHAT IS HAPPENING TO ME. I feel VERY upset!

I want to be strong! Strong! **STRONG!**

Onward Christian soldiers,
Marching as to war,
With the cross of Jesus

Junior High School Years
(1959-1962)

Humiliating

We are back from our summer in Denver. I love my new junior high. It is almost brand-new and is only a block down the street. Mommy laughed at me because I was afraid to go. I have never been in a building with two floors. I was afraid I wouldn't be able to find my way around since we change classrooms. Science class is in a large auditorium and on TV. The cafeteria has many yummy selections of food and huge desserts. I really like this school. I feel grown-up.

But I still don't like some of the things that happen to me at home. Last night my mommy gave me my first garter belt and nylons. She had me put them on and then told me to sit on the edge of her bed. Then she called my daddy to come see how "cute" I looked. He left in disgust. I felt completely humiliated. WHY did she do that to me? HOW could she do that to me? Sometimes I think she hates me and just wants to be mean, but other times she does nice things.

Last night made me think of when I had a terrible nightmare at Mom's house this summer. I dreamed I was at the zoo and a lion reached through the bars of its cage and grabbed Grandpa. I woke up screaming. My mother came immediately, but instead of comforting me, she told me to go get into bed with my FATHER and she took my cot in my and my sisters' room!

I felt so uncomfortable I could not sleep. I kept shaking. I laid very still and stiff. Then I moved to the very edge of the bed. When I got up in the morning and looked out the bedroom window at the willow tree, I felt sick to my stomach. All I could think was, "This will end when I grow up." I didn't understand where that thought came from or why I felt such intense nausea.

I often feel CRAZY because I do not understand my own head or my life. NOTHING makes sense to me – EVER! Only school; I LOVE school!

Mommy doesn't even need to play her music any more. I can hear it playing in my own head.

Jesus loves me this I know
For the Bible tells me so
Little ones to him belong
They are weak but he is strong

Yes, Jesus loves me
Yes, Jesus loves me
Yes, Jesus loves me
The Bible tells me so

I've got the joy joy joy joy
Down in my heart
Down in my heart
Down in my heart
I've got the joy joy joy joy

Parents!!!

Just when I thought I understood my religion and my parents, I am thrown for a loop, a BIG loop! Tonight is Christmas 1959. I am in the blue bedroom with my sisters. We are playing 45-rpm records our parents gave us today. What surprised me was that our record player came with Fabian's *Hound Dog Man*, Ricky Nelson's *Lonesome Town*, and Alvin and The Chipmunks *Christmas Song*. HOW does this make sense? Daddy tells me ALL rock and roll is be-pop from the devil and I will go to Hell if I dance. BUT now "Santa" brought popular music for us. I'm NOT complaining; I am just shocked and more than confused!

Oh, Yah! Mother started playing a popular radio station every morning. She even called the contest line to guess the name of a song in hopes of winning a prize. PARENTS! RULES ARE RULES except when they aren't!

At least they let us watch Dick Clark and *American Band Stand* after school now. Life is getting better. I am still trying to be a good Christian girl, if I can figure out what that is. Now we've got Mother's music along with Alvin, Ricky, and Fabian all at the same time.

I serve a risen Savior
He's in the world today.
I know that He is living,
Whatever men may say.
I see His hand of mercy;
I hear His voice of cheer;
And just the time I need Him
He's always near.
Hound Dog Man, Hound Dog Man, I wanna be a Hound Dog
Man!

He lives, He lives, Christ Jesus lives today!
He walks with me and talks with me along life's narrow way.
He lives, He lives, salvation to impart!
You ask me how I know He lives?
He lives within my heart.
Hound Dog Man, Hound Dog Man, I wanna be a Hound Dog
Man!

In all the world around me
I see His loving care,
And though my heart grows weary,
I never will despair;
I know that He is leading,
Through all the stormy blast:
The day of His appearing
Will come at last.
Hound Dog Man....

———

My family is driving home from my great-grandmother's house. She's the one who took me to Tennessee. Daddy is UPSET! He is telling us about some people who want laws that will stop teachers from spanking students. That sounds good to me.

"It is WRONG. Teachers MUST control students. What will happen to America if teachers stop spanking students?" He is also very much against television shows with loving fathers – *The Nelsons*; *Father Knows Best*. He says they undermine men's authority. Fathers are supposed to be STRONG. He likes Jackie

Gleason's *Honeymooners*. "POW! Right in the kisser Alice!" He's a smack 'em father; not a hug 'em father.

———

My father is a carpenter and a construction superintendent. He helps build hotels along Miami Beach. He talks about the Fontainebleau and the Eden Roc. He has been working on The InterContinental Hotel in San Juan, Puerto Rico. Mother and we girls had a REALLY FUN time while he was gone. It was SO nice and quiet. Happy!

Today is Valentine's Day 1960, and he just got back home. He brought each of us a heart shaped box of chocolate candy and a little alligator purse with a REAL little alligator head on it. He has NEVER been this nice to us before. I am very surprised. It feels good to have him be nice to me, but I also feel a little bit suspicious of him and awkward around him. He is talking funny.

"It was very beautiful there. I got to stay at a nice hotel, the Americana, and go to the beach. Every night I got to eat out and have a bottle of wine with my dinner."

That is REALLY unusual talk because as Pentecostal Full Gospel Christians, we are not allowed to drink ANY kind of alcohol!

"Children, honor and obey your parents that your life may be long. This makes God happy," I can hear my Sunday school teacher telling us. I will obey him and try not to think bad thoughts about him.

———

"Listen here sister! You do what I tell you to do and when I tell you to do it! No questions asked! Do you hear me? The problem with you is that you are strong – like MOM." (Yes, Daddy.)

Back to normal.

Jesus
loves
the
little

children
all
the
children
of
the
world!
Red
and
yellow
black
and
white
they
are
precious
in
His
sight

Children Obey Your Parents in All Things

"Pull your shorts and panties down and bend over the bed so I can spank you with Daddy's belt." (Yes, Mam.)

(Oh, Jesus, please help me. By His stripes we are healed. By His stripes we are healed. Saying my memory verses over and over makes the pain and humiliation go away!)

Programming Appearing as My Own Choice

When I feel sad, I go to Jesus in prayer. I ask Him to help me SURVIVE.

What a Friend we have in Jesus,
All our sins and griefs to bear!
What a privilege to carry
Everything to God in prayer!

ShaTterED DianA

O what peace we often forfeit,
O what needless pain we bear,
All because we do not carry
Everything to God in prayer!

Are we weak and heavy-laden
Cumbered with a load of care?
Precious Savior, still our refuge–
Take it to the Lord in prayer...

I just don't understand why God needs me to suffer so much! I just want to be normal!

Surprise

I
try
to
act
INVISIBLE
at
school.

THAT
is
why
I
am
very
surprised
when
good
things
happen
to
me.

I
got

nominated
and
elected
to
be
a
lady-in-waiting
to
the
Queen
at
my
school's
Valentine's
dance.

ME!

Mommy let me go as long as I promised NOT to dance. I LIED.

Damned If I Do And Damned If I Don't

I am now twelve and am finishing seventh grade in the Denver suburb of Westminster, Colorado. I am very happy to be back with my maternal grandmother, Mom. "Glory hallelujah!"

We are renting half of a very large 100-year-old house on Bradburn Boulevard. I like the stained wood stairs, spindles and banister; the two fireplaces; the large picture window in the living room that looks out toward the Rocky Mountains; and the huge, sunny, country kitchen at the back of the house. All of the rooms are huge. I share one VERY large upstairs bedroom with both of my sisters. There is brown wallpaper on the walls with ballerinas in pastel colors. I like it! I've never had wallpaper before.

The ninth-grade boys at school like me because I have a southern accent. I have a boyfriend. His name is Larry. His last name is German. "Never marry a German, Diana. They make their wives work hard. No man who loves you will ever ask you to work," my father tells me.

Some of the girls at school have invited me to join Job's Daughters. They said I have to be related to a Mason to join. I ask my parents. "Your paternal great-grandfather is a Mason, but that is a bad group. You cannot join."

Two days ago, I made everyone mad at me. "All Southerners hate Black people," my history teacher told the class. "I don't hate Black people," I said as I raised my hand. "I don't hate Black people, and I'm a Southerner." "Diana, go to the office immediately," he ordered me. "I will be having a meeting with your parents."

Now I have to eat my lunch in the vice-principal's office for the next two weeks with my southern girlfriend, Kathy. Nobody likes me anymore. They all believe the teacher. I feel sad. "What did I do wrong? All I did was tell the truth! I KNOW I was NOT disrespectful." My father did not defend me. He defended the honor of the South, but he did not defend me.

The best part of my new house is that the library is two blocks away. Hotdog! I read constantly now. *Gone with the Wind*, here I come!

Flunked For Using a Different Cursive Style

I still don't understand what comes over me, but sometimes I feel "different." I cannot quite explain it. When this happens, I even write differently.

It happened to me while I was doing homework last weekend. When I got my paper back, the teacher had given me an "F." I've never had an "F" since first grade "Unsatisfactory in arithmetic." (My Florida drafting teacher gave me a "D." I just couldn't understand 3-dimensional drawing.) So I went up to her desk and asked her why I received an "F."

"That is not your handwriting." "Yes it is," I replied. I even attempted to show her it was mine. But I was not feeling "that" way, so I could not do it exactly like my homework. So she did not believe me and I got an "F" even though I had done the work.

I don't think she was fair! I've never cheated. I would not lie to my teacher.

I often write differently depending on how I feel. Sometimes I slant right. Sometimes I slant left. Sometimes I make big fat letters like my girlfriend. Sometimes I make small and perfect letters like my mother's hand writing. That is how I wrote the assignment that my teacher flunked. It REALLY looked EXACTLY like Mother wrote it! I like to copy other people's style and pretend that I am them. I am still trying to figure out what other kids do that makes them OKAY.

Baby Sister Whipped Across Her Face

My youngest sister went to her elementary school principal to ask for help. She had red electrical cord marks across her face. He said it is a family problem, not the school's. MOTHER whipped her with an electrical cord! ACROSS THE FACE!

Our New Church

The church we go to across town is huge. It is where my parents met years ago. It looks like a big theater. I like this church better than the one in Florida. It is more sophisticated. We sing different kinds of songs, and the minister preaches standing still in back of a podium instead of marching back and forth across the platform carrying his microphone. He does not yell and scream like the pastor in Miami. He talks more like a teacher. And there is no big neon sign on top of the roof that says, "Jesus Saves" or "The wages of sin is death." It was embarrassing to go to that church in Florida!

The choir wears ivory robes and is very large, and I love when they sing the *Hallelujah Chorus* accompanied by the ebony grand piano and organ. They have lots of ministers, and all of their wives look like movie stars. Across the front of the church runs an altar, but they do not ask people to come down to be filled with the Holy Spirit and speak in tongues or to get healed. At this church, people sit still and are quiet. No one raises their hands or shouts out,

"Praise the Lord" or "Glory hallelujah!" They dim the lights when we pray. Someone told me it holds 1,500 people, and they have three morning services and one night service.

I know that I am too fat, ugly and stupid to ever get married; but if anyone asks me to marry him, I'm going to have that choir sing the *Hallelujah Chorus* at my wedding. The choir always sings the *Hallelujah Chorus* whenever the minister tells the congregation that we have reached our goal for the annual missionary pledges. ..

All of my churches stress the importance of missions – taking Jesus to "the world." The pastor tells us that everyone who does not accept Jesus as their savior will go to Hell. So it is our duty to give as much money as we can so that every person in the world gets to come to Jesus and be saved before Jesus comes back. This minister also talks about how we are living in the last days and that Jesus could come at any minute. That keeps me scared!

I don't feel completely comfortable at this church because everyone wears expensive clothes and drives newer cars than ours. I feel like I don't fit in. When I'm sitting in my Sunday school class, I am quiet. I just listen and smile if someone looks at me. I try to be invisible as much as possible. My teacher talks to us about walking with Jesus and tells us we need to be thinking about Jesus all the time.

I always have my memory verses memorized. I am still asking Jesus to help me be EXACTLY like him. I understand what sorrow, tears and agony feel like. I guess I am getting close.

Down from His glory
Ever living story,
My God and Savior came,
And Jesus was His name.
Born in a manager,
To His own a stranger,
A Man of sorrows, tears and agony.

O how I love Him! How I adore Him!
My breath, my sunshine, my all in all!
The great Creator became my Savior,
And all God's fullness dwelleth in Him.

What condescension,
Bringing us redemption;
That in the dead of night,
Not one faint hope in sight,
God, gracious, tender
Laid aside His splendor,
Stooping to woo, to win, to save my soul.

O how I love Him! How I adore Him!
My breath, my sunshine, my all in all!
The great Creator became my Savior,
And all God's fullness dwelleth in Him.

Without reluctance,
Flesh and blood His substance
He took the form of man,
Revealed the hidden plan.
O glorious myst'ry,
Sacrifice of Calv'ry,
And I know Thou art the great I AM.

O how I love Him...

Asking Jesus To Find Us A House To Buy

I am aware that when I'm in public and talk like my family talks at home, people look at me oddly or they gasp. So, I'm learning to stay quiet. I just listen. I simply do not know how to talk to people. That makes me very sad because I am very lonely.

It is 1961, and I am in ninth grade. I'm sitting in civics class. I really do not think I will ever need to know this boring stuff. I just want to get married and drive a car around all day like all the ladies I see when I look out the school bus window when I ride to school.

We are now in a house my parents bought in Arvada, Colorado. It is brick, very pretty and SMALL. BUT I have a tiny room of my own again. I really like that! I asked my mother if she would put some wallpaper on the walls for me. She agreed that I could have it on one wall. Mom came over and helped her. It is white with blue roses. I really like it, but I do not like the fact that they ran out of wallpaper and the last 10 inches of the wall is not covered. That really bothers me, but she says it is too expensive to buy more. I have hung lots of my stuff up on the other walls that are painted baby blue. I really enjoy decorating my little room. I have new furniture again. This time it is an early-American maple twin bed with a spindle headboard and a tiny kneehole desk with a matching chair and night stand. I never pick out any of my stuff; it just arrives! And all my other stuff just disappears!

The people next door and the people four houses away all go to our church across town. We moved here because my mother heard about it from one of the older ladies at church. Her son and daughter-in-law live next door. Everyone calls the older lady "Auntie." She is a very large woman and is known as a "prayer warrior." So my mother asked her if we should buy the house. Auntie prayed and told my mother, "Yes." It really is too SMALL for ALL of us! It does not make sense to me that God would not let us have a bigger house. I wanted a basement so badly.

———

Sometimes I feel very angry – so angry that I destroyed the beautiful doll that decorated my bed. I LOVED that doll! She is the one I saw in the bakery in Tennessee. My paternal grandmother bought her for Christmas. It was a wonderful surprise. But I ripped her apart one night. Now I feel bad and sad.

I have a blouse that has a print that depicts farmers harvesting. It has a quote, "Make hay while the sun shines." That is how I often feel. I never know any more how I will feel. Some days I am very sad. Other days I am okay but fuzzy-headed. So I try to get as much done as possible when I feel good.

———

I don't feel comfortable in my body. It feels like it is WAY TOO BIG for me. I feel clumsy in it. I don't feel connected to it most of the time.

I often get sick in algebra and have to go home. The teacher is the football coach, and that is what he talks about. When I can't follow him, I start to feel frightened. I don't want to flunk. I get

VERY sweaty. In that class especially, I feel light-headed and nauseous. I feel REALLY stupid, more stupid than normal, in THAT class. I need him to go slower and discuss less football.

High School
(1962-1965)

The Only True Church

Sunday school is where I am every Sunday morning. I am sitting in a little group of girls my age with an adult woman teaching us. I've learned that to be popular I need better clothes than what my parents give me, so I babysit to make money for clothes. I love buying adult hats to wear to Sunday school.

Today we are learning about how we are the true church and Catholics are wrong when they say that they are the first church. I really do not care. Something about all of this does not feel right to me. Sometimes God is mean and scary and kills people, and sometimes God is kind and gentle like Jesus and tells the little children to come to him and sit on his lap. But sometimes Jesus is mean and angry and kills people if they do not accept him before the end of the world.

My teachers always tell me that I have to have Jesus in my heart or I cannot do good. That confuses me because I have asked Jesus into my heart many times, and I try to be good. But it doesn't seem to me that my father tries to do good and he is the one who makes me go to church.

Something just does not seem right to me. My father is the one who hates Jews because they killed Jesus and hates colored people and Catholics. I do not think I hate anyone but myself.

Our memory verse is II Timothy 3:16 & 17: "All scripture is given by inspiration of God, and is profitable for doctrine, for reproof, for correction, for instruction in righteousness: That the man of God may be perfect, thoroughly furnished unto all good works."

There is power, power
wonder working power
in the blood of the Lamb!

There is power, power
wonder working power
in the precious blood of the Lamb!

Redeemed by the blood of the Lamb
Redeemed, redeemed

Trust and Obey

As I sit back in the plush stadium seat, our pastor is explaining tonight that "the world" asks: "Who am I?" "How did I get here?" "What is the meaning of life?" He says that true Christians do not have to ask these ridiculous questions because the Bible gives us all the answers. We are children of God if we have accepted Jesus into our hearts, and we are here on earth to do the will of our heavenly Father. That means that we are to obey Him and His word, the Bible, literally. Everything we need to know is in the Bible. Jesus and the Bible is all we need–ever! We are not like silly people in "the world," we have all the answers to all of life's problems. BUT part of ME thinks those questions are SMART questions.

I know I have asked Jesus into my heart many, many times, but my father says that if I commit one sin, He leaves. I cannot imagine losing Jesus. I would feel so alone.

I feel a strong urge pulling me to walk the aisle down to the front of this huge auditorium once again. The pastor says it is the Holy Spirit convicting me of my sin.

I am bending down on my knees in front of everyone at the wooden altar once again. I want Jesus to know I am serious about following Him. "Dear Jesus, I don't know what I have done bad, but I feel like a very bad person. Please, please come into my heart today to stay. I want to be good."

I hear the large choir singing:

Into my heart.
Into my heart.
Come into my heart Lord Jesus.
Come in today.
Come in to stay.
Come into my heart Lord Jesus!

As the choir sings this lullaby, I feel comforted. I feel warm. I feel loved. But I don't understand why that comforting and warm feeling does not last. As soon as I get into our cold car and my dad starts fighting with my mother, it disappears. I want to keep this good feeling all the time, but I can't. I don't know how. Everyone I see at church seems very happy all the time. They are always smiling and friendly. But I feel sad inside. I feel awkward. I feel lonely. I feel sooooo lonely. I feel frightened. I feel too evil to go up to other kids and be friendly.

I really don't understand. My Pastor tells me that all I need is Jesus and the Bible, but it seems to me that other people have more than just that. I cannot figure out what it is that they've got. I've been washed in the blood of the Lamb, but I am still just plain old, sad, awkward, and lonely scared me. I HATE myself. WHAT IS WRONG WITH ME?

When I walk down the halls in my high school, I feel fat, ugly and stupid. I feel like a huge, gargantuan monster, so I walk with my eyes looking down at the tiles on the floor instead of at my classmates. Even after asking Jesus to help me feel good about myself, I still feel like visual pollution. I do not want anyone looking at me. I don't want anyone talking to me. I feel like a creepy freak!

My mother will not allow my sisters and me to wear the popular fashions. I have to wear very full gathered cotton skirts that go three inches past my knees and saddle oxfords with very heavy white bobby socks that go all the way up to my knees. The other girls wear nylons and cute shoes called flats and short pencil skirts and sweaters. I wear white cotton blouses.

We are now in the car. OOOOOOOOhhhhhhhhhh, Jjjjjjjjiiiiiiiiilllllllllllllll! I wish my father would stop picking on my mother. WHY doesn't she leave him?

It feels weird that Mommy keeps track of our periods on a BIG calendar that hangs on the wall in our kitchen.

———

"Diana, I have given your mother beautiful jewelry and perfume and she will not wear it. I do not know what she has even done with it."

Why is Daddy talking to me like this? I feel VERY uncomfortable. I wish my mother would leave him and move into an apartment with us three girls. We could make it on our own. I KNOW we could! Mother is smart! Life would be so much happier without HIM. I do not feel sorry for my father.

———

"Diana, would you like to make chef salad with me tonight? We will stop after church and pick up Thousand Island dressing from the Old South chicken restaurant," my father is saying.

I don't understand why he is asking ME to help him instead of my mother! It gives me the creeps, just like when he asks to take my picture when we've come home from church and I'm all dressed up. He gets right up in my face – just inches away. CREEPY!

I also do not understand why my father keeps telling me these things. I HATE IT! He comes up alongside me and whispers a few words and goes away. YUCK!

"Do you know what your mother said to me? She said that she could call her brothers and they would take care of her."

He makes no sense to me. I just want him to STOP it! But my mother's statement does make me think of Jesus saying that he could have called ten thousand angels to protect him. In other words, HIS FATHER WANTED HIM TO DIE on the cross for my sins, and that is why he obeyed -- even unto death! He loves me so much that he was willing to die in my place.

Why doesn't my mother call her brothers? We need help! I sure feel like I am dying. Every day when I get off the school bus and walk home and into the house, my mother is sitting at the kitchen table reading her Bible. Every night, she cries as she washes and dries the dishes and then she sits in a chair and stares into space. We eat the same food week after week now. No more interesting ethnic recipes. No more barbeques on Saturday night. No more homemade ice cream. Sunday is pot roast, Monday is leftover pot roast, Tuesday is… She NEVER laughs or smiles.

———

It is all I can do to get through each day. Yesterday when I told her I am going to take shorthand next year, she told me I am not smart enough. I'll show her!

———

When my Aunt Bebe comes to town, she talks to me about demons and the devil. She thinks the devil is OPPRESSING me. That is different from demon possession. Whew! At least he's still on the outside of me, but I wish I could get rid of him!

———

Diana, come here, lean over my bed, and pull down your shorts and panties so I can spank you with your father's belt!"
(Yes, Mother.)
"By His stripes we are healed. By his stripes we are healed. By his stripes we are healed."
I am gone! No more pain! No more humiliation! No more heartbreaking betrayal! Gone!

Gone, Gone, Gone, Gone, yes! My sins are gone
Now my soul is free and in my heart's a song...

Teen Choir

I didn't want to join the teen choir. My parents made me, but I am enjoying it. There are about one hundred of us from high schools all over Denver. It is more fun than sitting home bored on Sunday afternoon. I sing alto. We are practicing two songs for next Sunday morning's early service.

"Man of sorrows," what a name
For the Son of God who came
Ruined sinners to reclaim!
Hallelujah! What a savior!

Bearing shame and scoffing rude,
In my place condemned He stood;
Sealed my pardon with His blood;

143

Hallelujah! What a Savior!

Guilty, vile, and helpless, we,
Spotless Lamb of God was He;
Full redemption–can it be?
Hallelujah! What a Savior!

Lifted up was He to die,
"It is finished!" was His cry;
Now in heaven exalted high;
Hallelujah! What a savior!

When He comes, our glorious King,
To His kingdom us to bring,
Then anew this song we'll sing
Hallelujah! What a Savior!

Fairest Lord Jesus!
Ruler of all nature!
O Thou of god and man the Son!
Thee will I cherish,
Thee will I honor,
Thou, my soul's glory, joy, and crown!

Fair are the meadows
Fairer still the woodlands
Robed in the blooming garb of spring;
Jesus is fairer,
Jesus is purer,
Who makes the woeful heart to sing!

Isolation: Church Is My Only Social Life

I am starting to meet more church kids my age, and church boys are taking me places, like out for a hamburger after church or to play miniature golf. I have been invited to a senior prom. I don't really know what that is because I am not allowed to go to the dances at my high school or join pep club. I'm not allowed to date anyone who does not go to my church because I'm still not supposed to mix with "the world." I really do not feel like I fit in anywhere, but I am more comfortable at church than at school. I still stay quiet wherever I go and smile.

I am very surprised the mother of a really cute guy at church called my mother to ask if he can take me to his high school prom. He is a letterman and a senior and has been nominated for prom king, so he needs to attend. I am a sophomore. My mother will let me go as long as he and I promise that we will not dance. "You need to stand for Jesus!" His parents make him promise also. My mother asked me, "What would Jesus think if he came back and found you dancing?" And, "What would Jesus think if he came back and found you sitting in a movie theater?"

(We danced, kind of. Neither of us knew HOW. It was fun, but I felt guilty and awkward. The restaurant was fancy, and I didn't know which fork to use. Ugh! I was shocked Mother bought me a beautiful formal. I have been buying or making most of my clothes since I began babysitting in junior high.)

———

My father is angry with me again. We have just walked into our little brick house after being in church all morning. I can smell my mother's roast beef cooking on the stove top. It smells good. I don't understand why my father is SO ANGRY with me. All I said was, "Our family needs love."

We just came from church, and that is what we talked about: God loving us so much he sent his son to die for us. Before I knew what happened, my father clinched his fist and slugged me in the face. My nose is bleeding. My heart is broken. "HOW could he do that to me," I ask myself.

As I run into my bedroom, I tell myself, "I know what is wrong with this family. Why won't he listen to me? Why does he always get so angry with me? Doesn't he want us to have a loving family?" I will not give up. I will find a way to communicate with him. I am determined to make him understand that we need love. Just love. That is all we need.

I hear my father yelling at me, "I give you a roof over your head! I give you the clothes on your back! I give you the food in your stomach! What more do you want?" I think to myself, "I need love. I need attention. I need help with school. I need guidance. I need hugs. I need to feel warmth." And besides, I BUY ALL OF MY CLOTHES AND SHOES NOW! Who wouldn't want their family to feel love, to feel the warmth other families have – instead of a cold windy vacuum?

Billy Graham's Gonna Rescue Me!

My family and I are at Billy Graham's crusade at Mile High Stadium. It is a beautiful evening with a light breeze. Billy has finished preaching, and everyone is starting to sing "Just as I am." I feel the Holy Spirit convicting me and pulling me to go down front. Maybe I can finally get Jesus to forgive me and come into my heart if I go forward and Billy prays for me. I wish I could figure out why I am so much more evil than everyone else.

Just as I am, without one plea,
But that Thy blood was shed for me,
And that Thou bid'st me come to Thee,
O Lamb of God, I come! I come!
Just as I am, and waiting not
To rid my soul of one dark blot;
To Thee whose blood can cleanse each spot,
O Lamb of God, I come, I come!

Just as I am, though tossed about
With many a conflict, many a doubt;
Fightings within, and fears without,
O Lamb of god, I come, I come!

Just as I am, poor, wretched, blind;
Sight, riches, healing of the mind;
Yes, all I need, in Thee to find,
O Lamb of God, I come, I come!

Just as I am, Thou wilt receive,
Wilt welcome, pardon, cleanse, relieve;
Because Thy promise I believe,
O Lamb of God, I come, I come!

Just as I am, Thy love unknown
Has broken every barrier down;
Now, to be Thine, yea, Thine alone,
O Lamb of God, I come, I come!

———

"Thy word have I hid in my heart that
I might not sin against thee."

"Thy word have I hid in my heart that
I might not sin against thee."
[Psalms 119:11]

School, Work And Dating

I am in eleventh grade and sixteen years old. I am still dating the same guy who took me to his senior prom last May. But I do not get to see him very often because he is in college in another town. Sometimes his parents invite me to go along with them to visit him, and sometimes he comes home, but not often. We mostly see each other in the summer. Sometimes we play putt-putt, go to a drive-in with his parents, or go to parties at church or at a church friend's house. His parents often invite me to have lunch at their house after morning church, and I enjoy that. They are very nice to me. They have a loving family – a FUN family.

Usually I get a letter from him once a week. Those letters mean so much to me because I feel alone and lonely without him. I am now working in a drug store after school because it gets me out of the unhappiness and tension in my house and gives me money to save for college. I want to become a business teacher. I get A's in shorthand!

At the drug store, I run the cash register and help at the cosmetics counter. Many of the women tell me I am beautiful. ME! I have never heard that before! I wonder if they are just being nice. Occasionally I help stock shelves. I really like stocking the tobacco shelf because it smells SO good!

After I get home from the store at 9:15, I do my homework and read my New Testament until I fall asleep. My house is a very lonely place because no one talks to me, and if I talk about what I learned in school, I make my father angry. So I try not to talk. Mother tells me "not to rock the boat." Reading my Bible and praying to Jesus helps me feel loved, especially on the days I do not receive a letter from my boyfriend.

My mother tells me scary stories about bad things that can happen to me if I date someone not from church or if I dance. I do not drink or smoke or dance. I am not even interested in drinking or smoking anyway. I don't want to start something that I may not be able to control. I want a good life. But I would like to dance!

Some of the guys from my high school come into the store and talk to the guy that works with me. One is really cute. I am too shy to say hello to him. I know that he dates the really pretty girls, so I don't want to embarrass myself by saying hello to him. But IF I could date someone from my school and IF I was good enough, he is the one I would want to date. I think he is the most handsome boy in our school.

———

I like this hymn. It comforts me because it puts very beautiful pictures in my head that make me feel good, relaxed. A beautiful peaceful garden at morning...lots of winding paths, ponds, streams, many varieties of trees to keep it cool, lots of flowers, mountains in the background...

I come to the garden alone while the dew is still on the roses...
And He walks with me and He talks with me
and He tells me I am his own;
And the joy we share as we tarry there
none other has ever known...

Or something like that. I sing it when I feel lonely. I sing it a lot.

I guess Jesus is my best friend. He and my maternal grandmother, Mom! I can call Mom any time. We often talk when I get home from the drug store.

Mom is the one who explained that I have whooping cough. EVERY NIGHT I have a hard time breathing after I've gone to sleep. I wake up making a HORRIBLE noise as I gasp for air. I sound like a barking seal! Even though I am next door to my parents' room, NO ONE ever comes to help me or gets me help. I don't know what I would do without Mom. I think I would die.

My paternal grandmother lives near me now, and she invites me over a lot. She is kind to me, but she is different from Mom – not as warm or interested in my life and boyfriends, but she sews for me. She is an expert tailor. She tells me to buy whatever pattern I want – even *Vogue* – and the material, and she makes it for me. NOW I have the BEST clothes! They are awesome. LOTS of beautiful suits and dresses!

———

I am home from school. It is not my day to work at the drug store, and I do not have a babysitting job today. I generally babysit only on Friday and Saturday nights now. (Babysitting taught me that children are not born evil or bad. They are sweet.) I have approached my mother as she stands in the kitchen where she is almost always to be found.

"Mother can we get my teeth fixed? I am embarrassed by my left eye tooth. It is a snaggletooth."

"Diana, you have the best teeth in the family. You have nothing to feel embarrassed about." "I know, I know," I think to myself. What I want is never important. We give our money to the church so the pastors' children can have whatever they need and want – satin gloves – the BEST of everything!

I don't understand God. Why is it that some get so much and the rest of us so little? Why can't I be one of His Chosen Ones? Why is it always about His will and my suffering? Why can't being good make a difference? I read my Bible and pray every day. I work so hard to be good, but nothing I do makes any difference.

Daddy Lies to Save His Reputation at My Expense: Evil

My father is angry with me again! I don't understand why. All I said was, "It feels so good when I go to my boyfriend's house. I wish we had love like they have." I thought that if he understood what it was like there, he would want it for us. I was wrong! VERY wrong!!

My father now has his red face close to mine. He is clinching his teeth and talking through them like he does.

"If you like them so much better, why don't you call Mr. Summers and ask him if you can live with them?"

My house still feels cold and tense. There is no warmth between my sisters and me or my parents and me. I do not think I can take any more. I am walking out of the living room while my father is speaking. "I give you…"

I walk down the short hall and pick up the telephone that is hanging on the wall across from the bathroom. I dial my boyfriend's house. I know he will not be home because he is in college. I am just a senior. I truly want to be away from my family, my father. There has to be a better way to live.

Mr. Summers answers the phone.

"Hello?"

"Mr. Summers, this is Diana."

"Hi! How are you?"

"My father just told me to call you and ask if I can live with you."

"He WHAT? May I talk with your father?"

I hear my father responding to Mr. Summers, "Oh, you know how she is. I never said that. Thanks for understanding, Barry. See you at church."

I am totally humiliated! My father just lied! I am shocked that he did not tell the truth! How will I face Mr. Summers again? HOW could my OWN father do this to me? All I want is love and happiness for my family. How can that be SO wrong? I've figured out that the reason our house feels like a huge vacuum is because the vacuum is where love should be. HOW can that be? We are Christians! Or is it just ME that feels it? Is it because I can't get Jesus to come into my heart to stay? Would I feel love then? Would everything be okay then? It must be me! I will keep trying!

BUT I KNOW Daddy tarnished my reputation to save his. I feel utterly betrayed, UTTERLY HUMILIATED!

And He walks with me and He talks with me
and He tells me I am his own...
What a friend we have in Jesus
all our griefs and sins to bear...

Children obey your parents that your days upon
the earth maybe long...

I need to read my Bible so I feel close to God and can feel safe and loved enough to get to sleep.

Mother

Used by permission, Olan Mills.

I have noticed my mother never smiles. Her mouth actually turns down. I am making myself a promise that I will never be like her. I will always smile, no matter what!

I have learned a song at church: "Smile awhile and give your face a rest!" They are always talking to us about how it takes fewer muscles to smile than to frown. I don't understand why my mother doesn't smile like other mothers.

I
don't
want
to
be
like
my
mother.

"Diana,
lean
over
my

bed,
pull
your
skirt
up
and
pull
down
your
panties."
(Yes, Mother.)

I can hardly feel the belt. I am so used to going into my head and repeating my verses.

"By His stripes we are healed."
"Children obey your parents…"
"And He walks with me and He talks with me and
He tells me I am His own…"
"Jesus loves me this I know for the Bible
tells me so."

I am WAY PAST SORROW and HUMILIATION. WHY is she doing this to me?

Intense Emotional and Verbal Abuse: Example of Locus of Control Shift

We are driving to Sunday school. We are almost to church. I am in the back seat with my two sisters. My Father is taunting me. "Diana is getting so big we will have to start buying her clothes at Denver Tent and Awning. Her feet are getting so big she will soon have to wear shoe boxes." Now he is calling my size seven feet "nigger flappers." We are minutes from Sunday school. I will myself not to cry by biting hard on my inner check and by digging my finger nails into my under wrist. Everyone is laughing…but me.

I remember when I was only eight or nine, I used to wish that he would never come home from fishing trips when he was late. I ALWAYS wished him DEAD. THEN I would feel guilty. I KNEW I was BAD. THAT is why Jesus cannot love me. I AM bad. So very, very bad. EVIL! I have to try harder to please Him!

Sunday Night Services

I love the Sunday night services. They are a bit more informal. And I like the boys. There are lots of them!

One of my favorite songs talks about how all of my sins are gone. That makes me feel so happy.

My memory verse this week was

> *Be careful for nothing; but in everything by prayer and supplication*
> *with thanksgiving let your requests by made known unto God.*
> *And the peace of god, which passeth all understanding ,*
> *shall keep your hearts and minds*
> *through Christ Jesus.*
> *[Philippians 4:6-7 KJV]*

I AM PRAYING and ASKING Jesus to take away my sins and give me peace and joy, but it still doesn't last. WHAT IS WRONG WITH ME? Try harder! Try harder! Try harder!

———

I still read my Bible every night before I go to sleep. I identify totally with the suffering Jesus, the misunderstood Jesus, the crucified Jesus. I long for my own resurrection and ascension. I try so hard to be a very good girl. I try to show love to my parents and sisters by buying them really nice gifts for their birthdays and Christmas, but nothing I do changes my life or my family. I just KNOW we could all be happy if my father and mother could understand that our family needs love. I often feel totally and completely overwhelmed with grief.

> *For it is God which worketh in you both to will*

and to do of his good pleasure.
Do all things without murmurings and disputings:
That ye may be blameless and harmless,
the sons of God, without rebuke, in the midst of a crooked and
perverse nation,
among whom ye shine as lights in the world.
[Philippians 2:13-15 KJV]

Oh, Jesus, please help me!

A sunbeam! A sunbeam!
Jesus wants me for a sunbeam!

Water Baptism Will Make Me Pure!

Now that I am in twelfth grade, I am ready to be baptized during the Sunday night service. This means a lot to me because it shows that I really want to be a good person. I am now in a white robe in the baptismal pool, and the senior pastor is asking me, "Diana, do you accept Jesus as your savior?" I shyly answer, "Yes." He then tells me that baptism symbolizes that I am sharing Jesus' death, burial and resurrection. He puts his hand on the back of my head and guides me into the water and back out as he says, "In the name of the Father, Son and Holy Spirit, I baptize you."

I feel I have done something very significant. It means everything to me. I really want to be a good person. I want to feel clean. Pure!

Now that I have been baptized, I am sure from now on I will be a happy person and I will feel like I fit in with everyone else. My head won't be foggy anymore. I won't get angry any more. I will always be sweet. THIS must be what has been missing in my life!

I am surprised that no one in my family says anything about it as we drive home. I thought it was supposed to be a REALLY BIG DEAL!

Amazing Grace

Amazing grace! How sweet the sound,
That saved a wretch; like me!
I once was lost, but now am found,
Was blind, but now I see.

'Twas grace that taught my heart to fear,
And grace my fears relieved;
How precious did that grace appear
The hour I first believed!

The Lord hath promised good to me,
His word my hope secures;
He will my shield and portion be
As long as life endures.

When we've been there ten thousand years,
Bright shining as the sun,
We've no less days to sing god's praise
Than when we first begun.

The congregation is singing *Amazing Grace* after the minister told us the man who wrote it had been a former slave trader. He felt gratitude that God forgave him. This tells me I am worse than a slave trader! I HATE what they did to people! No wonder I HATE myself! God cannot forgive me and take away my sins like he did the slave trader's!

We are driving home now, and my mother is asking me to please leave the living room alone. Every time she leaves, I move all the furniture and rearrange all of her knickknacks. I really think it looks better the way I do it. She doesn't.

"Most Men Lead Lives of Quiet Desperation"

"This is MY HOUSE. As long as you live here, you will do as I say." (Yes, sir.)

My father and I fight all the time now, but I really do not understand why. He tells me I cannot go to any state university. He will not pay unless I go to a church school – a Pentecostal church school.

I am saving all of my money from the drug store and from babysitting. I already have more than 500 dollars. I make 50 cents an hour. I have been accepted at three universities including Colorado State University in Fort Collins. That is where I will go. I will major in business. I want to be a business teacher like my teacher at school. I really like her; she is kind.

My mother drove me to Fort Collins, and I spoke with the head of the Food Services department. I have a job working in the kitchen serving food when I get there. I will not need any money from my parents.

I cannot explain why, but I know I do not want to go to a church school. There is something more, and I want to find it.

Trust in the Lord with all thine heart and lean not unto
your own understanding....

I feel God is leading me in a different direction from what my father is demanding. I'm going to trust God, not my father.

The Scapegoating Ritual

"Diana,
bend
over
and
pull
your
panties

157

down..."
(Yes, Mam!)

Man of sorrows what a name
for the son of God who came...

When she is exhausted, she stops. I leave. We act like nothing has happened. We never talk. Never!

This is why I was so surprised she gave me a GORGEOUS black chiffon cocktail dress for Christmas. It was exactly what I would want, but it was a size 9 and I am an 11. So I had to take it back. The elevens were gone. I went to the bargain basement and found a much cheaper black dinner dress.

She laughs in front of the family about me. She says that I am like a ham. "So firm and round and fully packed!" Nobody cares how I feel. Nobody cares about how hard I try. Only Jesus! He sees and knows everything I do!

When I darkened my hair, Daddy told me I looked like a prostitute – in front of my date.

I Surrender All: The Other Scapegoating Ritual

Here I go again. The lights have been lowered, the minister is telling us that we will feel the Holy Spirit pulling us toward the altar if we are sinners. I definitely feel that. The organist is playing, and the congregation of more than one-thousand people is singing softly,

> *All to Jesus I surrender,*
> *All to Him I freely give;*
> *I will ever love and trust Him,*
> *In His presence daily live.*
> *I surrender all,*
> *I surrender all.*
> *All to Thee, my blessed Savior,*
> *I surrender all."*

I am on my feet making my way to the altar. Again!

> *All to Jesus I surrender,*

Humbly at His feet I bow,
Worldly pleasures all forsaken;
Take me, Jesus, take me now.

I am at the altar crying. I still cannot figure out why Jesus cannot come into my heart and stay. Why am I so evil? What is it I am doing wrong?

All to Jesus I surrender,
Make me, Savior, wholly Thine;
Let me feel thy Holy Spirit,
Truly know that thou art mine.

Jesus, please forgive me. Please come into my heart again. I am so sorry I am such a bad person. Please help me be a good person. I ask you to control my life, now and always.

All to Jesus I surrender,
Lord, I give myself to Thee;
Fill me with Thy love and power,
Let Thy blessing fall on me.

Please, Jesus!

All to Jesus I surrender,
Now I feel the sacred flame.
Oh, the joy of full salvation!
Glory, glory to His name!

Thank you, Jesus. Thank you for saving me again.

Jesus Shows His Love for Mother at Luby's

I am with my family. We have just finished a meal at Luby's Cafeteria in the Lakeside Shopping Center. We are not alone. We have several families of relatives with us – ministers and their families on vacation. We've all been to church this morning.

When my mother got her check, it was for two people instead of this gang of people. She TOLD EVERYONE at the table what happened. She said, "Thank you, Jesus." And then she paid the check for two, and we all paraded out. No one said anything! I feel stunned. I guess I still do not understand Jesus! This feels wrong to me!

Trust
and
obey
for
there's
no
other
way
to
be
happy
in
Jesus
than
to
trust
and
obey!

My boyfriend is home for the summer. Hurray! He said his parents asked him what I do during the week that I need to keep going to the altar on Sunday evenings. He told them he didn't know. Hmmm. I thought EVERYONE could SEE how evil I am. I thought it was OBVIOUS!

Deeper and Wider

I'm standing in my university dorm suite combing my hair in front of the little sink and mirror when my roomy and our suite mate, also a Diana, ask me where I'm going. "I'm going to my midweek Campus Crusade for Christ meeting. They are teaching me that God has a wonderful plan for my life and that God wants me to have an abundant life. That is what I want." Flippantly, I add, "I am certainly getting an abundance of dates from the guys in the group. I'm finally having FUN!"

One of them pipes up, "Aren't you concerned this might be a cult?"

"Oh, NO! It is all about Jesus and the Bible! They are a very intellectual group. They have boiled down all the important Bible truths into just four verses, *The Four Spiritual Laws*. Let me show you."

My friends simply look at me and say nothing. Feeling elated, I grab my coat and walk out the door. One of the Crusade guys is waiting for me in his convertible at the entrance to my dorm. I get in and feel proud that I am on the right path to God and godly living. I just have to follow Jesus, let him lead me always, and Crusade will teach me HOW to do it. I am FINALLY going to get it right!

At the meeting, our male teacher is going over the *Four Spiritual Laws* pamphlet. He is pointing to a train diagram. The engine is labeled "Fact," and the coal car is labeled "Faith," and the caboose is labeled "Feeling." He is saying, "The train will run with or without the caboose. However, it would be useless to attempt to pull the train by the caboose. In the same way, as Christians, we do not depend on feelings or emotions, but we place our faith (trust) in the trustworthiness of God and the promises of His Word."

My Pentecostal religion is full of emotion. That is why this approach seems more intellectual and reasonable to me. I am trying to memorize the entire booklet, just as my personal Campus Crusade leader has encouraged me to do.

I don't know why, but my mind gets it all confused when I am not reading it. It is like my mind refuses it. I know that is Satan trying to keep God's word out of my mind. Just like it is Satan trying to trip me up when I feel uncomfortable sharing *The Four Spiritual Laws* with other students as I am supposed to do when my personal staff person takes me out witnessing.

I keep praying and asking Jesus to guide me and to help me defeat Satan's power in my life. I'm practicing Spiritual Breathing – that is what Crusade calls it. I breathe in God's Word and then exhale as I trust the Lord – the Holy Spirit – to guide me.

Exciting New Life In Jesus

I am in San Bernardino at the headquarters of Campus Crusade for Christ. It is summer 1966. Our teacher is teaching the book of John. Today we are in the fifteenth chapter.

I am the true vine, and my Father is the husbandman.
Every branch that beareth not fruit he taketh away:
And every branch that beareth fruit, he purgeth it, that it may bring forth more fruit....
Abide in me, and I in you, As the branch cannot bear fruit of itself, except it abide in the vine; no more can ye, except ye abide in me.
I am the vine, ye are the branches: He that abideth in me, and I in him, the same bringeth forth much fruit: for without me ye can do nothing.
If a man abide not in me, he is cast forth as a branch, and is withered; and men gather them, and cast them into the fire, and they are burned.
If ye abide in me, and my words abide in you, ye shall ask what ye will, and it
Shall be done unto you.
Herein is my father glorified, that ye bear much fruit; so shall ye be my disciples....
If ye keep my commandments, ye shall abide in my love; even as I have kept my Father's commandments,
And abide in his love.
[John 15:1-11 KJV]

According to the teacher, the way my father taught these verses to me is incorrect. (Thank goodness!) He said it is symbolic/metaphorical – not literal. According to my father and church, it is quite clear Jesus is teaching that one sin will send a person to Hell. A person who sins is like a dead branch that is pruned off and thrown into the fires of Hell. Black and white – and terrifying! This is the terror I have lived with every day of my life. I live in fear because I am afraid my father is correct. He says he is.

That is why I prefer this teacher and what he learned at Dallas Theological Seminary. Which is, "Once saved always saved" –

relax. What Jesus is teaching is that Christians are supposed to bear fruit and that means the fruit of the Spirit as defined in I Corinthians 13 – love, joy, peace, patience – but also we are to be studying our Bible and evangelizing the world.

Once again, I am in the position of asking myself, "What is true?" My father or the teacher? This is a very important decision for me. The wrong choice means I will burn in Hell. I feel very frightened and anxious!

––––––

The teacher has just instructed us to go outside on the grounds and study the relationship between vines and branches and to think of ourselves in this same relationship with Jesus. As I look at them, I see that they are one. The life-giving nutrients flow from the vine to the branches. And from Jesus to me!

Oops, Magical Prayers Are Not Answered: No Job, No University!

I thought Jesus was guiding me and "owned the cattle on a thousand hills" but things didn't turn out like I expected. I didn't go back to the university after I returned from spending the summer with Crusade because I had not worked and did not want to work in my dorm's kitchen again. Serving food felt humiliating since I was the only one on our dorm floor that had to work. I also didn't feel like I fit in at the university. I am more comfortable with church people.

I am working in downtown Denver at the phone company. I began as a long-distance operator. That was fun, but I keep longing to go back to school when I walk past the Colorado University extension building that is across the street. I know I am not smart enough to get a degree, but I think it would be fun to take classes just to learn. I am feeling bored even though I'm involved with the large college-age class at church, date different guys and still babysit.

After working as an operator for about a year, I got promoted to be a confidential stenographer in the state traffic office. I love it! My desk is on the ninth floor, and it faces a huge window that looks toward the Rockies. I am right under the window and have an unobstructed view. My boss gave me a raise because of my shorthand and typing classes, my year at the university and some other reasons. After working one year, I am on the five-year pay scale. I feel proud of myself!

Many people compliment me on my work ethic. I get the work done immediately and do a very good job. I am willing to run errands all over downtown. I also get complimented for being beautiful – that surprises me – and for my beautiful clothes. My paternal grandmother is still sewing for me. I buy very expensive fabrics now.

Recently, one of the bosses at work, a very nice woman, had me photographed for some marketing or training materials. THAT really surprised me!

I still live at home because Mother does not want me to pay rent, and I cannot afford to live on my own and I don't think I have the personality to live with girls. Mother says she wants to make up for all I missed as a child. I think that is kind, but she still will not accept ANY gift I give her. I bought her a GORGEOUS suit. She told me to take it back. I always cry because she rejects EVERY gift I give her. I don't understand why I can never please her.

Daddy is still Daddy. I stay out of his way. I am hardly ever home anymore. I just ordered my first car, a 1968 navy-blue Volkswagen bug with white interior. I can hardly wait for it to come! One of the younger neighbor boys across the street was excited for me. In workshop he made me a beautiful dark blue resin ball for the gear shift! It is gorgeous!

My youngest sister, my baby sister, just got married. She ran away from home. I do not blame her, but I feel frightened for her; she is only 16. The FBI agent who lives across the street from us told my parents how to stop her, but they did not even try. Isn't that weird? It's like they didn't even care; like they were glad she was gone. When she came back, they decided to give her a wedding.

We grew up hearing Mother, "Wait until the girls are gone!" And, "I just want to live long enough to see the girls married."

I have a nagging feeling deep inside my chest that tells me I will never marry. No one would ever want ME! I don't know how I know, I just know. But still I wish upon a star from time to time and pray and hope I am wrong. *...I wish I may, I wish I might have the wish...* "Dear Jesus, can't you help me find someone to love me?"

Postscript

(Based on my research and experiences in Book 5)

So where's my proof family trauma and Evangelical Fundamentalism made me psychologically and physically ill? Is there solid scholarly and scientific evidence beyond my childhood trauma art, two old letters to my grandmother, an old Sunday school handout from age four, a bunch of memories and a collection of hymns declaring human sacrifice blood purifies sins, Jesus lives and demands obedience, and the Bible is the "Word of GOD." Yes! Actually, this is quite a bit of evidence when viewed through the lens of research!

Our Brain Wires to Its Environment

We now know that the mental health symptoms I had are created by the kind of environments depicted in my memoir and supported by these documents. Criticism, hostile relationships, and intrusiveness (over-control) trigger the autonomic nervous system to send out stress hormones that prepare the body for fight or flight. When these conditions are a habitual part of one's environment, as I've described, the biological changes they create alters genes. Good genes get turned off and bad genes get turned on. In addition, when one is in a state of flight or fight, the immune system is switched off leaving the body vulnerable to many illnesses – including breast cancer.

In short, our brain wires to its environment. Frightening environments like those I describe keep stress hormones running 24/7. This prevents the hippocampus from growing which is important for memory and learning. Brain scans show that children who are neglected and abused have smaller brains.

When a person is kept frightened the fear center in their brain – the amygdala – grows bigger; thus, they are more easily frightened and more likely to be affected by the negative consequences of toxic stress hormones flooding through their brain and body on a regular basis. Our amygdala is our protector.

Harvard research psychiatrist, Bessel Van Der Kolk, MD, says it is like a smoke detector. It is always scanning our environment for threats. But it is not good if it is always in a hyper-alert state – as mine was due to my frightening family and frightening religion – because of the gene damage but also for this reason. Biologically, we cannot access our prefrontal cortex – the problem solving part of our brain – if our over-sized amygdala has hijacked our brain. This is what happens to military vets after they return home and cannot distinguish a car backfiring from a battlefield attack and they suddenly drop to the ground. Their thinking brain has been hijacked and they cannot think straight because their autonomic nervous system is in control – even when it only sounds like the battlefield and they are actually safe.

This protective response is automatic; it does not go through the problem solving part of the brain because the brain's most important function is survival. Fear responses are not choices! For those with a normal fear center, the problem solving part of the brain kicks in and makes the person aware, "Oh, it's only a car backfiring." But for those with over-sized fear centers, they are not able to easily sort this out and are also more easily triggered.

My Environment

Evangelical Fundamentalism's fear-based theology about end times, The Rapture, Armageddon, hellfire and brimstone preaching, along with, a frightening, demanding, violent, "god" who is "with us always" and who uses tornadoes, hurricanes and earthquakes to punish people and nations who disobey Him by accepting gays and/or allowing abortion, targets the amygdala! It keeps followers' brains traumatized and stress hormones flowing. This results in what scholars have observed: "Fundamentalists have been inoculated not to think" because they cannot access their prefrontal cortex while they are being kept frightened. Keeping them frightened and, thus, controlled and controllable, is the point of religion and church being the center of their lives. If true believers were not encouraged to isolate from "the world," they would learn from those not in fundamentalism that their fears are generally unfounded and they would probably leave their frightening religion, as did I, after I began to get more points of view. Followers, therefore, have not found freedom, as they are promised and assume; they are in bondage to those keeping them frightened.

[See: Marlene Winell, PhD, Leaving the Fold and journeyfree.org; Bessel Van Der Kolk, MD; The Body Keeps the Score; Vincent J. Felitti, Turning Gold to Lead study; Robin Karr-Morse with Meredith S. Wiley, Scared Sick: The Role of Childhood Trauma in Adult Disease; John Read, PhD, et al, Models of Madness; Norman Doidge, MD, The Brain that Changes Itself; Richard Davidson, PhD, The Emotional Life of Your Brain; Right-WingWatch.org; People for the American Way pfw.org; Southern Poverty Law Center]

Environment Not Genes – Post Traumatic Stress Disorder

Psychiatrists, psychologists and readers have known since 1957 that John Wesley-style fire-and-brimstone preaching – like I was subjected to at the time of my conversion – and weekly for years – creates what we now call Post Traumatic Stress Disorder. I will discuss this below in further detail in conjunction with my expose of Susanna's and John's childrearing advice.

[See: William Sargant, MD, Battle for the Mind: A Physiology of Conversion and Brainwashing; Kathleen Taylor, PhD, Brainwashing; John Read, PhD, et al, Models of Madness; Richard Davis, PhD, The Emotional Life of Your Brain]

Environment Not Genes – Bipolar and Schizophrenic Symptoms

Bipolar symptoms are due to methylated genes – genes that have been altered due to toxic stress hormones. Living in a frightening family with a frightening religion and frightening god who demanded purity and perfection, kept stress hormones flowing 24/7. Research at the University of Wisconsin found that children documented to have been abused did not have the gene turned on that enables everyone else to cope with stress. The inability to cope with stress is one of the traits of Bipolar Disorder. One of my psychiatrists taught me that "stress is to bipolar what sugar is to diabetes."

[See:http://www.waisman.wisc.edu/childemotion/pubs/2014-AssociationsBetwe enEarlyLifeStressGeneMethylationInChildren.pdf;http://onlinelibrary.wiley.com/ doi/10.1111/cdev.12270/pdf;http://www.nature.com/mp/journal/v13/n4/full/4002 001a.html]

Watching Jane Pauly's *Focus on Bipolar* (on WebMD) helped me understand my Bipolar symptoms reflected what my environment had done to my genes. Einstein University Bipolar researcher, Igor Galynker, MD, Ph.D., also director of Beth Israel's Bipolar Unit, explains there are three negative environmental traits that create Bipolar Disorder. They are criticism, over-control (intrusiveness) and hostile relationships. John Read, Ph.D., et al, report in *Models of Madness,* as do other researchers, that these relationship traits also create schizophrenia. It is emotional and spiritual abuse!

Both my family and Evangelical Fundamentalism criticized me constantly. I was the allegedly imperfect bad kid and the sinner GOD could not tolerate unless I was covered in the blood of his son. Both my parents and GOD had hostile relationships with me. My parents' was real. GOD's alleged rejection of me was a man-made construct – a lie – but I did not know I'd been deceived so I lived in terror. And both were over-controlling (intrusive). Both told me what I could and could not do, think and feel.

There is nothing more intrusive than the belief there is a GOD who sees everything one is doing and is also judging every thought, emotion, dream, behavior. I finally came to recognize *that* GOD was the original NSA! Crowd control! Everyone in that system is watching everyone else to make sure they are obeying GOD because no one wants to rock the boat! After all, that GOD uses natural disasters to kill people.

I could not have lived that life without adrenaline running 24/7 because I was allegedly being judged 24/7 by that GOD if not my parents. In short, I lived in terror and have experienced the reality of having been *Scared Sick!*

In addition, "…research consistently demonstrates a higher frequency of reports of childhood abuse and neglect compared with individuals in the general population" for patients diagnosed bipolar. Patients with bipolar report "higher levels of internalized shame" as adults in contrast to the general population. Shame is a normal response to any form of child abuse and neglect, including emotional child abuse and emotional neglect. Shame is the "what is wrong with me" feeling and "I am flawed" belief. that can hook victims into using destructive religion, alcohol, drugs, and other addictions to self-medicate if they do not get therapy.

[See: Jane Pauly's Focus on Bipolar, video on WebMD; Bessel Van Der Kolk, The Body Keeps the Score; Scared Sick: The Role of Childhood Trauma in Adult Disease by Robin Karr-Morse with Meredith S. Wiley; Childhood maltreatment and internalized shame in adults with a diagnosis of bipolar disorder by Fowke A, Ross S, Ashcroft K www.ncbi.nlm.nih.gov/pubmed/21557379]

Emotional Abuse Is More Destructive Than Sexual and Physical Abuse

In 2014 Dr. Viney sent me the following link to a March 31, 2014 article in *The Guardian, Emotional Child Abuse Has to be Banned: The Science Backs up our Instincts.* The author reviews a number of prominent studies that have found emotional abuse and neglect not only create psychotic symptoms such as Bipolar and Schizophrenia but are even more destructive to children than physical and sexual abuse! Children physically abused are 6 times more likely than non-physically-abused children to develop psychosis so imagine what emotional abuse does!

Emotional abuse is defined as, "exposure to behavior such as harshness and name calling by parents." "Emotional neglect implies lack of love and responsiveness" – not getting one's needs met.

In fact, one study found that children who suffered emotional abuse were 12 times more likely to develop Schizophrenia. In yet another study, scientists discovered 90% of children who suffered early childhood maltreatment suffered a mental illness. In a study of adolescents, if both parents were hostile, critical and intrusive,

1/3 of the subjects developed Schizophrenia in contrast to those who had only one hostile parent or no hostile parent. This information is shocking because we've been indoctrinated to think of Bipolar and Schizophrenia as genetic diseases thanks to the dominance of the medical model in psychiatry – not normal human reactions to psychologically traumatic experiences.

This article reveals that after 15 years of research, the Human Genome Project has not been able to link *any* genes to psychological traits. According to the author of this article, echoing John Bowlby, "The government is right. Children need love as much as they do vitamins – and a lack of it often leads to adult psychosis." Not surprising, my oncologist has incorporated "love heals" into his business marketing products because it is true.

[See: Oliver James, Not in Your Genes: The Truth About the Findings of the Human Genome Project;http://www.theguardian.com/commentisfree/2014/mar/31/emotional-child-abuse-banned-government-love-adult-psychosis]

Environment Not Genes – Dissociation

In addition to the autonomic nervous system's automatic fight or flight response, the other fear response is freeze. Freezing is dissociation. Dissociation is the inevitable result of trauma. Being emotionally overwhelmed for humans is like a power-surge for computers. It shuts down the system. The dissociative response is created in early childhood when infants and young children cannot escape traumatic environments. In order to survive, they must attach to their parents – no matter how abusive, neglectful or frightening. Dissociation enables the child to survive by splitting off the trauma from conscious awareness.

Dissociation is not a coping mechanism the infant *chooses*; it is an automatic protective response the brain makes to overwhelming, inescapable terror. Once the brain has wired in that response, it becomes an automatic habitual response whenever the person feels frightened and/or anxious. In essence, it is their "go to" app whenever they feel these emotions.

I was diagnosed as "highly dissociative"; it was difficult for me to remain in the present if a person, event or place left me feeling frightened or anxious – as most did because I'd been programmed by religion to fear the allegedly evil world and my family experiences left me paranoid and helpless. When triggered, I would simply be "gone" and unable to recall what triggered me. Understanding how dissociation affected me was difficult for many reasons.

Before and well into therapy I had no idea I was even doing it. It was my normal state of being. My body was present but not me! It took numerous years after therapy to connect the dots between how my then-teen daughter's contemptuous eye rolls triggered me to feel frightened, anxious, betrayed and demeaned, and her complaints that we'd had conversations I "pretended" not to recall. I couldn't recall them because my brain had automatically switched off.

An fMRI photo of a person's brain during a dissociative episode, in *The body Keeps the Score* by Bessel Van Der Kolk, MD, helped me finally understand this disability. Rather than showing brain activity, the scan is clear. [p. 71] There would be no way to recall what happened after I was triggered because the areas of the brain needed to create memories were not online.

Reading *Scared Sick* by Robin Karr-Morse with Meredith S. Wiley, helped me grasp that during dissociation the brain is in a state similar to some mammal's hibernation state after the autonomic nervous system triggers cortisol that in turn triggers the dorsal vagus nerve "to throw the freeze switch and regulate the freeze response: heart rate and breathing slow almost to a stop, we may collapse or become immobile. This is the mechanism that puts us in a state of dissociation, which is meant to provide protection when all else fails. But when this state continues, especially in humans, we can sink so deeply into a state of low oxygen and slowed pulse that we die. [p. 48]

[For more scientific detail see: Van Der Kolk and Karr-Morse]

How Dissociation Affected Me

Dissociation explains why my memories, as depicted in my book, do not tell the full story. It would take both eye witness reports, a licensed therapist and documents to help me fill in missing pieces. Sexual and physical abuse memories would have a beginning as I depict in my first vignette but then go blank just as I recall in that episode. It was my emotional response – terror – and my thought, "I don't like what happens next," that triggered that particular dissociative response in me.

Going blank explains why my drawings to my grandmother confused me. "Where is that hole?" In another memory, I recall only a gold watch, a pair of dark pin-striped trousers with an exposed penis, 2 separate locations and a sense I'd been hypnotized. Dissociation – compartmentalization – is what left me confused when my body became sexually stimulated in the afternoon and I "knew" I needed a wedding; my thought, "They will not like this," when I discovered my first pubic hair; and when I knew what was going on behind my parents' bedroom door but could not understand how I knew.

My trauma had been completely split off from my conscious awareness while another part of my mind contained information. Knowing what I couldn't possibly know, left me vulnerable to the belief that I could have Jesus, the Holy Spirit, Satan, and demons inside my head. In other words, I was being led to believe other entities could inhabit me. They were, in reality, dissociated parts – compartments – in my own mind. My own shattered mind!

In therapy, I came to understand I had a day child/night child split but it was not easy to accept. Only after reading my own memoir did I recognize that it was real and that it had set me up to believe really goofy religious stuff that made me sound crazy while my perpetrators were telling everyone I loved not to listen to me because I'd "always been a bad and hysterical child."

Childhood Art Tells the Truth

Based on research, my therapist explained the childhood drawings, that I drew compulsively, indicated I'd been a child with a dissociative disorder. My first grade drawing of flying trees, with their roots in the air, is a visual example of how a dissociative child feels – ungrounded. What "came over me" in first grade was my unconscious need to express my reality. It could be interpreted as the Night Child communicating. Today public school art teachers are trained to spot child abuse and neglect in students' art. One of my cousins, a former Miami vice detective confirmed, "Diana, children's art always tells the truth."

I learned my "stained glass drawings" depicted my mind that was compartmentalized just like my drawings. "It is a systems drawing," my therapist explained. This drawing also fits with my adult sense, after my breakdown began, that I was going through life looking through a kaleidoscope that kept turning. My mind would switch between compartments and each had a radically different perspective on any given topic. That, of course, left me feeling like I'd lost my mind and left me feeling both unstable and vulnerable until all of the different compartments were integrated into my adult mind and personality. This part of my breakdown was both terrifying and agonizing. I lived isolated because I could not tell what was true and real and what was not. I could have clarity one moment and lose it the next. Boxes of my therapy journals and therapy art confirm this was my reality.

I drew the drawings of the two coconut palm trees and the sailboat without a rudder compulsively during the years I now know I was being sexually exploited by two male relatives. The trees represent the two perpetrators. The sailboat without a rudder represents my helplessness. Helplessness – real or imagined – is what triggers dissociation.

I think it is possible the boat represented my Evangelical Fundamentalist understanding of Jesus' behavior in a boat during a frightening storm on a lake. He simply trusted his father and went to sleep. That matches my memory of how I coped when my father came to my bed during those years. I pretended I was asleep. My last memory of one event is that I stared intently off to the left at my bedroom window and repeated my memory verses until I was gone. I didn't want to see or feel what happened next.

After my memories began returning in the nineties, I'd be awakened at night by the sensation that someone was crawling into my bed. I lived alone. Terrifying! It happened repeatedly until I understood it was both an emotional and tactile flashback.

PTSD Flashbacks and Dissociation

Flashbacks can return as any of our five senses. I saw things that were not there, heard things that were not there, felt things that were not there in addition to living with paralyzing fear as I describe in Book 4.

Sexual abuse research has discovered that the closer the relationship between a perpetrator and victim, the less likely the victim will recall the attack because they have to interact with that person on a daily basis; however, they will experience the same psychological symptoms as someone stranger raped. This is why incest is so destructive. Symptoms seem to have no context. Dorothy Otnow Lewis, MD found that many families are willing to scapegoat the victim rather than tell the truth – even to save a child on death row. In fact, many victims would rather die than tell the truth about what their own family did to them and many do!

[See: Dorothy Otnow Lewis, MD, Guilty by Reason of Insanity]

Child Abuse in America

Child abuse and neglect are not the only causes of mental illness symptoms. Trauma from difficult births, operating on babies without anesthesia, prenatal stressors, war, natural disasters, and accidents also create symptoms but parental abuse is the most common cause of childhood trauma in America. In *Scared Sick*, the authors cite very troubling statistics. "Child abuse death rates in the United States are far higher than in all of the seven largest industrialized countries: three times higher than Canada and eleven times higher than in Italy. Just under five U.S. children die every day as the result of child abuse. Three out of four are under four years of age; nearly 90 percent of the perpetrators are the biological parents....Just over 20 percent (one in five children) either currently or at some point have had a seriously debilitating mental disorder. Thirteen percent of eight- to fifteen-year-olds have had a diagnosable mental disorder within the past year." [p. XV]

Americans are also the most religious industrialized country in the world. [See: Sam Harris, PhD, *The End of Faith*]. How can we be the most religious and the most abusive? I offer Susanna Wesley's letter to John regarding her childrearing methods as one example of abusive parenting committed in the name of GOD that has intergenerational ramifications for children and taxpayers.

[See supporting documents: Susanna Wesley's Letter; Miss America by Day, Marilyn Van Derbur; Trauma and Recovery by Judith Herman, MD; Guilty by Reason of Insanity, Dorothy Lewis Otnow, MD; The Body Keeps the Score, Bessel Van Der Kolk, MD; Trauma Model, Colin Ross, MD; Scared Sick: The Role of Childhood Trauma in Adult Disease, Robin Karr-Morse with Meredith S. Wiley]

Childhood Coping Mechanisms Became Adult Symptoms

I also used the little Samuel story to cope because "children," my therapist explained, "use whatever is in their environment to cope. If they only have comic books and TV, they will use characters from those in their coping strategy. For me, Samuel's, "Here am I, Lord," prevented me from knowing which god came at night. "Trust and Obey," "Children Obey Parents," as well as "I Surrender All" were part of my religious programming. My abuses and religious programming and use of fairy tales cannot be untwined easily.

I recited my memory verses in my mind to take me away, as well as, imagining fairy dust covering me until I felt no fear. Dissociation! But I also learned to self-hypnotize to escape by focusing intently. When my parents fought in the car, I self-hypnotized by focusing on the sound of the car engine and/or the sound of the tires hitting the road as I rested my head on the backseat arm rest.

During my breakdown years, I'd hear that sound which then triggered more terrifying flashbacks. I came to fear that sound because of what would happen next. When I accidentally set my house on fire Christmas 1998 and had to replace my kitchen, I ordered European appliances because they were the quietest on the market; my furnace and former American-made appliances switching on had triggered the engine-road noise and the cascade of frightening memories that followed. I would have done anything to prevent being triggered. During these years I wished I'd had a way to blow out my brains to stop the flashbacks!

After years of this particular sound hijacking my mind, I finally connected the dots and then it stopped. Hearing things that were not there was very unnerving because I'd had enough psychology to know that hearing things – at that point in time – meant Schizophrenia. And, supposedly, Schizophrenia was a genetic disease with no cure. Of course, I could not talk to anyone about these symptoms – not even my therapist. I couldn't bear learning my family and religion had been telling me the truth – I really was too evil to be saved.

Today all my symptoms are recognized as trauma symptoms and people can and do recover if they get the appropriate licensed therapies. My therapist later assured me that most trauma clients have the same fears I had had about being Schizophrenic. (Thanks medical model! We survivors really needed more undermining!)

When I made an appointment in 2015 to speak with the current medical director of "my" psych hospital, he informed me that they now tend to use the diagnosis "Dissociative Disorder" rather than Bipolar because Dissociative Disorder covers the same symptoms. He confirmed what I'd discovered, "with licensed therapies, patients can recover from Dissociative Disorder."

But, my god! How I suffered before I learned the truth!

[See: Colin Ross, MD, YouTube]

Tricks Used to Control Children's Minds

Hearing a shrill sound whenever I began to think logically and critically about my religion, as I describe when I was around nine, reveals I experienced Pavlovian conditioning. Pavlov used a tuning fork and that would match the sound I heard that left me confused and wondering if the noise was in my head or coming from "GOD." I was troubled when I watched the children's minister in the *Jesus Camp* documentary [see:

topdocumentaryfilms.com] pairing the breaking of cups with religious-political programing about breaking Satan's power in America. She was/is from the denomination I grew up in. That clip made me aware this type of deliberate programming does occur in children's "ministries."

I have broken memories of one of my great-grandfathers (not the barber) possibly hypnotizing me. I would learn in therapy that pedophiles have always used techniques to confuse the children they are exploiting. This is the back story of the hot dogs making me nauseated at their home. His wife was treating me like a fairy princess with my tin foil crown, robe and jewelry while he was exploiting me. (No wonder I had to accept Jesus in their church also!)

It is *possible* the weird mirror photo on my cover was used to confuse and disorient me – as it did – shock and awe – and to further push me from dissociative to full blown Multiple Personality Disorder as it did. I left realizing there could be more than one Diana!

Intentionally Creating DID/MPD

Making victims look and feel crazy provides a smoke screen for predators. I was surprised to learn I had had predators in my family simply because I'd been raised to believe we were GOD's chosen people and the only ones going to Heaven. I was equally surprised to learn there are some Christians who believe that if they have a conversion experience, they can do "anything" and still go to Heaven. "Once saved, always saved!" Eternal salvation! For some, this includes all sorts of exploitation including child abuse and pedophilia. They actually can point to biblical passages condoning sexual exploitation of various kinds.

Consider for example how easy it would be to trick a child who'd been brainwashed to believe the Bible is the word of GOD:

*Wherefore I give you to understand, that no man speaking by the Spirit of God calleth Jesus accursed: and that **no man can say that Jesus is the Lord, but by the Holy Ghost***
1Corinthians 12:3 [KJV; bold added]

*Whosoever is born of God doth not commit sin; for his seed remaineth in him: and **he cannot sin**, because he is born of God.*
1 John 3:9 [KJV; bold added]

This kind of programming leads to abuse of power. I really cannot imagine any context in which these verses would be true. They smack of cult programming.

[See: Robert Altemeyer's The Authoritarians; Judith Herman, Father Daughter Incest; John Read, PhD, et all, Models of Madness; Jesus Camp topdocumentaries.com; Pavlov's research using tuning forks; CIA Doctors and Military Mind Control by Colin Ross, MD]

One Loving Advocate Can Help a Victim Recover

I am including a signed interview with my supportive Aunt Bebe. She witnessed me being beaten by my father with his belt that left welts – after asking for light in my dark bedroom – when I was less than two. I had been frightened and knew how to solve the problem. My neuroscience prof taught me that one event changed the structure and function of my brain AND set me on the path to breast cancer!

I had no memory. If Bebe had not come forward I would not have had any context for some of my symptoms. And perhaps more importantly, after the vicious attack, Bebe is the one who comforted me. That may have saved my mind and life because babies and toddlers are dependent on the adults around them to help them calm down. They cannot do it on their own. My father would have left me abandoned to cry myself to sleep and my mother was so traumatized she was not able to help me.

Even Bebe had to get away as quickly as she could. Given the adults were traumatized, I would have been more traumatized because my brain was still wiring and developing my sense of self.

[See: The Body Keeps the Score, Bessel Van Der Kolk, MD; Turning Gold to Lead study, Vincent J. Filetti; Scared Sick: The Role of Childhood Trauma in Adult Disease, Robin Karr-Morse with Meredith S. Wiley; The Brain that Changes Itself, Norman Doidge, MD]

Diana Lee, M.A.

Sometimes It Takes Years to Confirm Childhood Trauma

I've also been able to confirm the context for a flashback that haunted me at the end of my marriage as I was sliding toward a breakdown and one that motivated my husband-at-the-time to falsely accuse the wrong person. So there is no doubt when I first had this flashback – before my divorce in 1994. My trauma art depicts a toddler me undergoing a weird genital "procedure" at the hands of my father on a white enamel table with red trim.

Before his death in 2013, my father's younger brother *finally* explained my great-grandfather, the local barber, was the one who circumcised older boys and girls on white enamel tables!

It is not unreasonable to conclude my father reenacted with me some of what he had been exposed to – especially after I received an email that talked about how my father's family would send the children on pretend errands before they killed their pet chickens. Clearly that is what motivated my own father's sadism regarding my and my sisters' pet Easter chickens. It also is not unreasonable to suggest my father was triggered when my mother purchased the table her family confirmed she had had.

In addition, whenever I'd   see a white enamel table in antique and collectible stores, I'd suddenly feel disoriented, light-headed, my eyes would dilate, my heart would start pumping, I'd feel sweaty and sick and too small for my body. I'd have to leave immediately. Of course, I felt awkward and crazy! Out of the blue, I'd suddenly no longer be me! "What has come over me," I'd wonder.

It was an awful experience to suddenly have my fight/flight response kick on after simply seeing that kind of table because I didn't know I had a fight/flight response or that terror triggered it. In my world everything was Jesus, Satan, demons at work or my sinful self. But now it makes total sense. It was a visual and emotional flashback. Those tables triggered terror that triggered my fight/flight response. But, my only frame of reference was to belittle myself and ask Jesus for help. In a similar manner, full moons left me feeling sick and falling down drunk. That took decades to resolve. It stopped only after I accepted I had witnessed at least one KKK event on a full moon as a young child. (Can you imagine experiencing this once a month for decades with no context? I'd run to the MD to be reassured I was fine!)

My terrifying early childhood traumas are well documented and for that I am deeply grateful to all who helped me collect and understand evidence; I no longer feel crazy because it all makes logical sense. But I did not have confirmation of the table incident until 20 years after my first memory because my Evangelical Fundamentalist relatives believed they'd go to Hell if they told what they knew. "Forgiveness" and "honoring parents" long dead preempted my need and right to know so I could save my mind and health – at least in their minds.

It took another several years before I connected the 1948 "ooo scaring me" photo to the table event. I was not yet one when the photo shows I made a fist and whispered this message into my mother's ear. She apparently thought it was funny because she wrote it in blue ink on the front of the photo's white margin preserving what I'd said to her. Even if I cannot prove that photo and saying match the white enamel table experience, it does prove I was being frightened as a young child and that is important due to what fear responses do to a child's brain.

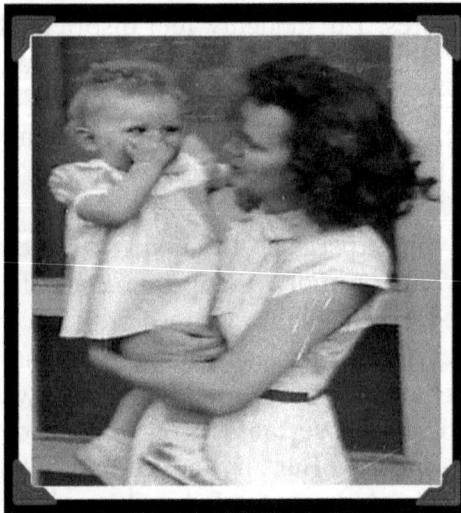

"Ooo scaring me" Fall 1948

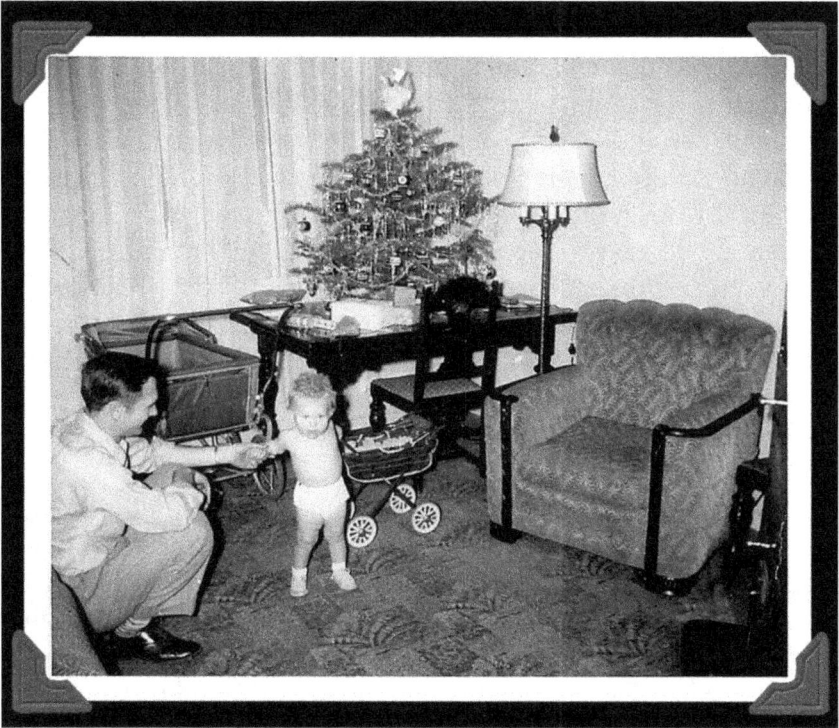

Already in Panties   Christmas 1948

Two years later, as soon as I saw the 1948 Christmas photo of me with my father, I exclaimed, "That's the little girl on the white enamel table!" Psychiatrists confirm that it is not uncommon for traumatized children to watch the scene from a distance and to not recognize the child as them self. I cannot prove this is what my exclamation reveals but it is certainly an interesting coincidence given my broken pieces of memory, my therapy art, my uncle's information, my dissociative diagnosis and especially given my reaction to my youngest sister's comments in the late nineties.

During my therapy years my youngest sister recalled what she felt was a "weird" memory. I had not remembered the incident. But as I listened to her description, I "saw" it play out in my mind but from across the room from where it happened. Her memory filled in a gap in mine and confirmed I had told my therapist the truth about the age I was when my father raped me.

My sister recalled that when she was "only six" our father sat all three of us down on a pink chaise we had in our Hialeah living room while our mother was away. "He told us that if we ever lost our maidenhead no man would ever want us! Wasn't that weird!" When my sister was six, I was nine. I had already told my therapist I believed I was around nine when my father raped me. Clearly as an adult it was easy to see what he was doing. Blaming his victim! No wonder my memory is dissociative, out of body I felt "evil to the morrow of my bones"– a common experience of incest victims, according to Marilyn Van Derbur, and that is why I needed religion to make me pure. But no amount of religious hocus pocus or abracadabra worked. Only telling and accepting the truth worked and feeling my pain, my rage and accepting reality.

In order to recover I had to give up my magical child beliefs in magical blood, magical water, magical people who speak for god, magical people with magical powers, and praying for what I need instead of letting real live people know what I need. I had to give up suffering in silence which is what I'd been programmed to do as an Evangelical Fundamentalist child (and wife). "Are you heavy laden...take it to the Lord in prayer." "Be careful for nothing; but in every thing by prayer and supplication with thanksgiving let your requests be known to God..." [Philippians 4:6]   Being neglected and abused – traumatized repeatedly – and feeling helpless triggered my mental illness symptoms including dissociation.   I had to learn to see what was there and hear what was there. I had to get into realty, learn how the real world works, and give up my imaginary friends that I had thought were real.

[In Book 5, I explain why Protestant Americans began circumcising older boys and girls in both the nineteenth and twentieth centuries; See: The Body Keeps the Score by Bessel Van Der Kolk, MD; The Emotional Life of Your Brain by Richard Davidson, Ph.D.; The Brain that Changes Itself by Norman Doidge, MD; Scared Sick: The Role of Childhood Trauma in Adult Disease by Robin Karr-Morse; Models of Madness by John Read, Ph.D., et al; Trauma Model by Colin Ross, MD; Miss America by Day, Marilyn Van Derbur]

Susanna Wesley's Letter to John Describing Her Childrearing Methods

The next piece of evidence is Susanna Wesley's letter to her son John, the founder of the evangelical movement, Methodism, documenting how she raised her children. John published it in his Methodist magazine and read it at her funeral. This is most likely how her childrearing "methods" became Evangelical Fundamentalist dogma that was then passed down inter-generationally. It appeared some families had mental illness genes instead of the same abusive frightening childhoods.

Susanna's complete letter follows my postscript. What she emphasizes is the need for religious parents to "conquer the will" of children at a very young age. In fact, both she and John advocated, "when turned a year old (and some before) they were taught to fear the rod and cry softly." Susanna did not allow her children to cry. Her house did not have the "odious" sound of crying children; it appears, because she spanked them until they cried softly – which one of my therapists explained would be the point at which the child was so emotionally overwhelmed the brain had dissociated to survive. Following this logic, a dissociated child is one whose will has been conquered/broken – a compliant child who would trust and obey Susanna and enable her to live in a quiet home as if no children lived there at all – an obedient religious child.

My maternal grandmother, Mom, shared that when I was born my father would not allow anyone to pick me up. He didn't want a "spoiled child." Susanna refused to give her children "anything they cried for." My father's unresponsiveness, apparently, was teaching me that crying would not get me the attention all babies need so I should not even go there. No wonder I grew up feeling abandoned and alienated – an emotion Evangelical Fundamentalists twisted into alienation from GOD – not alienation from my parents.

My father's authoritarian attitude links to my confrontations with him during my high school years when it was still not okay to ask for what I wanted and needed – love. Not getting what I desired explained my childhood memories of getting lots of

Christmas gifts – but never what I actually asked for. The issue was control, lack of empathy, creating a religious child – not a shortage of money. The 1948 Christmas photo makes clear that by the time I was one, I was wearing panties not diapers. My maternal grandmother had told me my father insisted that I be potty-trained before my sister was born eleven months after me. Daddy ruled with a rod of iron. Daddy got what Daddy wanted regardless of what it did to me – just like Roman Caesars ruled – with a rod of iron.

There are a number of parallels between Susanna's letter and how I was raised: beating infants and toddlers; withholding what children want if they cry; isolating them from peers; criticizing their peers; no snacks between meals; mother (parent) is authoritarian drill sergeant rather than a compassionate soft place to land; no playing in church or on Sunday; begin reading lessons with the Bible at Genesis 1 at age 4 or 5; children must eat whatever is given to them; the importance of obedience and silence; permissive compassionate parents condemned; no compassionate others are allowed to help the children; memorizing and reciting biblical verses and prayers; belief Bible is GOD's Word; "self-will is the root of sin"; children should obey parents – no questions asked; child must have perfected a lesson before he/she could move on; children are to be seen and not heard; spare the rod; the belief the parent is raising children for GOD – religious children – rather than for their own ego – or, perhaps, to be obedient cannon fodder.

In both homes authoritarian control was defined as religion. I could not help recall my mother's refusal to let us have after school snacks and her need to keep our home quiet – even our laughing was not okay, and her ridiculous assumption I'd be able to sew perfectly on my first attempt at hand stitching a tea towel hem at 5 or 6! (while dissociative no less!)

It is not hard to connect the dots and conclude that John's frightening fire-and-brimstone GOD was not the violent biblical eye in the sky war-god but his own traumatizing mother! Some are now beginning to recognize Susanna did not create a home environment conducive to raising healthy children; she created a boot camp environment! Psychologically breaking down recruits and rebuilding them into warriors is the point of boot camp. Boot camp is brainwashing.

It is because Susanna's childrearing methods harmed me, and are still considered godly and followed my many Evangelical Fundamentalist parents – along with the fact that she is also considered a heroine for some in the home schooling movement – I feel compelled to expose her methods for what they are: neglect and child abuse. Beating babies and children creates mental illnesses and can set them up for major physical illnesses as adults.

[See: Turning Gold to Lead, ACE Study, Vincent Felitti, MD; The Body Keeps the Score, Bessel Van Der Kolk, MD; Steph at www.whynottrainachild.com; Janet Heimlich, Breaking Their Will]

Evangelical Parents Manipulated into Making Their Own Children Ill

So what happens to children raised in boot camp-like environments as depicted in Susanna's letter and my book? It is not uncommon for them to dissociate to survive and to grow up with emotional problems. If they did not dissociate and shut down emotionally they would die. Beating and spanking infants and toddlers sends powerful chemicals/emotions and stress hormones surging through their brains that alters their genes, alters their brain circuits, alters the very structure of their brains – even the size of their brain – and determines how their brain will function – IF they survive! (Not all of Susanna's children survived and that is something that I think needs clarification. What exactly happened? Do we know?)

Every aspect of the child's brain is affected. Some areas get too big – like the fear center – and others do not fully develop – like the memory and learning center. Thinking logically is biologically impossible when the fear center is in control. Early childhood trauma and neglect prevents brain development and drastically affects one's physical, emotional, and intellectual quality of life. In school I thought I was stupid and in 1993 I tested as legally learning disabled. Completing licensed therapy decreased many of my symptoms.

Licensed therapy is like "micro-surgery" on the brain. Part of my therapy focused on increasing the function of my hippocampus and decreasing the influence of my amygdala. I emphasize "licensed" therapy because in Colorado pretty much anyone can hang out a shingle and claim to be a psychotherapist or counselor. Church counselors need no formal education or licensing and they often cite the Bible as their authority – not scientific research – and can keep their victims bumping around in the dark. In short, there are many charlatans and I've found they charge more than licensed therapy!

[See: *Breaking Their Will, Janet Heimlich; The Body Keeps the Score by Bessel Van Der Kolk, MD; The Brain that Changes Itself by Norman Doidge, MD; Scared Sick by Robin Karr – Morse with Meredith S. Wiley; Everything by Alice Miller; Everything by Bruce Perry, MD.; The Emotional Life of Your Brain, Richard Davidson, PhD; Steph at www.whynottrainachild.com says that all of the Wesley children had emotional problems and Wikipedia indicates that was true of John; homeschoolersanonymous.com]*

Battle for the Mind: A Physiology of Conversion and Brain-Washing

The next piece of evidence is psychiatrist William Sargant's *Battle for the Mind* [1957]. Sargant was Britain's top mind control expert after WWII. Based on the diaries of the founder of Evangelicalism, John Wesley, along with Pavlov's trauma research, and Sargant's own WWII battle field observations, Sargant was able to document how Wesley was able to convert so many – including skeptics. Wesley followed an ancient, but now common cult, political, military and Evangelical Fundamentalist conversion formula: Terror – hellfire and brimstone preaching – traumatized the brain and then Wesley offered his converts quick relief (from the trauma symptoms he had just created – intense fear and anxiety) by offering his converts a "personal relationship" with Jesus and a ticket out of Hell.

In short, Wesley was not leading people to GOD or Jesus or any other deity. He was creating Post Traumatic Stress Disorder in them and making them vulnerable to his particular Bible-based theology. His conversions were brainwashing. Methods he learned at home.

Three Core Mind Splits

Colin Ross, MD, literally wrote the book on dissociation. He was on the DSM-IV Dissociative Disorders committee, directs two trauma model psych hospitals and has published extensively. Ross explains that when a child is in a chaotic, inescapable traumatic environment and his/her brain dissociates to survive, the mind splits into three core dissociated identities: a protector part, a traumatized child part, and a part that blames the victim for having been victimized. "If you'd just kept your room clean Daddy would not have moved out." In our Judeo-Christian culture, according to Ross, these three core splits are experienced as God, Jesus, and Satan (in other cultures these splits have other names).

Thus, when Wesley was emotionally and spiritually battering potential converts with his hellfire and brimstone preaching and claiming they needed a "personal relationship" with Jesus, it is *possible* he was unwittingly reenacting his own early childhood traumas, as well as, describing his own compartmentalized mind – not reality. And/or perhaps he was describing his own sense of emptiness created by dissociation from his own inner child. In that case, he'd assumed, or been led to believe, that vacuum could be filled by the biblical Jesus. One of the insights one of my licensed therapists taught me is that all adults act out their childhoods until they become aware.

(Wesley's psychology is a dissertation topic for the right person and that person is not me. But as a survivor of the authoritarian child rearing and beating-babies trauma described by Susanna and Evangelical Fundamentalism, I know this is a topic someone needs to research – as well as looking into infant mortality rates among Puritans, Evangelicals, Evangelical Fundamentalists. How many babies died because they were beaten?)

Once I understood the yammering critical voice in my mind was not Satan, a demon, or Jesus/God convicting me of my sin, it stopped after I was able to *accept, love and integrate that part into my adult personality and awareness.* It was the part of me that worked very hard to be good enough and perfect enough, as a child and wife, so the bad stuff would stop. By the time my therapist helped me integrate her, she was past exhaustion. I now let my conscience direct me and I am happy! I no longer have the sense GOD is watching every move I make and judging me. I no longer live in fear and with generalized anxiety.

Ross also notes that in his experience, behind every Satan is a traumatized child. In other words, the still-current belief in demon possession is inaccurate! This teaching is still common within some circles in traditional Catholicism and Evangelical Fundamentalism. The so-called blaspheming demons and Satan are the split off child part of the traumatized mind that blames the victim-Jesus part for having been victimized.

Psychiatrists and psychologists trained in trauma recovery recognize it is the "locus of control shift." It is a response to trauma the brain makes. It is not a choice, the shift functions to give the helpless child a sense of power in a powerless situation. For me, it gave me the sense that all would be well if I was the best Evangelical Fundamentalist little girl and wife that I could be. Of course, nothing I did made any difference. The problems were within my parents and within their religious belief system and later my husband; I had no control over their stuff. But because of my locus of control shift I dug in deeper and tried harder until I understood what was going on and accepted reality It was not evil!

[See: *The Trauma Model* by Colin Ross, MD; *The Body Keeps the Score* by Bessel Van Der Kolk; *Models of Madness* by John Read, Ph. D.; *The Emotional Life of Your Brain* by Richard J. Davidson and Sharon Begley; everything by Bruce Perry MD; everything by Alice Miller; Lundy Bancroft, *Why Does He Do That?*]

Listening to Elders Helped Me Put Puzzle Pieces Together

More evidence. When my family spent Christmas in Miami during my high school years, my paternal Evangelical Fundamentalist great-grandfather (the barber) was proud to show me the wide leather razor strap he used to beat my paternal grandmother. It was hanging on the back side of his bathroom door. No one is talking but it seems pretty obvious, my grandmother reenacted what was done to her and I suspect my grandfather did also since it was his mother who smacked me in the face in Tennessee. Acting out one's history is not uncommon. Memories are wired in even if they are unconscious. "Neurons that fire together, wire together."

Bebe's mother, my Evangelical Fundamentalist maternal grandmother, Mom, admitted to me not long before she died in March, 1989 that she had beaten my mother as a very young child just as she had been beaten. We have a long history of Evangelical Fundamentalism and intergenerational child abuse. At least now I know whose parenting advice they were following. It was not Rousseau's or their innate human parenting instincts!

[See: Mariette Hartley, Breaking the Silence. Hartley is J. B. Watson's granddaughter. He is the father of behaviorism. His mother was "very religious." According to Hartley, her mother and other family members suffered greatly due to his child rearing advice. I came to recognize Evangelical Fundamentalists were practicing behaviorism before Behaviorism was recognized. Reward and Punishment. Heaven and Hell.]

Looking for What is There and What is Not There

I did not find it difficult to locate examples of the experiences that create mental illnesses – even Bipolar and Schizophrenia – in my family-of-origin memories, as well as, my marital memories. I think a close reading of Susanna's letter reveals she was critical/judgmental, over-controlling, and, definitely, a hostile mother to her infants and toddlers. She is not the paragon of virtuous motherhood or the child rearing role model many Evangelical Fundamentalists today assume. *Never* should her early childhood methods be employed! They need to be exposed and rejected by everyone who cares about children.

Attorneys have taught me to look at what is not there. What I found lacking in Susanna's child rearing letter is empathy for her children. It appears, based on this important letter that she was definitely not the nurturing mother her present-day followers have been led to believe. She comes across as authoritarian, cold and cruel. As research is proving, neglect, the lack of love and responsiveness, is a child's ticket to mental illness and is more harmful than physical or sexual abuse.

[See: www.whynottrainachild.com; Robert Altemeyer's, The Authoritarians, posted online free.]

From my point of view these mental-illness-making traits are also evident in the biblical God's relationship with his allegedly sinful children but also toward his own son whom he offered as a human sacrifice even though the gospels allege Jesus begged not to be sacrificed. And this is where the rubber hits the road. Evangelical Fundamentalist parents have been brainwashed and manipulated into sacrificing their own children on the altar of their religion – a religion of obedience – as their understanding of Jesus modelled. Obedience unto death!

It was my dear friend, Lovey, raised on a ranch, who made me aware of how unnatural my story, religion and Susanna's parenting was. "Diana, animals fight to the death to protect their offspring!!" Yet, in Evangelical Fundamentalism, parents are conditioned to attack and, too often, destroy their own children!!!

Spare the Rod and Spoil the Child

A quick review of "spare the rod and spoil the child" on Wikipedia taught me it was coined in a 17th century poem by Samuel Butler and was based on Old Testament passages. The phrase is not literally from the Bible as many assume. ReligiousTolerance.org taught me conservatives trace this concept back to Solomon and his parenting proverbs whereas liberals point out the proverbs were written long after the dating for Solomon and also point out his son was hated when he ruled.

Either way, the Judeo-Christian culture has a long history of child abuse and neglect. Susanna did not create child abuse. She was a woman of her own culture that included her own Puritan roots. **Her story and legacy reveals what happens when parents are taught to elevate any ideology, including religion, over their**

own human parenting instincts. The ideology of obedience trumped human parenting – and children and taxpayers have paid the price.

[See: Breaking the Will, Janet Heimlich; The History of Childhood, Lloyd deMause; YouTube Gabor Matte, MD; YouTube Colin Ross, MD; YouTube, Robert Sapolsky, Ph.D., Stress: Profile of a Killer; Bessel Van der Kolk, MD, The Body Keeps the Score. Vincent Felitti, MD, Turning Gold to Lead, Adverse Childhood Experiences study that revealed the relationship between early childhood abuse and neglect and major illnesses in adults.]

How Can Evangelical Fundamentalism Make a Person Mentally Ill?

For psychological and physical health, the brain needs truth. Evangelical Fundamentalist dogma is deceptive and manipulative because it is not what it claims to be and the Bible is not what they claim it to be. It is, therefore, a direct assault on a young child's sense of self, sense of integrity, and sense of reality because it does not match what children observe and it does not feel right. It turns reality on its head and uses fear to dominate its victims. Up is down and down is up. It makes children feel crazy! It is a form of gaslighting. Intentional or not, it is a method that destabilizes children and makes them dependent on authoritarian leaders, who are often blatant sociopaths or psychopaths, because converted children are unable to think for themselves after they experience this Jesus. Children are, literally, "Sheep led to the slaughter."

Exposing Evangelical Fundamentalism's Shaky Foundation

The easiest and quickest way to expose Evangelical Fundamentalism's faulty theological foundation that proves it is deceptive and manipulative is by watching the documentary (or reading the book) *The Bible Unearthed* by University of Tel Aviv archaeologist, Israel Finkelstein, and historian Neil Ashur Silberman.

Finkelstein was the first to do a comprehensive *scientific* archaeological study of the "Holy Land." What he discovered is that the facts on the ground do not match the facts in the Old Testament! All the great epic stories that I, and millions, have been taught are historical accounts of the Israelites and their one true god, are in fact, propaganda!

They were written in the 7th century by King Josiah's priests – beginning with the book of Deuteronomy. In short, the literature was written in Judah – not Israel – and the goal was to present Josiah as the promised political and military savior (messiah) who would unite the land between the Euphrates (Iraq) and the Nile (Egypt) – now known as "The Holy Land" by some.

Josiah's aspirations were based on the fact that both the Assyrians to the north and the Egyptians to the south were in decline. There was a political vacuum and at this time Judah had experienced tremendous growth due to an influx of citizens who'd escaped the Assyrian devastation and relocation of Israel. Organization was definitely needed. And the Yahweh-only group seized power.

The mythical stories depict who is in (followers of Yahweh) and who is out (those demonized to justify taking their land, their harvests, their cisterns and slaughtering them with the exception of young virgins) as Josiah begins beating his war drums. The biblical cultural laws that created a new culture in Judah were based on a simple formula, "If they do it, we don't" and this is how others were demonized and allegedly deserving of death. The point was conquest – not spirituality!

Palestine is filled with archaeological evidence that proves Judah and Israel were just like their neighbors – polytheistic and goddess worshiping – until the rise of the Yahweh-only faction in Judah in the seventh century BCE. In short, Finkelstein and Silberman discovered historical and archaeological evidence does not support the biblical stories depicting massive slavery of Hebrews in Egypt, a massive Exodus, or wandering in the Sinai by massive numbers of Hebrews for 40 years – nor is there any evidence for Joshua's conquest of Canaan or that his god and trumpets made Jericho's walls fall down.

What their scientific study found is that those in Judah were Canaanites also. They'd been Bedouin herders who had finally settled in Jerusalem and were an insignificant tribal kingdom at the time of David and Solomon – not the center of the world as I'd been taught. Probably tents not grandiose palaces at that point in time! They were ordinary people just like their neighbors until the Yahweh-only group seized power and began creating a hierarchical, patriarchal, misogynistic, warrior culture centered in Jerusalem, which conveniently, was under their political, religious and economic control.

Unfortunately, for the world, I would say, after Pharaoh Necho killed – or had – Josiah killed at Megiddo (Armageddon), his propaganda lived on and echoed down the halls of time as it morphed into what my family and religion taught me was "GOD's Word." Yep! I was taught that propaganda – and not just propaganda – but war propaganda –- was the Word of God!

I was taught I should deny my own sense of self, my own conscience, my own intuition, my own emotions, my own observations and logical thinking, my own healthy needs and wants, in deference to this alleged god – and give him my children – or fry in Hell. This denial of self-process – psychological, emotional, spiritual and physical sacrifice – makes people sick and vulnerable to being puppets controlled by authoritarian leaders. Actually, that had been the point in the 7th century BCE! They were creating warriors for Josiah's army. He is "the Lord."

Psychologist Marlene Winell, PhD, is a former Evangelical Fundamentalist-missionary-child from my same exact denomination. Her painting, "He Must Increase, I Must Decrease," provides a visual depiction of the Evangelical Fundamentalist brainwashing process that she has coined Religious Trauma Syndrome.

"He Must Increase," mixed media, 1991. This piece illustrates my loss of identity I experienced at age sixteen as I tried to emulate Christ. The title is from the words of John the Baptist: "He must increase, I must decrease."

Used by permission.

The goal of destructive religion is to create a cult self – a "part"– that functions to hijack the normal human personality. In other words, leaders create an alter personality that can be manipulated by the "right person" to do whatever that person wants them to do – including thinking and acting like sociopaths and psychopaths – in The Lord's Army!

[See: Marlene Winell, PhD, Leaving the Fold and journeyfree.org; Stephen Hassan's Combatting Cult Mind Control and Releasing the Bonds: Freeing People to Think for Themselves; Colin Ross, MD, CIA Doctors and Military Mind Control; Cults & Consequences, Rachel Andres and James R. Lane, eds.; James B. Pritchard, ed., Ancient Near Eastern Texts Relating to the Old Testament; Raymond O. Faulkner, trans., Ancient Egyptian Book of the Dead]

Religious Documents

Documenting I was born into a destructive religion and experienced cultic programming shows the importance of my returned Sunday school handout from age four and all the hymns glorifying human sacrifice and military obedience.

My Sunday school paper is a very important primary source document. It reveals how young I was when I was being indoctrinated into Evangelical Fundamentalism. Given the stories are propaganda; there is no other way to view it than as cult programming. Did you notice the cover story taught me at a very young age that GOD's people follow clouds? And that "GOD" kills people? Scary! (So could my violent dad!) And on the inside I learned the same "GOD" is always with me and I should not be afraid. Yikes! No place to hide!

This is emotionally too overwhelming for a four year old child to cope with. Given my early beating set me up to dissociate, I probably compartmentalized the information so I could stay in my four-year old skin! "God is love." "God kills people." "God is scary." "Daddy is scary." "God is with me always." "I cannot escape from God." "I cannot escape from Daddy." "I am not afraid."

I lived with terror until therapy in my fifties. I was so well indoctrinated that I truly believed that god saw everything I did and was judging me 24/7. I now understand what living with that terror as well as the terror of my family did to create mental illness and cancer in me.

[See: *Scared Sick* by Karr-Morse]

Yahweh Was a War God

I am grateful Elaine Pagels, PhD, taught me Yahweh was a tribal war god and told me to check out Exodus 15:3 "The Lord our God is a man of war." The fundamentalist belief that God is a righteous warrior justified in slaughtering the so-called unrighteous – as defined by them – explains why the songs I was being taught were militaristic cultic programming. "I'm in the Lord's army!" "Onward Christian soldiers." And, "The B*I*B*L*E yes! That's the book for me, *I stand alone on the Word of God* the B*I*B*L*E!"

There is so much blood in fundamentalist theology because it is, at its core, a warrior - military religion created by Josiah and later exploited by the Romans – who were also a militaristic authoritarian government. This Jesus has a lot in common with Mithraism the warrior religion of the Roman army. One point of obvious similarity being, Roman soldiers literally washed in the blood of a bull that represented their god Mithra. No wonder it felt like I was born into *Star Wars*!

Marlene Winell, PhD, calls Evangelical Fundamentalism a death cult. I agree! It is easier to manipulate warriors to offer their lives on the battlefield if they have been conditioned to believe it is not only a hero's death but one that merely precipitates the next stage of life – not death. It was actually no different for me. I was raised to believe that as a warrior in Jesus' great cosmic battle between good and evil, I had no rights in this life. This life was a vale of tears. A time of testing whether or not I was good enough for Jesus and Heaven! If I endured I would receive my rewards in Heaven. Suffering was not proof something was radically wrong but proved I was, indeed, a child of THE KING of KINGS.

Who's Jesus?

Okay, so what happened to the real Jesus if Wesley's Jesus might have been one of his own dissociated "parts"? As a fundamentalist I was shocked to learn there is actually no solid historical or archaeological evidence, outside the Bible, that confirms Jesus and Paul ever existed. Evidence suggests they were literary characters created by those in power, just like Moses was created by Josiah's priests – to justify his political agenda – and theirs. Many of us have heard the biblical stories so many times – and often beginning in childhood – that we never question their historicity. But we should. "Where's the evidence?" Evangelical Fundamentalists have no credible evidence and that is why their religion is built on "faith" and not evidence.

Upon close scrutiny it becomes obvious the New Testament is the voice of Rome – an oppressive military empire that enslaved most people to some degree and ruled with a rod of iron – not that of a loving teacher and his band of fishermen, women and slaves. This explains why Jesus and Paul taught everyone to obey and pay their taxes and why Romans 13:1&2 make it clear that if you don't, you'll be damned:

Let every soul be subject unto the higher powers. For there is no power but of God: the powers that be are ordained of God.

Whosoever therefore resisteth the power, resisteth the ordinance of God: and they that resist shall receive to themselves damnation. [KJV]

Two other translations, NIV and NASB, often used by Evangelical Fundamentalists, make it clear the higher powers are the "governing authorities." Both demand that everyone must submit and claim that it is God who gives these people the "authority" to rule over the rest. In other words, this god is a god of hierarchy – not a god of equality, as many assume.

Most people are shocked to read these words by the gospel Jesus:

Do you think I came to bring peace on earth? No, I tell you, but division. From now on there will be five in one family divided against each other, three against two and two against three. They will be divided father against son and son against father, mother against daughter, daughter against mother, mother-in-law against daughter-in-law, and daughter-in-law against mother-in-law.
Luke 12:51-53 [NASB]

Actually, this is an example of Roman military strategy. When the army went into new areas they pitted men and women against each other as a way of destabilizing the area to make it easier to conquer. Divide and conquer!

It is not difficult to find wonderful people born into the numerous spin-off denominations of Evangelicalism that are shunned by their family when they do not accept the sect's beliefs – based on this verse and others! In such brainwashed families, following warrior Jesus is more important than happy human family relationships. In other words, dysfunctional families are normalized and considered divine. This is one example of the sociopathic character of these sects. They turn reality on its head. The gut-wrenching pain and suffering for those ejected is beyond words.

Fundamentalist ideology eventually even severed my once loving relationship with my Aunt Bebe. Someone asked me point blank if I still believed the Bible is the Word of GOD. When I said no, based on evidence, that person went to her. It was an act of cruelty not godliness! But this is an example of how Evangelical Fundamentalism functions like the old KGB or NSA. Everyone spies on everyone else because everyone lives in terror of what that GOD will do them if they do not obey and force others to obey. They are clearly reenacting their own traumatized childhoods and/or brainwashing. It is bizarre and provides a window into how crowd control works within these often-now-considered-mainstream denominations.

Neurological Impact of Shunning

How could one not live in fear? Even after I began connecting dots, it was years before I could challenge my "elders" because I knew what the "punishment" would be – shunning and I simply could not bear it yet! I needed to develop my adult self and a close circle of friends first.

Brain scans reveal that shunning is experienced by the brain as literal physical pain. And chronic pain undermines the immune system. Once again, another example of how cults and Evangelical Fundamentalism make people ill!

[See: The Pain of Exclusion, by Kipling D. Williams]

Many Disturbing Passages in the New Testament Also

Actually, there are many disturbing images and passages in the New Testament that most adults are simply unaware of because they've been indoctrinated to believe the Bible is all about love and so they do not bother to check it out for themselves. But there is a very dark cultic side and that is the stuff Evangelical Fundamentalists dwell on because they are authoritarians. No matter how inhumane, illogical, or frightening the stories, I was taught it was all the Word of God and everything was part of His plan. Now I know kings and Caesars were the gods. In addition one can easily pick up sociopathy in verses that claim those who have Jesus cannot sin and that no one can call Jesus Lord but by the Spirit! [Yah! Right!]

As a former ancient history major, I found it refreshing to read Christopher Hitchens *God is not Great*, Joseph Atwill's *Caesar's Messiah,* and first century Jewish-Roman historian Josephus' *War of the Jews* because I had nagging questions. In my Ancient Rome class, for example, I learned the tax collectors were hated by the people because they were allowed to extort whatever they could get beyond what Rome expected. Yet the New Testament teaches people to submit and pay their taxes or be damned. If most people were enslaved, whose houses were the first churches held in? Given it was a patriarchal slave society, where did the female followers get their money to support Jesus? Where did the church hierarchy come from? Who, exactly, were the Church Fathers? Why did they hate women?

Hitchens points out many troubling biblical passages in both the Old and New Testaments that helped me open my eyes. Have no concern for tomorrow? Just trust GOD to take care of you?

Atwill and Josephus made me aware Jewish elites (the Alexanders and Herod's family) sided with Rome against the rebelling political messianic movement – Zealots and Sicarii – and may have been instrumental in creating Christianity as a way to undermine that element within Judaism. Josephus realized, upon his capture, that Yahweh's messiah was now Rome and in the person of General Vespasian – soon to be Caesar. .

There can be no doubt the alleged "end times" prophesy concerning the coming Son of Man who will destroy Jerusalem and the Temple is describing Titus the Roman general who destroyed Jerusalem in <u>exactly</u> the way described in the gospels and at the exact time as it was allegedly prophesied to happen – within a generation of Christ's crucifixion. (An interesting aside. Herod's granddaughter was both Titus' mistress and a widow of one of Philo of Alexandria's relatives.) Thus, the coming Son of Man was Titus – not a returning-to-Earth Jesus – who fulfilled the alleged prophesy in 70 CE – not in the 21st century.

BUT Evangelical Fundamentalists cite this text as proof Jesus is returning to earth "any day now"– and some of their leaders have access to our White House as advisers! As interpreted by

Evangelical Fundamentalists these verses are used to keep Evangelical Fundamentalist amygdalas in over-drive, their thinking brains shut down, and money pouring in to charlatans as they kowtow to warmongers. Alleged divine insider information about "end times" is one of the ways Evangelical Fundamentalists suck in those who do not know history or the Bible and divert taxpayer monies to their projects.

This so-called Evangelical Fundamentalist "end times" prophetic passage is not about the biblical Jesus returning to earth to wreak vengeance on Jews for rejecting him as messiah! Actually, it was written after the first century Roman destruction of Jerusalem to make it appear prophetic and to give the gospel Jesus prophetic power. Other gospel Jesus stories are elements from pagan agrarian and solar religions: Isis and Horus; Demeter and Dionysus; Mithra – along with Old Testament prototypes. I was taught the "light of the world" is Jesus but, in reality, it is the sun.

Like my father, my religion scrambled my brains and left me sounding crazy! It is easy to trick Evangelical Fundamentalist adults because they have been brainwashed to reject all secular education when it contradicts the Bible so they do not know what everyone else knows. And that is why I didn't as a child. I was in a parallel universe created by mind control!

Reading Josephus made it clear to me that "salvation" was about "surrendering" to Rome – not to Jesus – as I had been taught before my weekly trips to the alter during high school and after.. Before Titus destroyed towns in Galilee, he gave them an opportunity to save themselves. They had a choice. They could continue to rebel against Rome or they could submit, obey and pay their taxes. If they trusted Titus' offer and repented, they were saved from destruction that often included death by catapulted rocks, famine and fire. THIS is the Evangelical Fundamentalist god and salvation. Titus not Jesus! War not eternal life!

After reading numerous scholars, it became obvious the Old Testament was the blueprint for much of the New Testament and shared the same motive: controlling and exploiting the masses by using religion to create and justify sociopathic hierarchies. Hierarchy in the original Greek means "sacred rule" or "rule by the sacred." ("Says who?" "Their warriors!")

Today those who feel entitled to control and exploit others are called sociopaths and psychopaths. But most of us have been conditioned to not even recognize them. Being in a sociopathic system makes people feel crazy because everything is backwards or upside down and out of sync with normal perceptions, values, motives, empathy and strategies.

My friend Paul Weis, made an astute observation about Evangelical Fundamentalism when he commented, "It would be like going through life looking in a mirror; everything is backwards." I literally felt like I was trying to stand up like the Vitruvian Man inside a four-square ball while others dribbled, kicked and threw it! Out of control! Helpless! Terrified! Dissociated.

[See: Randel Helms, Gospel Fictions; Randel Helms, The Bible Against Itself; Richard Elliott Friedman, Who Wrote the Bible?; Gregory J. Riley, One Jesus Many Christs; Tom Harpur, The Pagan Christ; Thomas Paine,Tthe Age of Reason; Joseph Campbell, The Goddesses; James George Frazer, The Golden Bough; Riane Eisler, The Chalice and the Blade]

Trust Your Guts

Whereas healthy people know to trust their guts when making decisions, Evangelical Fundamentalists are taught to defer to dogma as my memory (and their literature) of the campus ministry makes clear. I was shocked when I took their tract to my PhD psychologist a few years ago. She did not even look at it! "There is nothing true in that tract, Diana." (She did not care if she hurt my feelings!) Her immediate and firm response turned out to trigger a major healing in my life as I began researching to understand what she knew that I did not! Lots!

Ignoring my emotions as they were teaching me to do in deference to the Bible left me without a sense of self just as Winell's painting portrays. Without our emotions online, we have no sense of self, no conscience and no empathy. We feel empty! Perhaps that is why Evangelical Fundamentalists like to quote Pascal, "Everyone has a god-shaped vacuum" and they assume it is their biblical Jesus who can fill the vacuum – not one's own emotions. Living numbed out puts true believers on the narcissism-sociopathic continuum and might explain why a surprisingly large percentage of true believers think they can do "anything" after their conversion experience. Their conscience is not online!

Given that one of the symptoms of child abuse is numbed emotions, it is hard to know how to separate out the chicken-egg cycle between fundamentalist theology and child abuse. Which came first? Does Evangelical Fundamentalist parenting create Evangelical Fundamentalist theology? I would argue yes. There is no doubt in my mind that both experiences reinforce and justify each other.

[See: Robert Altemeyer, Ph.D., The Authoritarians (free online); Martha Stout, The Sociopath Next Door; James Fallon, The Psychopath Inside; 2012 DOJ FBI Bulletin for Law Enforcement: Psychopathy; Marlene Winell, Leaving the Fold and journeyfree.org; Riane Eisler, The Chalice and the Blade]

The Evangelical Fundamentalist Jesus is the Old Roman Political Warrior Jesus

More evidence against Evangelical Fundamentalism surfaces when one explores what happens when the personal Jesus morphs into a political Jesus. Jeff Sharlet's *The Family* and *C Street*, Frank Schaeffer's *Crazy for God* (and numerous online interviews), Max Blumenthal's *Republican Gomorrah*, Katherine Stewart's *The Good News Club: The Christian Right's Stealth Assault on America's Children*, and Chris Hedge's, *American Fascists: The Christian Right and the War on America*, and Sean Faircloth's *Attack of the Theocrats* all document the Evangelical Fundamentalist political agenda.

This personal savior Jesus has an alter ego also! He is a he-man Jesus who expects his followers to return America to its alleged moral Evangelical Fundamentalist roots. Jesus is now often portrayed as a radical right-wing warrior with his own Christian assault weapons. "Real men love Jesus" is the refrain in a new country western song. This new imagery is possible because, as Atwill has made clear, one of the Gospel Jesus' is the Roman

General Titus who just happened to be Caesar at about the time scholars believe the gospels were written. Coincidence?

This Jesus is the biblical Jesus who Evangelical Fundamentalists claim will return and who will kill all who do not convert – just like his "father" warrior-god Yahweh – did in the Old Testament. (There is definitely a family resemblance!) This Jesus is the dark side of Christianity that most know nothing about. This returning-to-earth warrior Jesus during "end times" is also the one who, allegedly, will correct any environmental problems mankind may have created in his absence – before or after his believers hijack the American Constitution and "reconstruct" it to conform to their authoritarian understanding of the Bible and God! Their politicians are not kidding! Listen to them.

The current Evangelical Fundamentalist movement is like the many-headed Hydra. I cannot help but recall, the KKK was resurrected by Christians who believed they were doing God's work – as did Hitler!

[See: Book 5 goes into more detail. Also see: instrinsicdignity.org; intrinsicdignity.wordpress.com; intrinsicdignity.com;shame.goodnewsclubs.info; topdocumentaryfilms.com has a number of very good documentaries about this movement: Jesus Camp and The Lord's Next Army are good places to start. Hitler's Children is a good place to end. Don't miss BBC, and Vice documentaries exposing Evangelical Fundamentalist anti-gay and witch-children influence in Uganda; PEW polls have found that White church-going Americans are more likely than other groups to support torture. Jeremy Shahill notes it shows 'White evangelical Protestants were the religious group most likely to say torture is often or sometimes justified–more than 6 in 10 supported. Coincidence?; Mikey Weinstein, militaryreligiousfreedom.org]

KKK

Okay, I came to understand Evangelical Fundamentalism is a mix of propaganda and destructive psychology. "But how does the KKK fit into this mess," I wondered? Anyone can Google and get a brief history. The KKK was resurrected in the 20th century by a Methodist Minister in Georgia. Uncles on BOTH sides of my family told me "they did good work" and Aunt Bebe was not surprised to learn I'd been exposed to the KKK.

Many Protestant Christians joined after viewing the first-ever-movie-blockbuster *Birth of a Nation* [1915] that presented Klansmen as American saviors during Reconstruction in the South. This led to increased racism and lynching primarily of Blacks. At the same time, more European Catholics and Jews were immigrating to America. In the 1920s the Klan was very active in Colorado politics. Coloradoans had a Republican KKK governor who was known for his extreme anti-Catholic stance. [See: Wikipedia] This is why I did not trust any white people when my KKK memories began surfacing – I was in Colorado and knew its dark history. I lived in terror fearing KKK people would discover my memories were returning!

There is more than one Klan but the KKK dot com makes it clear they are a Christian organization.

[see: Dick Lehr – The Birth of a Nation]

A Brief History of Evangelicalism

I thought Methodism was always a mainstream progressive religious movement and that is why I had to read some history. After Darwin published *On the Origin of the Species* and after the Scopes Trial, evangelicals had a major split. Those who accepted evidence-based science turned their religion into what has been known as the social gospel based on the Golden Rule. (And that is why they know nothing about the dark side of the Bible! It was ignored. Science and conscience were their authorities – not the Bible science was discrediting.)

Those who rejected science and believed the Bible was the inerrant word of God created the Evangelical Fundamentalist movement. Dwight L. Moody, Billy Graham, Oral Roberts, Pat Robertson, Jerry Falwell, Francis Schaeffer are just a few – along with numerous disgraced televangelists and disgraced faith healers – who helped create American Christian fundamentalism – that now often overlaps with the prosperity gospel that has fueled the megachurch explosion. But if one pays attention, one will notice, their authority is always the Bible – not conscience – and is often linked with "end times" terror.

Like every human group, Methodists have had their share of unhealthy people. A Colorado Bishop recently revealed that prominent Colorado members were not only part of the Sand Creek Massacre but may have engineered it. Manifest Destiny is anchored in Puritan thinking and Puritanism is part of Susanna Wesley's background and appears to have been part of John and Charles ideology when they came to Georgia with Oglethorpe given Charles was his Indian Affairs Agent.

My understanding is that Methodism was the largest religious movement during the 19th century and many of the current denominations are spin offs from Methodism. Many of the old hymns were penned by Charles Wesley and/or written in the nineteenth century. But unlike the Wesley's, most of their ministers were not educated at Oxford – if at all. But even the Wesley's were viewed as fanatics at Oxford. My understanding is that pretty much any young man could feel called to preach the gospel and Wesley's methods – which I now understand were anchored in trauma and mind control – not reality or spirituality.

Wesley Influence

"How did Wesley's get so much influence," I wondered? Like most religious leaders – by aligning with political elites. Oglethorpe brought both John and Charles to America when he came to establish the colony of Georgia. Hard to believe, but the Wesley evangelists had some problems with women, and other issues, and soon headed back home. But from what I've read, it appears the plan was for them to convert Native Americans and bring them under control. African Anglican Bishop and activist Desmond Tutu has been credited with saying, "When the missionaries came to Africa, we had the land and they had the Bible. They said, 'Let's pray.' When we opened our eyes they had the land and we had the Bible." Whether or not Tutu was the first to say this – and even if he never did – the history of missionaries confirms the gist is accurate. Missionaries and religion have often paved the way for exploitation of native peoples and common folks by the elite.

[See: Howard Zinn, A Peoples' History of the United States; Jeff Scharlet, The Family]

Good Stuff in the Bible

"Diana, there is good stuff in the Bible – like the Ten Commandments and the Golden Rule. Where did they come from if the Bible is not divine," some have asked me.

Evidence shows us the Ten Commandments were in the Egyptian *Book of the Dead* (Spell 125) centuries before there was a Judah. Writers of the Old Testament adopted them. The major difference between the two versions is that there is no vain, jealous war-god telling people, "Thou shalt not." In the Egyptian version. people were expected to live by the rules of the Goddess Maat. "The way things ought to be." Upon death their heart was weighed against her feather. If their heart was heavier it was fed to a crocodile and that was the end of them. In other words, the dead tell the god of the underworld, "I have not lied. I have not…" All ancient cultures had rules of civility. Martha Stout in *The Sociopath Next Door* describes how some tribes took sociopaths hunting and they always had an unfortunate accident.

We still encourage one another to "follow your heart." "Trust your guts." "Trust your inner wisdom." "Follow your conscience." Those are scientifically valid ways to live but the opposite of cult control. Cult control is external control. Healthy people listen to what their emotions are teaching them. In the words of Stanford neuroscience professor, Robert Sapolsky, "We are emotional machines that think." Bessel Van Der Kolk tells readers to "trust your guts." In my non-credit neuroscience classes I learned why this is important. There are approximately one million neurons in our guts that function just like the neurons in our brain.

[See: Bessel Van Der Kolk,MD, The Body Keeps the Score; Molecules of Emotion by Candace Pert, PhD]

The Bible is a Man-made Document

Every culture has a Golden Rule. Evidence shows this social code also predates Judah and those who wrote the Bible. There are enormous amounts of evidence that some biblical laws and the creation story and flood story were borrowed from much older Mesopotamian literature created in Sumer and Babylonia – not by Yahweh – as I had been brainwashed to believe.

That the Bible is a man-made document – propaganda – that flipped healthy ways of being on their head – and is not a divine document – explains why following it as though it was the word of the one and only creator GOD made me ill. As Swiss psychologist, Alice Miller, wrote, "The brain needs truth!" The Bible is not true when read literally as the word of God. Never was I a sinner. Never did I need Jesus' atoning blood to make me pure! Human sacrifice! Ugh!! There is no heaven or hell! Those are man-made manipulative constructs! Behaviorism.

The Garden of Eden

The Garden of Eden story is not what I was taught. Like many ancient myths it reflects the conquest of the patriarchal warrior god over the goddess-centered cultures. All this, and more, is why – and how – Evangelical Fundamentalism made me ill. I was not living in reality! I had been programmed into *Star Wars*! It was quite a shock to figure out <u>that</u> GOD is actually a psychopath! Fortunately, at the time I was connecting the dots, I happened to meet a university literature professor in Barnes and Noble who was also discovering <u>that</u> GOD is a psychopath! So I knew I was not crazy! At least two of us had figured it out! And if we had surely others had. But I wondered why no one was talking about this momentous discovery. That opened the door for me to read Hitchens.

The Bible is crazy-making when read as the literal, infallible word of God for all people in all times and places because of what Finkelstein discovered. Biblical cultural laws – those beyond the Ten Commandments and Golden Rule – were based on the formula, "If they do it, we don't." If they eat this, we don't. If they do this, we don't. There is massive evidence the gentiles, pagans, whatever we call them, lived in harmony with nature and generally with each other. They were not originally warriors. Sinful was a political construct. This is the point of the Cain and Able story. The herder is the good guy because Yahweh was the herder's god. The herders' god was replacing the agrarian gods so the agrarians and their gods had to be demonized.

Biblical priests using cult formulas basically flipped realty on its head – everything went upside down. And that is why my sisters and I finally figured out, "We learned everything upside down!" There was a reason. We were not bad or idiots. We were in a destructive religion committed to scrambling our brains so we could never escape their political and financial control. We would live controlled and exploited forever – or so they hoped but we three escaped.

Victim/Perpetrator/Rescuer Triangle

The biblical drama in both the Old and New Testament is built upon the victim/perpetrator/rescuer triangle just like Cinderella! Cinderella is the victim. Her sisters and stepmother are the perpetrators and Prince Charming is the Rescuer. It would not surprise me if this formula is our number one cultural paradigm! It is everywhere – including Madison Avenue, Hollywood and politics – not just in religion and literature. Some call it the sociopathic triangle.

The Yahweh-only priests demonized everyone whose land Josiah wanted to integrate into his kingdom in Judah and his invisible man-made war-god, Yahweh, conveniently justified what he wanted – including genocide. And his warriors complied. It is not hard to see how the propaganda myths cast Judah as the victim with Josiah as the rescuer (messiah) and the polytheist agrarian cultures as evildoers in the sight of Yahweh who, therefore, deserved death.

In a similar way Jesus as messiah plays out the rescuer role. All humanity is allegedly the victim of Satan or Yahweh depending on how you look at it. But according to the New Testament and Josephus, the Jews are evil, Rome is the victim and Titus/Jesus is the savior. Divide and conquer! It is, as Colin Ross, MD, points out. The victim, perpetrator, rescuer triangle/formula is analogous to the three core splits of traumatized minds: GOD, Jesus, and Satan in the Judeo-Christian culture. Given how traumatic life has been under psychopathic leaders it is pretty easy to see why and how this formula feels like a psychological architype. Many have been forced to live it since 3,500 BCE!

The problem, my therapist explained, is that once a person (or group) gets on this triangle they will go around and around it without ever getting their needs met. And they will play each of the roles. This is how early childhood neglect and abuse fuels rage that gets acted out on innocent people.

[See: Riane Eisler, The Chalice and the Blade; Howard Zinn, The Peoples' History; everything by Alice Miller]

Deuteronomy

When I read Deuteronomy from cover to cover in one sitting after my recovery, I not only felt sick to my stomach, I picked up this formula immediately and then experienced numerous pictures from Jonestown on the screen of my mind. My understanding is that my thinks-in-pictures mind recognized the cult parallels. The Yahweh-only elites forced their hierarchy and war god on the rest of those in Judah so they could control everyone from Jerusalem. Rural gods and rural local control were no longer acceptable because the Yahweh people were creating a male-dominated totalitarian theocracy with a conquest agenda. Yahweh was in, Ashura, Ishtar, Isis, Tiamat and Eve were out!

This is the point of the biblical conflict stories between Yahweh and the nature gods the people preferred. The stories reveal how the Yahweh-only religion was used to impose the political agenda of the Yahweh-only king, priests and their warriors. It is not, as I was taught in Evangelical Fundamentalism, examples of spiritual battles between Yahweh, the real creator god, and all the evil false gods. None of the gods were real! ALL were only projections of the people who created them in their image. The pagan gods represented aspects of nature. The Yahweh-only god – conveniently – spoke for the elites: Josiah, his priests, and their warriors had the power to enforce their laws and agendas on the rest of the people by using terror and a terrifying god.

[See: Finkelstein & Silberman, The Bible Unearthed; The Chalice and the Blade by Riane Eisler; When God was a Woman by Merlin Stone; all of UCLA archaeologist Marja Gimbutus' books; Joseph Campbell's Goddess book; Robert Graves, Greek Myths; everything by Barbara G. Walker]

Incest in Christian Families?

"But, but, but how does incest fit into this picture," I finally wondered. Incest, according to former Miss America, Marilyn Van Derbur, affects every area of a person's body and life. "Incest is like adding a drop of red dye to a gallon of white paint." "The worst part of incest is the shame it creates in victims." "Incest victims feel evil to the morrow of their bones!" "Incest families are vicious."

Sexual abuse is a huge problem in America. My chief of police told me that most police work is involved in sex crimes. The shame incest created in me was the hook that kept me tied to Evangelical Fundamentalism as I assumed there was something wrong with me because their hocus-pocus-covered-in-Jesus'-blood cures were ineffective at removing my sense of shame.

I assumed I was simply too evil for even Jesus to forgive and so I doubled down and tried harder and harder. I was like a hamster in its wheel. Working hard but going nowhere! All the time getting sucked deeper into the insane world of Evangelical Fundamentalism! Deeper and Wider!

I could not see the obvious because I'd been brainwashed since early childhood not to see the obvious: There was something terribly wrong with Evangelical Fundamentalism – not me! Smoke and mirrors at my psychological and financial expense! All of my shame and other mental illness symptoms were common consequences of what had been done to me and my brain. NEVER had I been evil!

Fundamentalism disguised and redirected my shame back onto me by claiming my normal human reactions (especially my rage) were sin – not symptoms of incest and other abuses and neglect. By turning the tables on me – in sociopathic style – this smoke screen provided perpetrators a perfect out.

Fortunately, not long before my mother's early death to breast cancer in 1973, she told me, "He had a vasectomy so it was okay." At the time, I was in my early twenties and my memories were completely split off from my conscious memory. I had no idea what she was talking about at the time. It literally came out of the blue. I now suspect it was a reaction to a conversation we'd had earlier that I describe in Book 2.

She apparently never understood the damage she and my father and their religion had done to me. She didn't know it was so traumatic my brain had hidden their evil secrets – miraculously just like Evangelical Fundamentalists claim – "as far as east is from west." From my point of view, my parents' sins were "white as snow." They literally did not exist because my memories were still repressed.

Now it is obvious why I never felt loved and always sensed there was a wall between us that I could not destroy no matter how hard I tried. That wall was most likely their shame and guilt that got projected onto me as well as their own compartmentalized mind filled with walls. Feeling unloved and rejected is our inter-generational child rearing tragedy that has nothing to do with a real live Satan or an "evil world."

[See: Miss America by Day by Marilyn Van Derbur; The Body Keeps the Score by Bessel Van Der Kolk, MD; Trauma and Recovery by Judith Herman, MD.; Marlene Winell, PhD, Leaving the Fold]

For more detailed information regarding how I continued to be controlled and how I recovered, see my remaining books, 2-4. For more information regarding the history of Evangelical Fundamentalism's advocacy of hostile and abusive childrearing as well as the experiences that enabled me to escape it, see Book 5.

Susanna Wesley, Bebe, and Me

Susanna Wesley's Letter to John Regarding Her Child Rearing Methods

July 24, 1732

Dear Son,

According to your desire, I have collected the principal rules I observed in educating my family: which I now send you as they occurred to my mind, and you may (if you think they can be of use to any) dispose of them in what order you please.

The children were always put into a regular method of living, in such things as they were capable of, from their birth: as in dressing, undressing, changing their linen, etc. The first quarter commonly passes in sleep. After that they were, if possible, laid into their cradles awake and rocked to sleep: and so they were kept rocking till it was time for them to awake. This was done to bring them to a regular course of sleeping; which at first was three hours in the morning and three in the afternoon; afterwards two hours, till they needed none at all.

When turned a year old (and some before), they were taught to fear the rod, and to cry softly; by which means they escaped abundance of correction they might otherwise have had, and that most odious noise of the crying of children was rarely heard in the house, but the family usually lived in much quietness as if there had not been a child among them.

As soon as they were grown pretty strong, they were confined to three meals a day. At dinner their little table and chairs were set up by ours, where they could be overlooked; and they were suffered to eat and drink (small beer) as much as they would; but not to call for anything. If they wanted aught they used to whisper to the maid which attended them, who came and spake to me; and as soon as they could handle a knife and fork, they were set to our table. There were never suffered to choose their meat, but always made eat such things as were provided for the family.

Mornings they had always spoon-meat; sometimes on nights. But whatever they had, they were never permitted to eat those meals of more than one thing, and that sparingly enough. Drinking or eating between meals was never allowed, unless in case of sickness; which seldom happened. Nor were they suffered to go into the kitchen to ask anything of the servants when they were at meat; if it was known they did, they were certainly beat, and the servants severely reprimanded.

At six, as soon as family prayers were over, they had their supper; at seven the maid washed them; and beginning at the youngest, she undressed and got them all to bed by eight; at which time she left them in their several rooms awake, for there was no such thing allowed of in our house as sitting by a child till it fell asleep.

They were so constantly used to eat and drink what was given them that when any of them was ill there was no difficulty in making them take the most unpleasant medicine; for they durst not refuse it, thou some of them would presently throw it up. This I mention to show that a person may be taught to take anything, though it be never so much against his stomach.

In order to form the minds of children, the first thing to be done is to conquer their will, and bring them to an obedient temper. To inform the understanding is a work of time, and must [with children] proceed by slow degrees [as they are able to bear it]: but the subjecting the will is a thing that must be done at once–and the sooner the better. For by neglecting timely correction, they [will] contract a stubbornness [and obstinacy] which is hardly ever [after] conquered; and never, without using such severity as would be as painful to me as to the child. In the esteem of the world they pass for kind and indulgent whom I call cruel parents, who permit their children to get habits they now must be afterwards broken. [Nay, some are so stupidly fond as in sport to teach their children to do things which in a while after they have severely beaten them for doing.

Whenever a child is corrected, it must be conquered; and this will be no hard matter to do if it be not grown headstrong by too much indulgence. And when the will of the child is totally subdued, and it is brought to revere and stand in awe of the parents, then a great many childish follies and inadvertencies may be passed by. Some should be overlooked and taken no notice of, and others mildly reproved; but no willful transgression ought ever to be forgiven children without chastisement, less or more, as the nature and circumstances of the offence require.]

I insist upon conquering the will of children betimes, because this is the only [strong and rational] foundation of a religious education [, without which both precept and example will be ineffectual]. [But] when this is thoroughly done, then a child is capable of being governed by the reason [and piety] of its parent[s], till its own understanding comes to maturity [, and the principles of religion have taken root in the mind].

I cannot yet dismiss this subject. As self-will is the root of all sin and misery, so whatever cherishes this in children ensures their after-wretchedness and irreligion; whatever checks and mortifies it promotes their future happiness and piety. This is still more evident if we [farther] consider that religion is nothing else than the doing of the will of God, and not our own; that the one grand impediment to our temporal and eternal happiness being this self-will, no indulgences of it can be trivial, no denial unprofitable. Heaven or hell depends on this alone. So that the parent who studies to subdue it in his child works together with God in the renewing and saving a soul. The parent who indulges it does the devil's work, makes religion impracticable, salvation unattainable; and does all that in him lies to damn his child, soul and body, forever.

This therefore I cannot but earnestly repeat: break their wills betimes. Begin this great work before they can run alone, before they can speak plain, or perhaps speak at all. Whatever pains it cost, conquer their stubbornness: break the will, if you would not damn the child. I conjure you not to neglect, not to delay this! Therefore: 1. Let a child from a year old, be taught to fear the rod and cry softly. In order to do this, 2. Let him have nothing he cries for, absolutely nothing, great or small; else you undo your own work. 3. At all events, from that age, make him do as he is bid, if you whip him ten times running to effect it: let none persuade you it is cruelty to do this; it is cruelty not to do it. Break his will now, and his soul will live, and he will probably bless you to all eternity.

The children of this family were taught, as soon as they could speak, the Lord's Prayer, which they were made to say at rising and bedtime constantly; to which, as they grew bigger, were added a short prayer for their parents, and some collects; a short catechism, and some portions of Scripture, as their memories could bear.

They were very early made to distinguish the Sabbath from other days, before they could well speak, or go. They were as soon taught to be still at family prayers, and to ask a blessing immediately after, which they used to do by signs, before they could kneel or speak.

They were quickly made to understand they might have nothing they cried for, and instructed to speak handsomely for what they wanted. They were not suffered to ask even the lowest servant for aught without saying, "Pray give me such a thing."; and the servant was chid if she ever let them omit the word. Taking God's name in vain, cursing and swearing, profaneness, obscenity, rude, ill-bred names were never heard among them. Nor were they ever permitted to call each other by their proper names without the addition of brother or sister.

None of them were taught to read till five years old, except Kezzy, in whose case I was overruled; and she was more years learning than any of the rest had been months. The way of teaching was this. The day before a child began to learn, the house was set in order, everyone's work appointed them, and a charge given that none should come into the room from nine till twelve, or from two till five; which, you know, were our school hours. One day was allowed the child wherein to learn its letters, and each of them did in that time know all its letters, great and small, except Molly and Nancy, who were a day and a half before they knew them perfectly; for which I then thought them very dull; but since I have observed how long many children are learning the hornbook. I have changed my opinion. But the reason why I thought them so then was because the rest learned so readily; and poor Brother Samuel, who was the first child I ever taught, learned the alphabet in a few hours. He was five years old on the 10th of February; the next day he began to learn and as soon as he knew the letters began at the first chapter of Genesis. He was taught to spell the first verse, then to read it over and over, till he could read it off-hand without any hesitation; so on to the second, etc., till he took ten verses for a lesson, which he quickly did. Easter fell low that year;

and by Whitsuntide he could read a chapter very well; for he read continually, and had such a prodigious memory that I cannot remember ever to have told him the same word twice.

What was yet stranger, any word he had learned in his lesson he knew wherever he saw it, either in his Bible or any other book; by which means he learned very soon to read any English author well.

The same method was observed with them all. As soon as they knew the letters, they were put first to spell; and read one line, then a verse, never leaving till perfect in their lesson, were it shorter or longer. So one or other continued reading at school time without any intermission, and before we left school each child read what he had learned that morning; and ere we parted in the afternoon, what they had learned that day.

There was no such thing as loud talking or playing allowed of; but everyone was kept close to their business for the six hours of school; and it is almost incredible what a child may be taught in a quarter of a year by vigorous application, if it have but a tolerable capacity and good health. Everyone of these, Kezzy excepted, could read better in that time than the most of women can do as long as they live.

Rising out of their places, or going out of the room, was not permitted unless for good cause, and running into the yard, garden, or street, without leave, was always a capital offence.

For some years we went on very well. Never were children in better order. Never were children better disposed to piety, or in more subjection to their parents, till that fatal dispersion of them after the fire into several families. In these they were left at full liberty to converse with servants, which before they had always been restrained from; and to run abroad and play with any children good or bad. They soon learned to neglect a strict observation of the Sabbath and got knowledge of several songs and bad things, which before they had no notion of. That civil behavior which made them admired when at home by all which saw them was in great measure lost, and a clownish accent and many rude ways were learned, which were not reformed without some difficulty.

When the house was rebuilt, and the children all brought home, we entered upon a strict reform; and then was begun the custom of singing psalms at beginning and leaving school, morning and evening. Then also that of a general retirement at five o'clock was entered upon, when the oldest took the youngest that could speak, and the second the next, to whom they read the Psalms for the day and a chapter in the New Testament, as in the morning they were directed to read the Psalms and a chapter in the Old, after which they went to their private prayers, before they got their breakfast or came into the family. And I thank God this custom is still preserved among us.

There were several by-laws observed among us, which slipped my memory, or else they had been inserted in their proper place; but I mention them here, because I think them useful.

1. It had been observed that cowardice and fear of punishment often led children into lying, till they get a custom of it which they cannot leave. To prevent this a law was made, that whoever was charged with a fault , of which they were guilty, if they would ingenuously confess it, and promise to amend, should not be beaten. This rule prevented a great deal of lying and would have done more if one in the family would have observed it. But he could not be prevailed on, and therefore was often imposed on by false colours and equivocations, which none would have used (except one), had they been kindly dealt with. And some, in spite of all, would always speak truth plainly.

2. That no sinful action, as lying, pilfering, playing at church, or on the Lord's day, disobedience, quarrelling, etc., should ever pass unpunished.

3. That no child should ever be chided or beat twice for the same fault; and that, if they amended, they should never be upbraided with it afterwards.

4. That every signal act of obedience, especially when it crossed upon their own inclinations, should be always commended and frequently rewarded, according to the merits of the case.

5. That if ever any child performed an act of obedience, or did anything with an intention to please, though the performance was not well, yet the obedience and intention should be kindly accepted; and the child with sweetness directed how to do better for the future.

6. That property be inviolably preserved, and none suffered to invade the property of another in the smallest matter, though it were but of the value of a farthing, or a pin; which they might not take from the owner without, much less against his consent. This rule can never be too much inculcated on the minds of children, and from the want of parents or governors doing it as they ought proceeds that shameful neglect of justice which we may observe in the world.

7. That promises be strictly observed; and a gift once bestowed, and so the right passed away from the donor, be not resumed, but left to the disposal of him to whom it was given, unless it were conditional, and the condition of the obligation not performed.

8. That no girl be taught to work till she can read very well; and then that she be kept to her work with the same application, and for the same time, that she was held to in reading. This rule also is much to be observed; for the putting children to learn sewing before they can read perfectly is the very reason why so few women can read fit to be heard, and never to be well understood.

Susanna Wesley: The Complete Writings, edited by Charles Wallace, Oxford Press, 1997, pp. 369ff. [I am using it under fair use laws given the importance of the content for public awareness and I have applied for permission to publish. I typed this copy.]

Signed Interview With Aunt Bebe:

December 2010

I am chatting on the phone with one of my maternal aunts, Bebe, who is now seventy-five. Everyone remarks about how sharp her mind is – especially her ability to recall great detail. She is always supportive, warm and loving. The kind of mom everyone wishes they had.

Bebe is helping me understand some of my forgotten childhood experiences. I've just told her about my father's bizarre attack on me at his mother's viewing. It does not surprise her. I listen…My aunt's voice softens and begins to quiver:

"I was only fourteen. It was in the fall. Your parents were living in Mrs. Goldberg's basement. Your sister was just learning to pull herself up in her crib. So she was probably around ten months. That would make you around twenty-one months [September 1949]. Your parents and I were playing Monopoly in their living room. You and your baby sister had been put to bed for the night. But you opened your bedroom door and asked if you could have the door open for some light. You were frightened of the dark and your sister was making noises in her crib. You said, 'I'm scared.' Your father got up and slipped his belt off. He doubled it over, made you lie on your tummy and held you down on your bed with his left knee on your legs. I saw him spank you so hard on your bare bottom!

I felt like I'd witnessed a horrible car wreck. Your mother looked like she had been slapped in the face and she began gasping for air. Tears rolled down her cheeks. That was the first time I ever saw him act like that but it probably was not the first time for her.

When he came back to the game he shook his finger at me and said, 'This is my house. I will correct my children as I want.'

He sat down as though nothing had happened to finish the game but I was too traumatized to play Monopoly. I called my mother and asked her to come and get me.

I went in to your room and you were sobbing. 'Bebe! My daddy boom-boomed me!' You had raised welts on your bottom and legs. You were crying hysterically. You could not stop sobbing! You were hurt physically and emotionally! I tried to calm you down by rubbing your back and telling you not to cry. You did not want me to leave. 'Bebe! Don't leave me Bebe!' I promised I would come back.

Your baby sister settled down after she saw what happened to you. I was young but I knew it was wrong and so the next morning I went to the Humane Society and reported what I'd seen. The Humane Society used to be for children and animals. They sent an officer. But your mother would not press charges. We did not hear from your mother for several weeks. We didn't know what happened to you. Your father never let us see him spank you after the officer almost threw him into jail....

———

In February [1949], your father decided he wanted to be in Florida. It was snowing. His car was not working right. But he insisted that you four leave right then. You, your baby sister, him and your mother! I don't know what they did with their furniture. Your mother made him bring her home so she could say goodbye to us. Your dad was in the car and just you and your mom came inside.

He yelled out, 'If she is going she'd better get in the car!'

Your grandpa said, 'He needs to have someone talk to him' and he was going to go out and talk to your dad. It was late at night. But your mother stopped him.

'No Dad! He has a gun and is foolish enough to use it!'....

[I think this may be the trip mother talked about many times as I was growing up. She said they were driving to Florida and Daddy fell asleep at the wheel and my baby sister cried just in time for him to awaken before we hit a bridge abutment. My mother believed The Lord Jesus caused my sister to cry and save our lives!]

When you were three [1950] your mother flew home from Florida with you and your sister. She was pregnant with your youngest sister. They were about to break up. She could not take it any more....

———

Diana, imagine how your mother must have felt to have her husband attracted to her daughter and without the information we have today. I think that is why she beat you so hard and was so stern with you. Today she would have done things differently. She felt threatened…. Your father was trying to destroy you!….

I am not surprised you were exposed to KKK. Your mother told us in the fifties that uncle was KKK. I remember hearing them talking about 'coon hunting'…."

Before we hang up Bebe reassures me, "Diana, always remember I love you!"

"I love you too! You saved my mind and life by telling the truth!"

————

I typed up Bebe's interview and she signed it knowing it would be in my book. She told me she said what she knew she could testify to in a court of law.

————

My neuroscience professor explained what the trauma of just that one beating did to my brain and health – especially because I was so young and my brain was still wiring! It wired my brain to survive under extreme stress. It set me up not only for mental illnesses but also cancer! (BINGO!) Because stress hormones were running 24/7 due to my chronically violent and frightening environment! Both my family and Evangelical Fundamentalism were keeping me frightened. This undermined my immune system and prevented my NK cells (natural killer cells) from destroying the cancer before it could colonize.

In addition to many beatings that also left welts and bruises, my immune system was undermined by the toxic stress of living with a husband who later admitted in writing that he had lied, manipulated me and our children, sabotaged me, withheld whatever I wanted, etc. In other words, emotional battering! That was, without a doubt the worst trauma because I couldn't figure out what was going on due to the religious halo hovering over his head. And that is why my therapist made me aware I would have found myself in a psych hospital even if I'd had the perfect childhood because of how he had treated me.

Reversing My Child-Self's Locus of Control Shift: Holy Father [2012]

The locus of control shift is like an evil transfusion. All the evil inside the perpetrator has been transfused into the self, making the perpetrator good and safe to attach to–the locus of control shift helps solve the problem of the attachment to the perpetrator...When you really reverse the locus of control shift, then you really get it that mom and dad weren't there for you, and didn't protect you. This throws you into the fundamental work of therapy: mourning the loss of the parent you never actually had.

[Colin Ross, M.D., The Trauma Model]

Why have I not understood this before now? Did I need Daddy to die last month to be able to get it?

I REALLY WAS carrying HIS guilt and shame–like the biblical scapegoat–when I walked the aisle to the altar those many times during my high school years (and after) to ask Jesus to forgive ME! for whatever unrecalled horrible thing I had done to feel so dirty and evil. So guilty! So ugly! So angry! So unlovable! So unworthy of life on planet earth!

HOW could he have sat there and watched my agony week after week and not felt compassion? Not told the truth? Not begged My forgiveness? HOOOOOOOOW?

RAPE!
THAT is the true word!
Incest ever so politely hides the ugly ravagingly violent demeaning word
RAPE!

The word incest has a lilt of softness that blurs the edges of reality and made it harder to accept!
The word rape does not!

Rape sounds like what it is:

228

Diana Lee, M.A.

Intense!
Sudden! Aggressive! Unexpected! Terrifying! Humiliating!
Betrayal!
Abandonment! Painful!

MY father RAPED me!
That focuses my attention!
Perks up my ears!
Makes my blood boil!
Curdles my soul!
Makes me sob!

Whereas the word incest stays stuck in my head
or just kind of lays on the ground looking pathetic.
Perhaps it is the two syllables that slow it down!
But RAPE energizes me!
Makes me wanna fight!
Kick the bastard in the balls!

When I say incest I feel drugged like falling asleep.
Oh, yah! I did fall asleep! Not really! I pretended!
I actually turned my head to the left, focused on my window then
closed my eyes
so I wouldn't have to watch.
I focused intently on God
and my biblical memory verses until I went away into my head.
Gone!
"Casting all your cares upon Him for He careth for you."

My–FATHER–raped–ME!!!!
I did not ask for it.
"Ask and ye shall receive."

I did not provoke it!
"Blessed are the pure in heart."
I did not have any evil power that made him do what he did to me.
"Whiter than snow."
My mother called him oversexed.

ShaTterED DianA

"I beseech you abstain from fleshly lusts which war against the soul."
She told me to do whatever he told me to do!!
"Wives submit to your husband as unto the Lord."

He was an adult who made the choice to rape me because it met his needs!
"The devil is like a lion roaming the earth seeking whom he may devour."
HE called it, "Teaching me how to be a good wife!"
"Fathers do not provoke your children to wrath."

He never considered how it would affect ME!
"Jesus wept."
I was ONLY a little girl!
"Suffer the children."
HIS little girl!
"Children are a blessing from the Lord."

Daddy could do whatever he wanted to do because the Bible told him so!
"Children obey your parents in all things."
He took me to church so that I would learn that he told me the truth!
"Trust and obey for there's no other way to be happy in Jesus than to trust and obey!"

Then he told everyone I loved that I was a bad little girl who lies and is mentally ill and that is why he had to spank me hard to break my will and spirit!
"Appears as an angel of light."

And then he took me back to church so that I would learn that being a bad little girl means that I am a sinner that even God could not love and that I really deserved to die.
"The wages of sin is death!"

When my mommy beat me with the belt and left long bruises on my
arms, legs, and back, I could hardly feel it because I'd learned so
well how to go away into my head to numb out my shock,
humiliation, anger and suffering!
"Present your body as a living sacrifice unto the Lord."

I became very good at disconnecting from my body's pain
and choosing not to see what I saw or hear what I heard
or think my own thoughts.
"Trust in the Lord and lean not unto thine own understanding."

In my mind I quoted my memory verse, "By his stripes we are
healed!"
I knew mommy was taking away my sin and helping me be a good
little girl
not taking out her fear, frustration and rage on me and my body!

"Honor thy father and thy mother that thy days may be long upon
the earth."
Well, I tried not to know what she was really doing but my mind
and body
knew the truth I tried to ignore while silently quoting my memory
verse!

"Thy word have I hid in my heart that I might not sin against
thee."
But the truth cannot be ignored! I could only pretend I didn't
know!
"The truth shall set you free."

That is the kind of man my REAL father was…
"Our father… who art in heaven…"
And that is the truth about how my mommy coped–not so good!
"Let he who is without sin cast the first stone."

They both blamed me and so did that phony-baloney warrior god–
and–even me myself!!!!
"For it was the woman who was deceived…."

231

ShaTterED DianA

If the bad happened because I was such a bad little girl,
I knew that if I tried my hardest to be a good little girl
then all the bad would go away!
"Be perfect as I am perfect."
"

But after 50 years of striving to be perfect and failing and
still meeting loving, kind and helpful people, I finally figured it out.
"You shall know them by their fruit!"

The bad happened to me because he was bad–not me!
"For all have sinned and fall short of the glory of God."
I don't have to be perfect after all!
"Love your neighbor as your self."
Whew! Empathy and sympathy!
NOT perfection is all I need!

I am glad he is finally dead!
"A whitened sepulcher filled with dead men's bones."
He was an evil man!
"The devil is the father of lies!"

I loved him and I hated him!
"Love the lord your god."
He was my hero.
"The bright and morning star."
He took me fishing.
"I will make you fishers of men."
And he broke my heart.
"Weeping, wailing and gnashing of teeth."

He was my father AND my worst enemy!
"Your adversary the devil…"
All I wanted was a normal father's love!
"Love is kind."

Not only did he hurt me,
"I am weary of my crying."
he hurt my children,

"Such is the kingdom of heaven."
because he shattered me
"Strong crying and tears"
and devastated my mother.
"O Lord how long shall I cry?"

Crushing my mind and spirit is one thing!
"Here am I Lord."
Harming my children is a completely different matter!
"Whoever shall harm one of these little ones...
it is better for him that a millstone be hanged around his neck
and he be cast into the sea!"
There is NO forgiveness for harming my children!
"The unpardonable sin!"

Christian fundamentalist mutigenerational incest family!
"The Lord visits the sins of the parents...unto the fourth
generation."
What an unbelievably ugly reality!
"Oppressed by the devil."
That is the truth I could not see!
"He opened the eyes of the blind."
Well...I knew what was happening I just didn't know what to call
it!
"God is not the author of confusion."

I was only nine, after all!
"Out of the mouths of babes."
It was awfully confusing....and scary!
"Resist the devil and he shall flee."
How could I stop them?

"I must be about my father's business."
A drink!
"And when he took the cup."
A trance!
"Pray without ceasing."
A man!

ShaTterED DianA

"He a rose!"

Oh dear god help me dear god!
"Thou shalt not commit adultery."
HELP MEeeee!
"The second woe is past; and behold the third woe
cometh quickly."
Jesus! Jesus! Jesus! Jesus!

"And the veil of the temple was rent in the midst."
I am gone!
"The Lord knoweth how to deliver the godly out of temptations,
and
to reserve the unjust unto the day of judgment to be punished."

I now know that heaven and hell are just systems of control:
reward and punishment
meted out like rats in a cage.
Behaviorism!
Press the bar and get a pellet little mouse.
Run out the door and you will get an electric shock Mr. Rat.
Isn't that too bad!!!!
"Hallelujah!"

And so these words have echoed through every relationship since
Daddy,
"HOW could you do that to ME?"
Until the truth set me free!
I was an innocent helpless dependent child!
NEVER a sinner!
"Amen"
"It is finished!"

SUGGESTED READING

Neuroscience, Psychiatry and Psychology:

The Body Keeps the Score, Bessel Van Der Kolk, MD

The Trauma Model, Colin Ross, MD

Scared Sick: The Role of Childhood Trauma in Adult Disease, Robin Karr-Morse

The Emotional Life of Your Brain, Richard Davidson, PhD

The Brain that Changes Itself, Norman Doidge, MD

Turning Gold into Lead, Vincent Felitti, MD (online free)

For Your Own Good, Alice Miller (all her books)

Leaving the Fold, Marlene Winell, PhD

Battle for the Mind: A Physiology of Conversion and Brain-Washing, William Sargant, MD

Brainwashing: The Science of Thought Control, Kathleen Taylor, PhD

Child Abuse, Narcissism and Psychopathy:

Breaking Their Will, Janet Heimlich

Miss America by Day, Marilyn Van Derbur

The Sociopath Next Door, Martha Stout, PhD

The Psychopath Inside, James Fallon, PhD

Why Does He Do That?, Lundy Bancroft

ShaTterED DianA

Why Is It Always About You?, Sandy Hotchkiss

The Authoritarians, Robert Altemeyer, PhD (online free)

The Political Face of Evangelical Fundamentalism:

The Family: The Secret Fundamentalism at the Heart of American Power, Jeff Sharlet

C Street, Jeff Sharlet

Republican Gomorrah, Max Blumenthal

Crazy for God, Frank Schaeffer

The Good News Club: the Christian Right's Stealth Attack on America's Children, Katherine Stewart

American Fascists: The Christian Right and the War on America, Chris Hedges

Attack of the Theocrats, Sean Faircloth

Archaeology, History, Mythology:

The Bible Unearthed, Israel Finkelstein and Neil A. Silberman

The History of Childhood, Lloyd deMause

The Chalice and the Blade, Riane Eisler

A Peoples' History of the United States, Howard Zinn, PhD

Everything by Marija Gimbutus, UCLA

The Goddesses, Joseph Campbell

Book Club Readers' Guide

Book One: Downloading Malware

1. Looking at my 4-year-old Sunday school paper, what are the lessons I was being taught?

2. What would be the normal emotional response to learning God kills people? And then learning God is watching you? Isn't "do not be afraid" teaching children to discount and dissociate from their normal human emotions? How would a child assimilate the contradictory instructions of fear and don't fear?

3. Children are concrete thinkers. They believe what adults tell them. How does my experience with the fire truck relate back to the lessons in my Sunday school paper?

4. Can you identify the Sunday school songs that separate Evangelical Fundamentalism from so-called liberal denominations/churches?

5. What are examples of fundamentalist magical thinking being reinforced by my mother?

6. What are examples of ways I learned to numb my emotions, dissociate from my body, and escape my traumatic reality?

7. Psychological dissociation is the separation of one's awareness and emotions from one's body. This can be accomplished through trauma or by being hypnotized or by self-hypnosis. Singing, chanting, hand clapping, and focused attention can be used to hypnotize. Dissociation can also manifest as compartmentalization of the mind and as amnesia barriers or walls that disconnect conscious awareness from traumatic events. List examples that reveal how I dissociated due to trauma. List examples that reveal how I was hypnotized and how I self-hypnotized.

8. How did compartmentalizing set me up to believe in demon possession?

9. Would you call my conversion experience at age six a free-will decision?

10. What do you feel when you compare my early sunbeam pictures with the family portrait taken when I was in high school?

11. What was compelling me to walk the aisle to the altar every Sunday night during my high school years? At Billy Graham?

12. How were religious ideals about purity being reinforced in my family? Does the following quote from Evangelical Fundamentalist psychologist Dr. James Dobson broaden your understanding? "Pain is a marvelous purifier."

13. How were religious ideals of perfection being reinforced in my family without any understanding of normal child development?

14. How were fundamentalist religious ideals of suffering and sorrow being reinforced through my family's treatment of me?

15. Cults maintain control through fear. Now we know that living with chronic fear not only reshapes the brain it also undermines one's immune system. What are the many ways I was kept frightened in my family and religion?

16. Who are the real satan's and demons in my life?

17. During my college religious cult experience, what was I calling Satan and Satan's power?

18. Why am I unable to keep that groups simplistic literature in my mind?

19. What was the effect of the double onslaught of family trauma and fundamentalist dogma on my internal dialogue about myself?

20. In what ways could that internal dialogue set me up to become a true believer and eventually clinically depressed and suicidal?

21. How do you feel when you read that an abused child was taught to turn to Jesus rather than to adults who could help her?

22. What was your reaction to what happened to my youngest sister when she had the courage to talk to her elementary school principal in Colorado in 1960?
23. In what ways did fundamentalist dogmas prevent me from seeking help?
24. What are examples of how my father's and mother's treatment of me reinforced fundamentalist dogma?
25. How did fundamentalist dogma set me up to blame myself for what my family did to me?
26. What is my uncle asking my father when he asks him if he is ready to go coon hunting?
27. Why do you think my mother did not allow me to keep Mark Twain's *Tom Sawyer* and *Huckleberry Finn*?
28. List ways my father is actually an exemplary manifestation of Yahweh/Jehovah/God.
29. What is the primary lesson Evangelical Fundamentalism teaches young children?
30. Would you say fundamentalism is promoting unity, brotherhood and love, or something else? What makes you think so?
31. To what degree is my mother a free agent?
32. Art is communication. Children's art can reveal if they are being traumatized. What does my SOS art to "Mom" when I am six communicate? What message does my stained glass convey? The floating trees? What about the beach and coconut trees?
33. What do you think is going on with the worm checks? What created my real-live, naked-lady dreams? What compelled me to pose spread eagle, then semi-spread eagle, for my grandfather's photograph in the Smokey Mountain stream?
34. Some experiences, like rape, are so traumatic that even adult victims can have no memory of them and cannot understand why their life begins to fall apart or why they become suicidal? Give examples that indicate I experienced sexual abuse even though I had no conscious memory of it as a child or adult.

35. What explains the fact that I heard a shrill noise that no one else heard when I was thinking critically about my family and religion? (This continued way into therapy decades later.)

36. In 1994, I met a minister's son who told me on the dance floor, "Fundamentalism crushes spirits." After reading my memoir, would you agree?

37. Would you call what I experienced religion, child abuse, or religiously sanctioned/justified child abuse?

38. Do you think this is what the Founding Fathers had in mind when they secured the right of all citizens to practice the religion of their choice or no religion at all?

39. What would anyone feel given they are a dependent child in my family of origin?

40. Do you know our environment and our thoughts literally shape our brain and how it functions?

41. Do you know our culture determines what we do and do not see? What was my Evangelical Fundamentalist culture conditioning me to see and not see?

42. Did my story help you understand why psychologist, Marlene Winell, says Evangelical Fundamentalists/biblical literalists are confused? What makes them confused?

43. In what ways is fundamentalism emotionally destructive? In what ways is it intellectually inaccurate?

44. Give examples of how I was taught the political face of fundamentalism without my awareness.

45. Even if a person has a bipolar gene, they will not get bipolar disorder unless they experience criticism, over-control and hostile relationships – chronic unbearable stress. Give examples of how I experienced all of these conditions day-in and day-out in both my family and evangelicalism.

46. One of the traits of bipolar disorder is sleep disturbance. In what ways was I conditioned by my family and evangelical dogmas to fear going to sleep?

47. Robert Sapolsky, Ph.D., Stanford neuroscientist, found that living with chronic stress "marinates" the brain in

glucocorticoids (cortisol), the stress hormones that the body needs when faced with life-threatening situations to empower us to fight or flee. However, when chronic psychological stressors are a way of life, the excessive hormones kill neurons in our hippocampus. The hippocampus is important for learning. Give examples of how my family and evangelicalism kept my brain bathed in glucocorticoids by keeping me terrified. [There are numerous lectures by Sapolsky online. He authored *Why Zebras Don't Get Ulcers*]

48. Bipolar disorder can have psychotic features. Evangelicalism became my psychological defense mechanism simply because traumatized children use whatever is in their environment to survive. For me, that was fairy tales, a literal understanding of the Bible and Evangelical-Pentecostal-Fundamentalist religion. List psychotic features inherent in Evangelicalism-Pentecostalism-Fundamentalism that I was conditioned to believe are reality.

49. Those with Bipolar I struggle with suicidal ideation and attempts. Many take their own life. In what ways did actions and thinking in my family and fundamentalism set me up to conclude suicide is a logical choice and that I "deserved" to die?

50. What made me feel isolated from the world?

51. What caused me to feel stupid?

52. Why didn't I know what other kids knew?

53. How did keeping me isolated protect my predators?

54. How many ways did my religion protect predators at my expense?

55. One of my favorite Marilyn Van Derbur quotes is, "Incest families are vicious." It is not uncommon for families to turn against the one who blows the whistle. They circle the wagons and abandon the whistleblower. It is not uncommon for siblings to claim, "I would have known if that was going on at night." Which two memories of mine prove siblings do not always know what happens in their own home at night while they are asleep?

56. How was I being conditioned by my family and religion to live in fear and to have the fear response of adrenaline running 24/7? Would there have been any way I could have felt comfortable living a normal life "in the evil world"? Does it make sense to you that I lived with high levels of anxiety 24/7 and especially as I pushed the boundaries of my cult life and began moving toward higher education? Which family members pulled the rug out from under me?

57. We now know that paranoia is a consequence of one's history. What aspects of my history set me up to appear paranoid if I told someone my story?

58. In what ways have you been affected by Evangelical Fundamentalism?

59. Do you think it is time Americans define religion? How do you define religion? How do you define God?

Recently I made an appointment and spoke with the current medical director of "my" psych hospital. He explained they are now more conservative about using the bipolar diagnosis because of the harm it has caused patients in the past. My insurance premiums reached $1,500/mo. many years ago. I still had copays. My daughter told me I would never recover and decided to move on with her life sans me. Friends deserted me. I was told I had a genetic disease and would be on all 5 psychotropic meds the rest of my life.

The Medical Director told me they now use the diagnosis "Dissociation" because it includes bipolar symptoms. "Patients can recover from dissociation." And I did because the brain can recover with licensed therapies IF the patient does the work.

Song Credits for *Shattered Diana* Series:

All hail the pow'r of Jesus' name
Lyrics: Edward Perrronet
(1726-1792)
Music: James Ellor
(1819-1899)
Hymnal.net

All to Jesus I surrender
Lyrics: Judson W. Van de Venter
(1855-1939)
Music: Winfield Scott Weeden
(1847-1908)
Hymnal.net

Amazing Grace
Lyrics: John Newton
(1725-1807)
Music: Traditional American
Arranged by: Edwin Othello
(1851-1921)
Hymnal.net

A mighty Fortress is our God
Lyrics: Martin Luther
(1483-1546)
Translated: Frederick Hedge
(1805-1890)
Hymnal.net

Are you washed in the Blood?
Lyrics and Music by Elisha A. Hoffman (1839-1929)
Cyberhymnal.org/htm/a/r/aruwashed.htm

Blessed Assurance
Lyrics: Fanny Jane Crosby
(1820-1915)
Music: Mrs. Joseph F. Knapp
Hymnal.net

Cowboy Hymns and Songs of Inspiration
Gene Autry
The Old Rugged Cross

Deep and Wide
Chorus and lyrics: Rev. Sydney Cox
Hymnal.net

Do Lord/Way Beyond the Blue
Author unknown
Traditional African-American Spiritual
Gospelsonglyrics.org/songs/do_lord_remember_me.html

Down from His glory
Lyrics: William E. Booth-Clibbon, 1921
Music: Eduardo. di Capua 19th century
Originally O sole mio "My Sun"
Later recorded by Elvis Presley, "It's Now or Never"
Hymnal.net

Essential Gene Autry
Here comes Peter Cottontail
Lyrics: Gene Autry

Fairest Lord Jesus
Lyrics: German 17th century
Music: Schleisische Volkslieder 1842
Arranged by: Richard Storrs Willis
(1819-1900)
Hymnal.net

Give me oil in my lamp
Childbiblesongs.com

Heavenly Sunlight
Lyrics: Henry J. Zelley 1899
Music: George Cook 1899
Hymnal.net

He leadeth Me! O blessed thought
Lyrics: Joseph Henry Gilmore
(1834-1918)
Music: William Batchelder Bradbury
(1816-1868)
Hymnal.net

Diana Lee, M.A.

He's got the whole world in His hands
Traditional American Spiritual
Wikipedia

I Can hear my Savior calling
Lyrics: Ernest W. Blandly
Music: John Samuel Norris
(1844-1907)
Hymnal.net

If you're happy and you know it
Childbiblesongs.com

I love to tell the story
Lyrics: Katherine Hankey
(1834-1911)
Music: William Gustavus Fisher
(1835-1912)
Hymnal.net

I'm in the Lord's army/I may never march in the infantry
Sundayschoolsources.com/songs.htm
Based on Ephesians 6:10-20

In the Garden
Lyrics and Music by C. Austin Miles
Nethymnal.org

I serve a risen Savior
Lyrics and Music by Alfred Henry Ackley
(1887-1960)
Hymnal.net

It is Well
Lyrics: Horatio Gates Spafford
(1828-1888)
Music: Philip Paul bliss
(1938-1876)
Hymnal.net

I've Got the Joy In My Heart
Lyrics: George Willis Cooke
(1848-1923)
Wikipedia
childbiblesongs.com

I will sing the wondrous story
Lyrics: Francis Harold Rowley
(1854-1952)
Music: Peter Philip Belhorn
(1865-1936)
Hymnal.net

Jesus love me
Lyrics: Anna Warner 1860
Music: William Batchelder Bradbury 1862
Wikipedia

Jesus loves the little children
Lyrics: C. Herbert Woolston (1856-1927)
Music: George Root (1820-1895)
Cyberhymnal.org

Just as I am
Lyrics: Charlotte Elliott
(1789-1871)
Music: William Batchelder Bradbury
(1816-1868)
Hymnal.net

Leaning on the Everlasting Arms
Lyrics: Elisha Albright Hoffman
(1839-1929)
Music: Anthony Johnson Showalter
(1858-1924)
Hymnal.net

Low in the grave He lay
Lyrics and Music: Robert Lowry
(1826-1899)
Hymnal.net

Man of sorrows, what a name
Lyrics and Music: Philip Paul Bliss
1836-1876
Hymnal.net

More about Jesus would I know
Lyrics: Eliza Edmonds Hewitt
(1851-1920)
Music: John Robson Sweny

(1837-1899)
Hymnal.net

My Hope is Built on Nothing Less
Lyrics: Edward Mote (1797-1874)
Music: John Stainer ("Magdalen")
www.lutheran-hymnal.com

Nothing but the blood
Lyrics and Music: Robert Lowry
(19ᵗʰ century)
Cyberhymnal.org

O Be Careful, Little Eyes
*Lyrics: from children's Bible songs taught in church, Bible class, Vacation Bible School (VBS) Printed from **ChildBibleSongs.com***
Childbiblesongs.com/son-12-be-careful-little-eyes-shtml

Oh, how I love Jesus
Children's song
Hymnal.net

Onward Christian Soldiers
Lyrics: Sabine Baring-Gould 1865
Music: Arthur Sullivan 1872
Wikipedia

Redeemed–how I love to proclaim it
Lyrics: Fanny Jane Crosby
(1820-1915)
Music: William James Kirkpatrick
(1838-1921)
Hymnal.net

Rescue the perishing
Lyrics: Frances Jane Crosby
(1820-1915)
Music: William Howard Doane
Based on Luke 14:23

Rock of Ages, cleft for me
Lyrics: Augustus Montague Toplady
(1740-1778)
Music: Thomas Hastings
(1784-1872)
Hymnal.net

The Battle Hymn of the Republic
Lyrics; Julia Ward Howe
Music: William Steffe 1856
Wikipedia

The B*I*B*L*E
Traditional
Makingmusicfun.net

The Old Rugged Cross
Lyrics: George Bennard 1913
Library.timelesstruths.org/music/The_Old_Rugged_Cross

The wise man built his house
Childbiblesongs.com

There is a fountain filled with blood
Lyrics: William Cowper
(1731-1800)
Music: 19th century camp meeting song
attributed to Lowell Mason
hymnsite.com

There is power in the blood
Lyrics and Music: Lewis E. Jones 1899
Cyberhymnal.org

Tis so sweet to trust in Jesus
Lyrics: Louisa M.R. Stead
(Circa 1850-1917)
Music: William James Kirkpatrick
(1838-1920)
Hymnal.net

Trust and Obey
Lyrics: John H. Sammis
(1846-1919)
Music: Daniel B. Towner
(1850-1919)
Hymnsite.com

What a Friend we have in Jesus
Lyrics: Daniel Webster Whittle
(1840-1901)
Music: James McGranahan
(1840-1907)

Hymnal.net

When we all get to Heaven
Lyrics; Eliza E. Hewitt (Pentecostal, 1989)
Music: Emily D. Wilson

When the roll is called up yonder
Lyrics and Music: James Milton Black
(1856-1938)
gbgm-umc.org/HolcombUMC/whentheroll.htm

When we survey the wondrous cross
Lyrics: Isaac Watts
(1674-1748)
Music: Gerogrian Chant
Arranged by Lowell Mason
(1792-1872)

Diana Photos

Turning Gold to Lead
Vincent Felitti, MD
[See: Adverse Childhood Experiences Study]

Early childhood abuse increases a girl's chances of getting breast cancer as an adult.

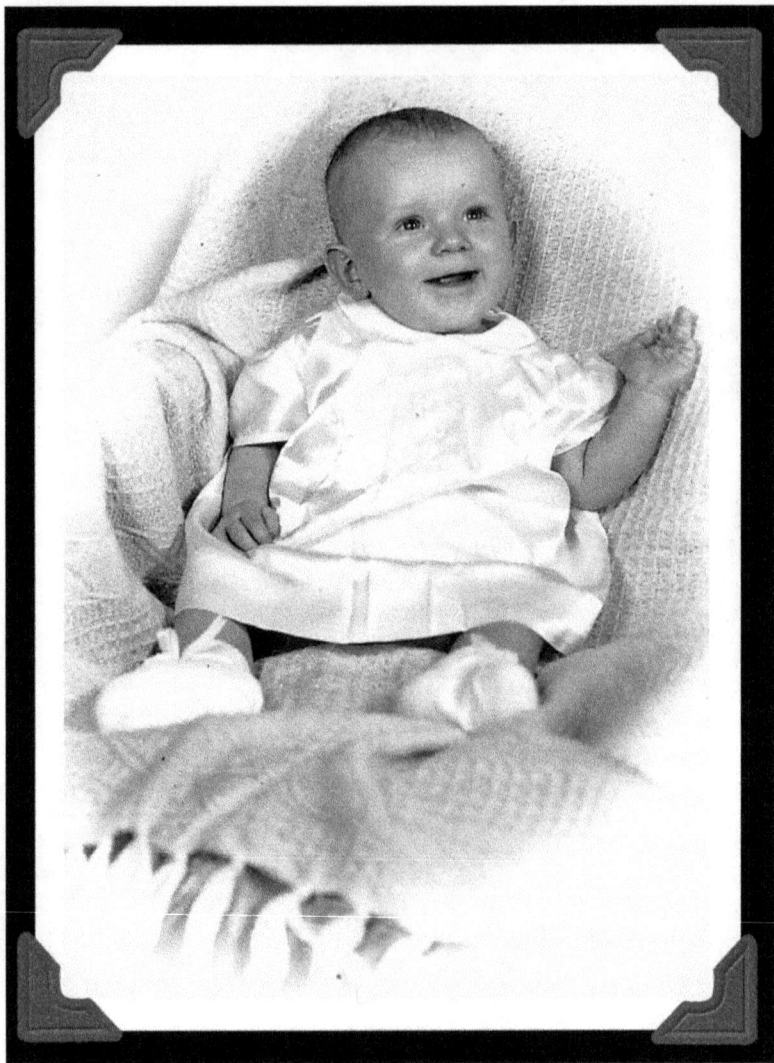

Happy Baby 3 Months 1948   Family Photos

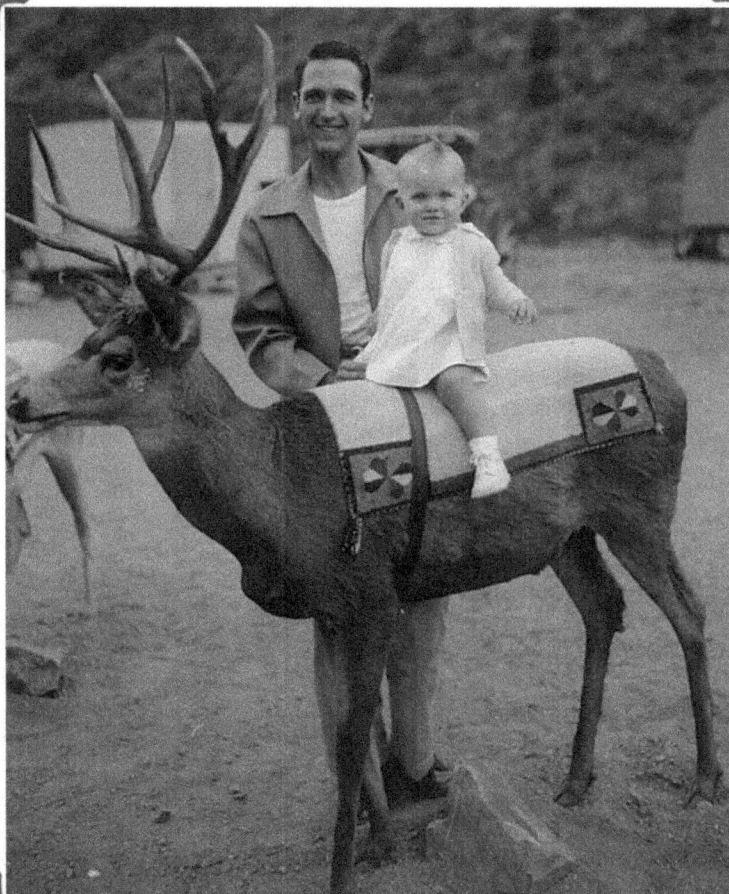

Daddy and Me on Berthoud Pass   Family Photo

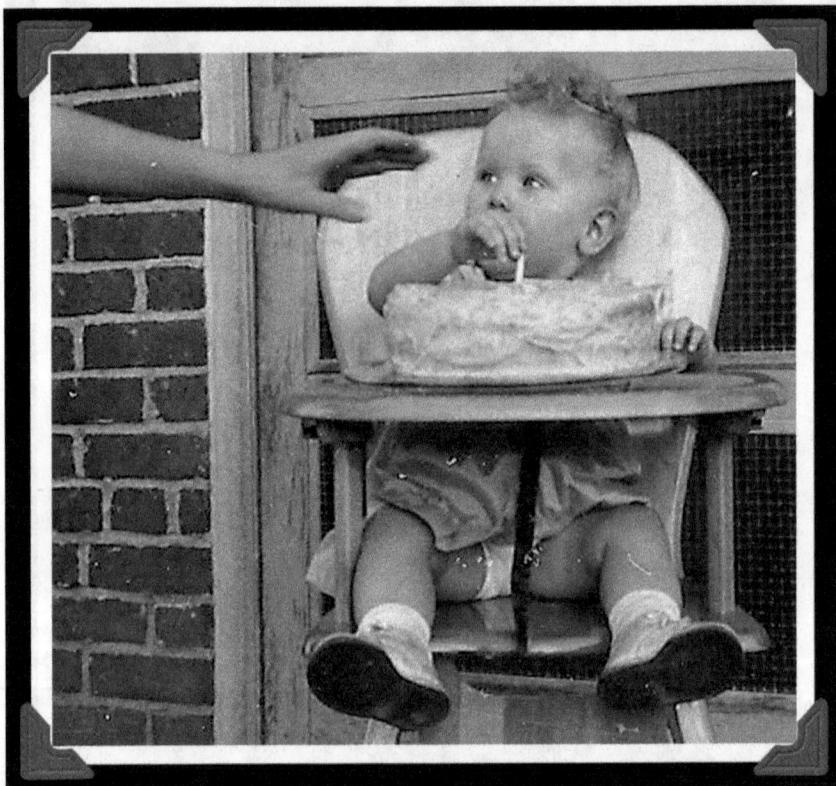

First Birthday "Don't Touch" Family Photo

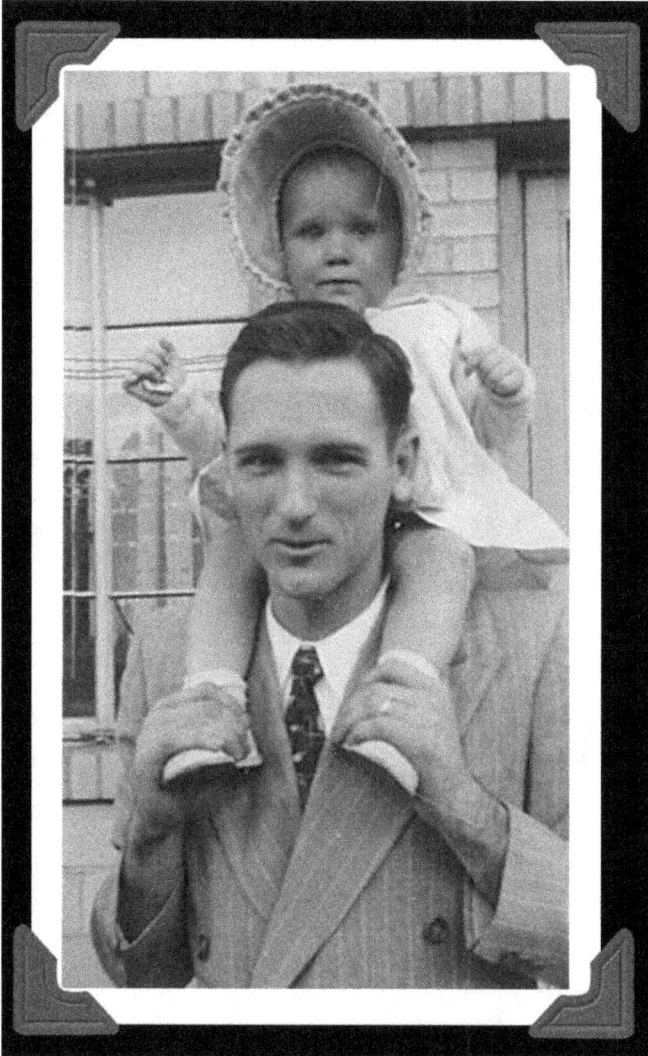

Daddy and Me   Family Photo

I see fear on my face.

Evangelical Fundamentalists generally discount/ignore/numb
emotions in self (and others).

Hard to tell if I am frightened being up so high or if I didn't feel safe because of
him "hauling me out of church to spank me when I cried."

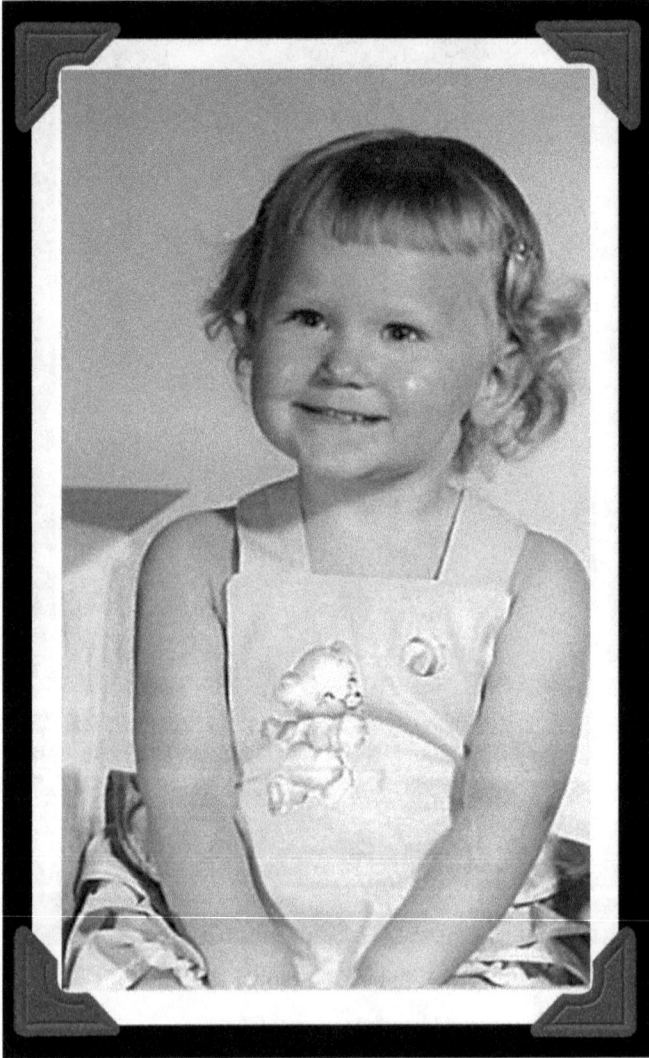

18 months   Family Photo

Who could "spank" this baby "hard" for asking for light?

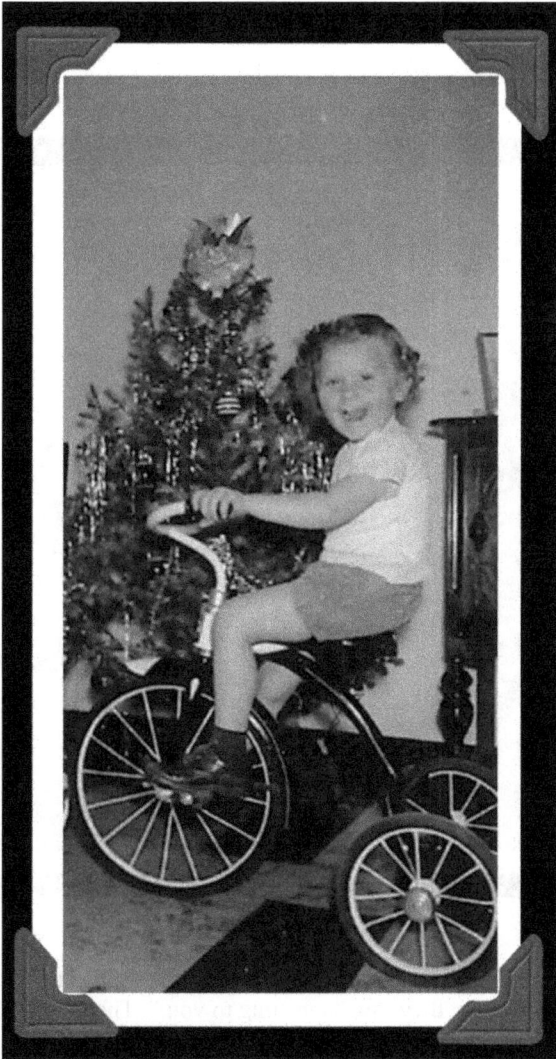

1951   Family Photo

Four: and living near Cherry Creek where Daddy plays mind games and where I put my hand into Mother's wringer washing machine out of curiosity.

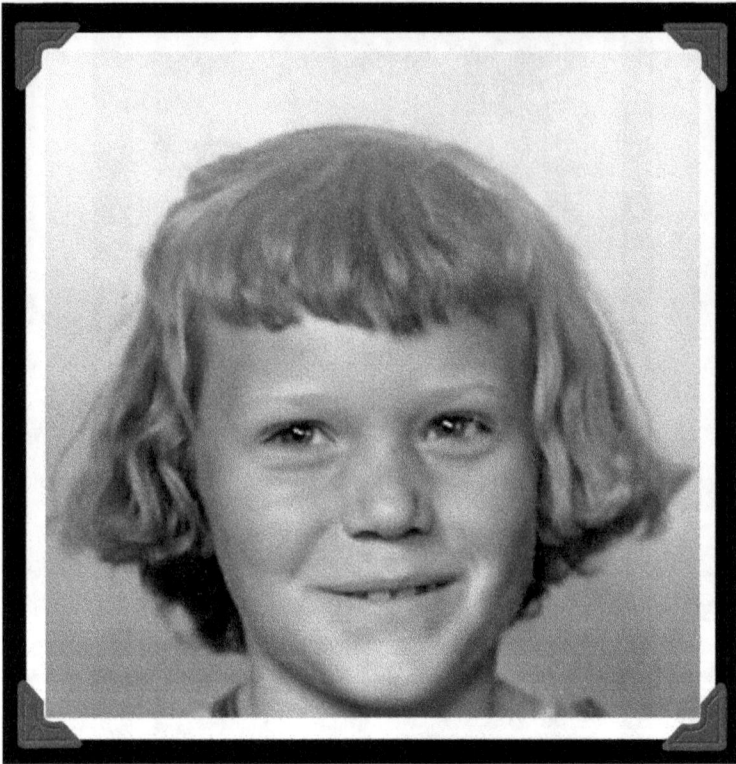

Second Grade School Photo

"They had to destroy you because you would have spilled the beans. Your sisters learned by what they saw happening to you." Therapist and Aunt Bebe

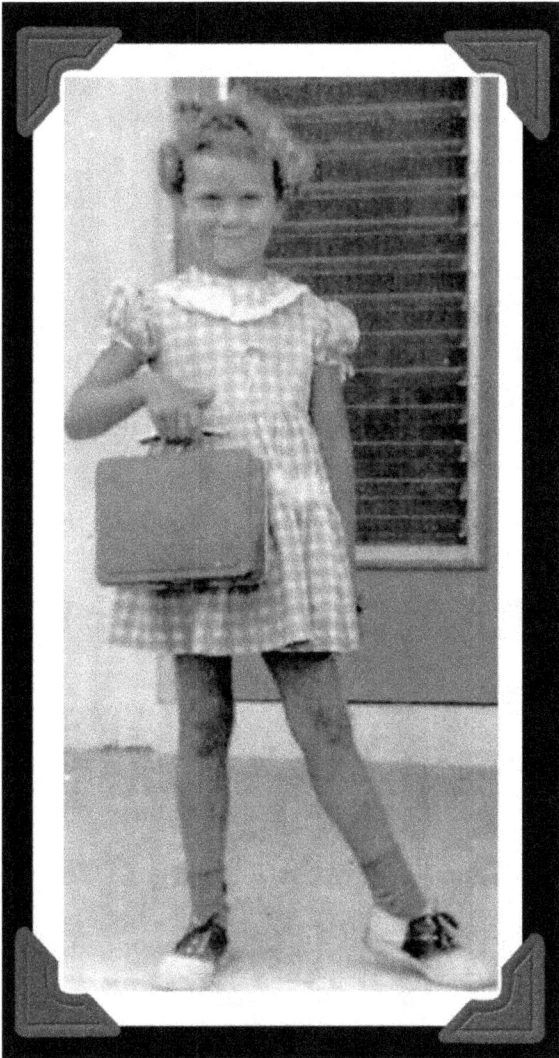

1954 Second Grade Model (Family Photo)

ShaTterED DianA

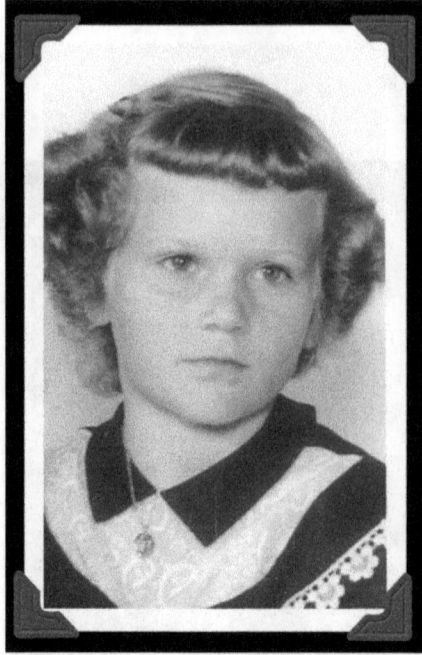

1955 Christmas (months after the mirrors photo). Photographer: Anonymous
What did the others look like if this was the keeper?

Eight years Old Sexy Modelling

January 1957   Fourth Grade,
Nine Years Old   Family Photo

Bess Myerson Modeling.   Now feel like a grown up woman.
Notice my protective left arm.

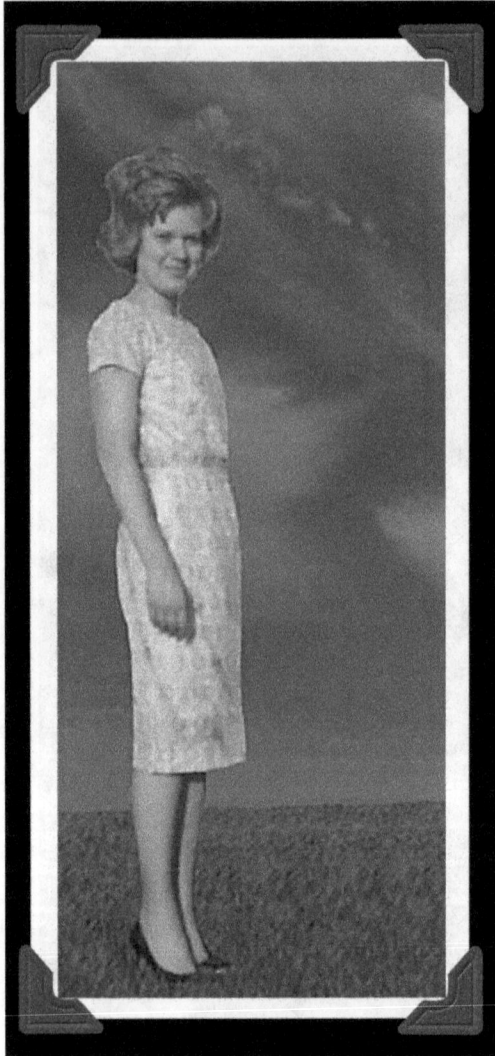

"Ha! Ha! Ha!
Diana's getting so big she's going to have to buy her
clothes at Denver Tent and Awning!" Her feet are so big…"
[Emotional Abuse]

Senior Photo One
Credit: Piper Studio, Denver

Senior Photo Two
Credit: Piper Studio, Denver

Two very distinct sides of my personality but in both
I am modeling not authentic.
Emotional abuse causes adolescents to dissociate.
[See: Scared Sick]

Diana Lee, M.A.

Family Photos

Four generation maternal family   Photographer Anonymous

"Mom"   "Ma"   "Me"   "Mother"

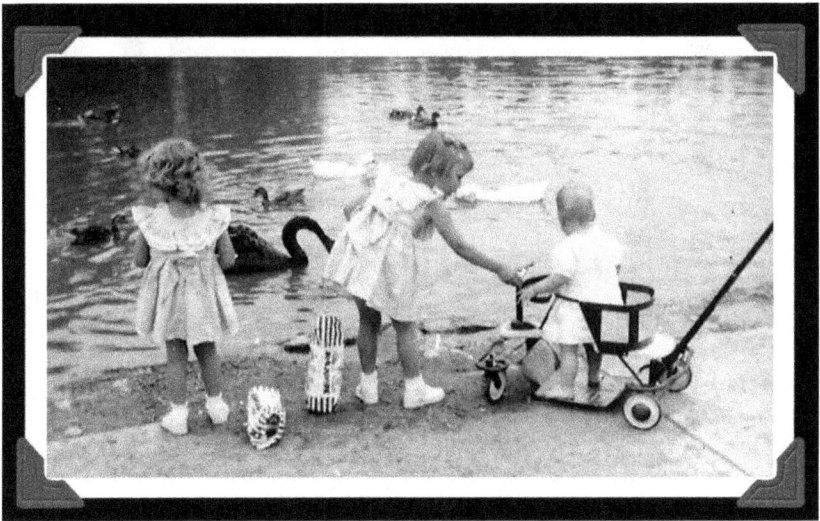

City Park, Denver   I'm four and in the center helping baby sister

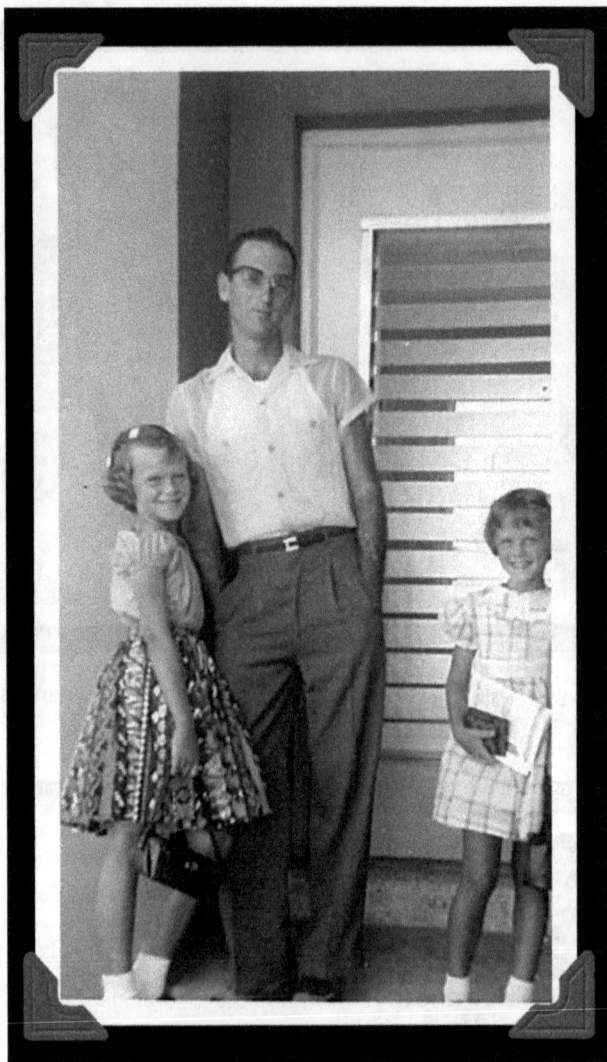

When my adult son dated
an MSW she told us this is
a "classic" incest family photo.

Taken by Mother before church.

Fall 1955. Possibly evidence of "grooming."

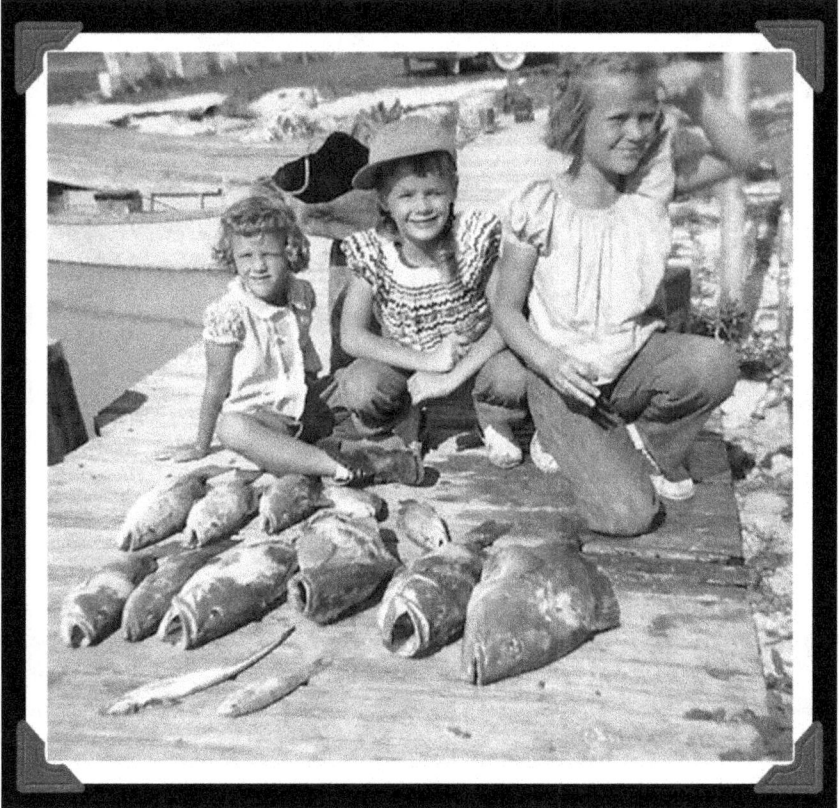

Fishing in the Florida Keys   Family Photo

Thanksgiving 1955. At the rental dock; notice rental boat on left top.

1957. I am on the far left. Taken by "Mom."

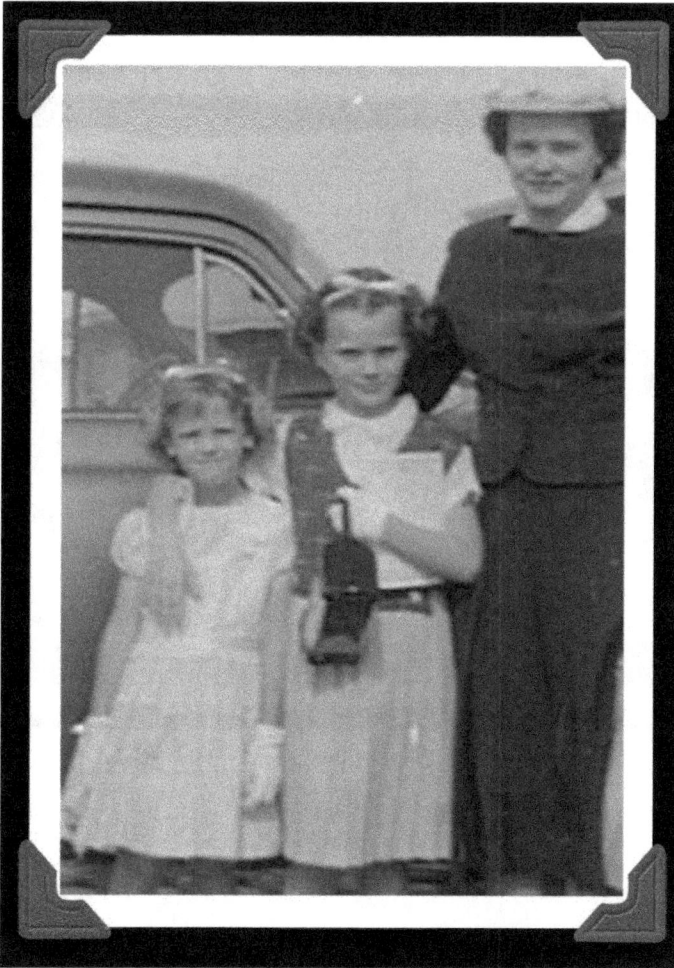

Easter 1957.   Taken by "Mom"

Always new dresses, new hats or ribbons, new gloves,
clean and shiny car and our Bibles.
I'm in the middle with my protective arm around baby sister

1964   Olan Milles used by permission

"Most men lead lives of quiet desperation and go to the grave with the
son still in them." ~ Thoreau
I am on the far right; baby sister is front middle.

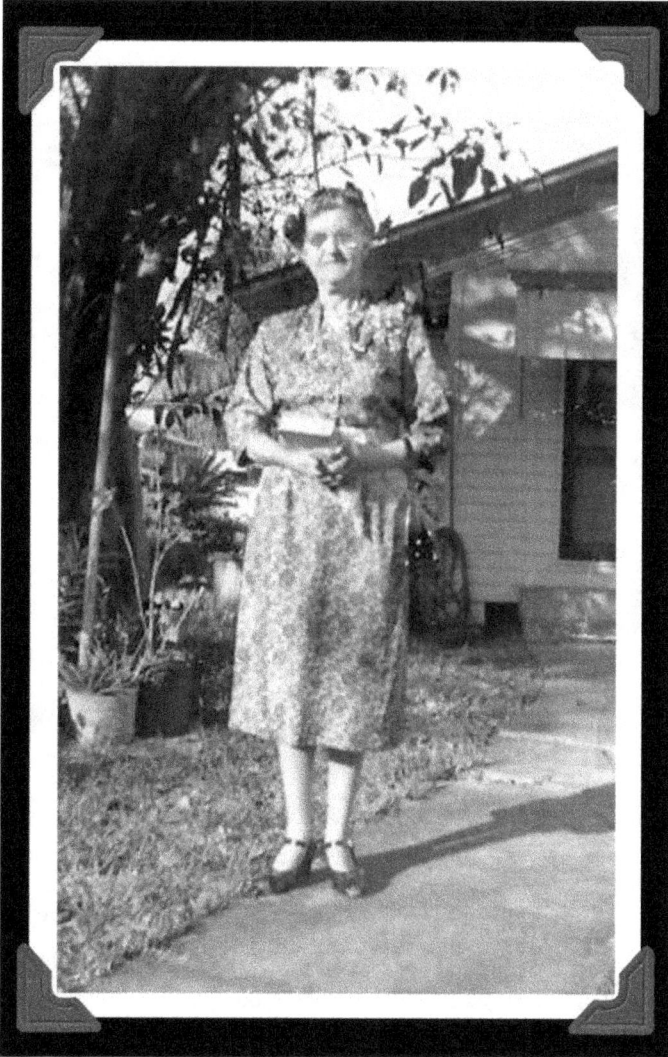

Paternal Great Grandmother

What she looked like when we went to Tennessee in 1957.

Our homes were always perfectly clean with manicured lawns
Room on right is the window I stared at to survive and also
the window where I made my vow to survive. Coincidence?

Window on left is the pink room which had a window on the side by the door so
I could always see "More Paternal Great Grandparents" arriving to take me
home with them.